THE EXTRAORDINARY FORM OF MARRIAGE ACCORDING TO CANON 1098

THE CATHOLIC UNIVERSITY OF AMERICA
CANON LAW STUDIES
No. 348

THE EXTRAORDINARY FORM OF MARRIAGE ACCORDING TO CANON 1098

A HISTORICAL SYNOPSIS AND A COMMENTARY

A DISSERTATION

Submitted to the Faculty of the School of Canon Law of the Catholic University of America in partial fulfillment of the requirements for the degree of Doctor of Canon Law

BY
REV. EDWARD ANTHONY FUS, A.B., J.C.L.
Priest of the Diocese of Brooklyn

THE CATHOLIC UNIVERSITY OF AMERICA PRESS
WASHINGTON, D. C.
1954

Nihil Obstat:

CLEMENT V. BASTNAGEL, J.U.D.,
Censor Deputatus.

Washingtonii, die XXII Maii, 1954.

Imprimatur:

✠ THOMAS EDMUNDUS MOLLOY, S.T.D.,
Archiespiscopus—Episcopus Bruklyniensis.

Bruklyni, die XXV Maii, 1954.

Printed by
THE PAULIST PRESS
401 WEST 59TH STREET
NEW YORK 19, N. Y.
51

TABLE OF CONTENTS

CHAPTER V

CHAPTER VI

CHAPTER VII

FOREWORD

Ever solicitous for the eternal happiness as well as for the temporal welfare of the souls committed to its care by its Divine Founder, the Church has always given marriage and the marriage contract its special care and attention. Realizing that fallen human nature is not averse to regarding matrimony as a mere human institution, dissoluble at will, and further, realizing also the many heartaches that are a result of broken marriages and new alliances, the Church has, in order the better to establish the fact of marriage, prescribed certain formalities which are to be observed in the contracting of marriage.

The Church is fully aware of being the custodian of the sacraments and the official interpreter of God's laws. Legislating for the sacrament of matrimony, the Church has always taken care not to encroach on the natural right of marrying that each man has. What is more, the Church has always championed that right. Inasmuch as these formalities will at times be impossible of observance, one is led to believe, and rightly so, that some provision must have been made for such eventualities. It will be, then, the purpose of this dissertation to investigate the canonical institute known as the "extraordinary juridical form of marriage."

The treatise is divided into two parts: the first will deal with a historical synopsis of the development of the extraordinary form of marriage, and the second will be devoted to a canonical commentary on this institute.

The writer wishes to take this opportunity to express his heartfelt gratitude to His Excellency, the Most Reverend Thomas E. Molloy, S.T.D., Archbishop-Bishop of Brooklyn, for the special privilege of being allowed to pursue post-graduate studies in Canon Law and for his kind generosity in making this publication possible. The writer wishes also to express his sincere appreciation to His Excellency, the Most Reverend Raymond A. Kearney, S.T.D., J.C.D., Auxiliary Bishop and Chancellor of the Diocese of Brooklyn, for his kindness in suggesting the topic for this dissertation and for his continued interest in it and for his helpful encouragement. He is deeply indebted indeed to the members of the Faculty of the School of Canon Law for their helpful suggestions and their scholarly direction and assistance in the preparation of this dissertation.

Part One

Historical Synopsis

INTRODUCTION

ANY appreciably complete effort to trace the history of what canonical commentaries have termed the "extraordinary form of marriage," or the juridic form of marriage in "extraordinary cases," as appertaining to the form of marriage described in canon 1098 of the Code of Canon Law,[1] must of necessity delineate the historical development of the Church's doctrine as to what is essential in the formation of the marriage contract and simultaneously in the reception of the sacrament of matrimony, for among the baptized one cannot exist without the other.[2] That the Church has this right to declare what is required can be gleaned from the fact that it is the custodian of the sacraments and the official interpreter of God's law. Logically, one must first show what has been and what is now considered the *ordinary form* of marriage before one may satisfactorily describe the development of the *extraordinary form* of marriage.

It seems mandatory at the very outset to note in exactly what sense the term *form* is to be understood. It is not to be taken in the philosophical sense as specifying a thing in its species, e.g., in marriage, an association of man and woman as husband and wife, and not an association of any other type; nor, in the theological sense of *form,* as in the sacrament of matrimony, i.e., the mutual acceptance of the two parties in words or signs of each one's rights over the other's body for the performance of acts which of themselves are suited for the begetting of children, which rights are being given at the time of their acceptance.[3]

[1] *Codex Iuris Canonici Pii X Pontificis Maximi jussu digestus Benedicti XV auctoritate promulgatus, Praefatione, Fontium Annotatione et Indice Analytico-Alphabetico ab Emo Petro Card. Gasparri Auctus* (Romae: Typis Polyglottis Vaticanis, 1917; Reimpressio, 1934).

[2] Canon 1012.

[3] P. Gasparri, *Tractatus Canonicus de Matrimonio,* editio nova ad mentem Codicis Iuris Canonici (2 vols., Romae: Typis Polyglottis Vaticanae, 1932), I, n. 34 (hereafter rited Gasparri); Cappello, *Tractatus Canonico-Moralis de Sacramentis* (5 vols., Vol. I, *De sacramentis in genere,* 5. ed.; Vol. V, *De Matrimonio,* 5. ed., Romae: Marietti: 1947), V (*De Matrimonio*), n. 30 (hereafter

It is to be taken, rather, in the juridic sense, i.e., with reference to what is necessary for the formation of the marriage according to the law of the Church, or in respect to what is requisite for bringing marriage into existence for a man and a woman. Inasmuch as marriage is a contract,[4] one may explain the *form* as that which will be necessary to "close" the contract, that which is required for making the marriage contract a real entity. To put it in still another way, looking at it from the point of view of the contracting parties, one may regard the *form* as that which is essential for them to do in order to contract marriage in the eyes of the Church.

The Code of Canon Law states that marriage comes into being by the legitimately manifested consent of the persons capable in law of entering marriage.[5] Since by divine law, whether natural or positive, there is not prescribed any type of substantial form according to which the matrimonial consent is to be expressed,[6] the Code explains what is meant by a "legitimately manifested consent," viz., the matrimonial consent must be exchanged in the presence both of a lawfully deputed minister (bishop or priest) and of two witnesses.[7] This, then, is what is known today as the *ordinary form* of marriage.

The aim of the historical conspectus will be to trace the development of the canonical or juridic form of marriage from the beginning of the Church through the Middle Ages to the Council of Trent, in which, for the first time, there was decreed, under the pain of nullity, a universally prescribed form of marriage. With this as a background, one can trace the development of the canonical institute of the *extraordinary form of marriage* through the intervening centuries to the publication of the Code of Canon Law.

cited *De Matrimonio*); Wernz-Vidal, *Ius Canonicum* (7 vols. in 8, Vol. V, *Ius Matrimoniale,* 3. ed., a Philippo Aguirre recognita, Romae: Apud Aedes Universitatis Gregorianae, 1946), n. 43 (hereafter cited *Ius Matrimoniale*).

[4] Canons 1012, 1069, 1070, etc.

[5] Canon 1081.

[6] DeBecker, *De Sponsalibus et Matrimonio Praelectiones Canonicae* (2. ed., Lovanii, 1903 cum appendice *Commentarius in Legem Novam de Forma Sponsalium et Matrimonii,* a. 1913), p. 87.

[7] Canon 1094.

CHAPTER I

THE DEVELOPMENT OF THE FORM OF MARRIAGE UNTIL THE DECREE OF GRATIAN (CA. 1140)

STRUGGLING for its very existence during the first three centuries of the Christian Era, the Church enacted few statutes in regard to marriage. The early Councils of the Church, e.g., Elvira (305),[1] Ancyra (314),[2] and Arles (314),[3] to mention just a few examples, dealt more with the problems of adultery, bigamy, incestuous relations and mixed marriages than with a code of marriage laws. The Church tried to inculcate a clear comprehension of morality in marriage relations, busying itself with the indissolubility of marriage, the inadmissibility of divorce, and the enactment of impediments unknown to Roman Law.[4]

In leaving it the sacraments, the Church's divine Founder did not postulate any definite, external form of marriage. Accordingly, there was room for a free development regarding the form of marriage.[5] Besides, the Church was just beginning its missionary labors, converting different peoples, each with customs of its own as to the formation of marriage. It found one type among the Romans, another among the Jews, and still another among the Germanic peoples. Not wishing to do violence to these and thereby alienate these peoples, the Church adapted its practice to the existing customs wherever

[1] Concilium Eliberitanum—Bruns, *Canones Apostolorum et Conciliorum Saeculorum IV-VII* (2 vols., Berolini, 1839), II, 9 (hereafter cited Bruns); cf. also Mansi, *Sacrorum Conciliorum Nova et Amplissima Collectio* (53 vols. in 60, Parisiis, 1901-1927) II, 14 (hereafter cited Mansi); Hardouin, *Acta Conciliorum et Epistolae Decretales ac Constitutiones Summorum Pontificum* (12 vols., Parisiis, 1714-1715) I, 256 (hereafter cited Hardouin).

[2] Bruns, I, 68; Mansi, II, 525; Hardouin, I, 276.

[3] Bruns, II, 208.

[4] Feine, *Kirchliche Rechtsgeschichte* (2 vols., Vol. I, Weimar: Herman Böhlaus Nachfolger, 1950), I, 112.

[5] Freisen, *Geschichte des canonischen Eherechts bis zum Verfall der Glossenliteratur* (2. ed., Paderborn, 1893), pp. 121 ff.

it found them and accepted them, keeping whatever was not contrary to Christian principles of doctrine and morality, purifying others and adding customs of its own.[6] It realized that there were civil effects as well in regard to marriage, such as the legitimacy of the children, the right of inheritance, and the like. Therefore, it counseled the faithful to observe the civil customs and laws of marriage.[7]

When Christianity came in contact with the Romans, it was customary to have marriage preceded by a betrothal.[8] However, this was not essential for the validity of the marriage that was to follow. Mere consent was sufficient to constitute the espousals or betrothal.[9] Even though the girl had to yield to the all powerful *patria potestas* of the *paterfamilias,* the law simply invoked the presumption that she consented if she did not resist her father's wishes in the matter.[10]

Great legal value was placed on these betrothals in the later Roman Law. Justinian (527-565) declared that marriage was constituted when sexual relations followed upon a betrothal. No formal consent was required by Roman Law. The consent of the betrothal was considered as passing automatically into a consent to an actual marriage because a *maritalis affectio* was adjudged to be present.[11] The presence of this *maritalis affectio* was so essential for the Romans that once it was lost, the marriage was at an end.[12]

Marriage itself was not considered a contract in Roman Law. It was completely devoid of form. Gaius (second century) in treat-

[6] Sägmüller, *Lehrbuch des katolischen Kirchenrechts* (2 vols., Freiburg im Breisgau, 1900), I, 491; Freisen, *loc. cit.*; Joyce, *Christian Marriage* (2. ed., London: Sheed & Ward, 1948), p. 40.

[7] Pollock and Maitland, *History of English Law (before the time of Edward I)* (2. ed., 2 vols., Cambridge: University Press, 1895), II, 369.

[8] Buckland, *Textbook of Roman Law, from Augustus to Justinian* (2. ed., Cambridge: University Press, 1932), p. 112.

[9] D. (23.1) 4.

[10] D (23.1) 12.

[11] N. (74.5). This law gave rise to great disputes among the medieval canonists as to the exact moment when the betrothal consent passed into marital consent.

[12] D. (24.1) 3; (32.13).

ing of *manus* [13] stated that in prior times, i.e., prior to the second century A. D., *manus* could be acquired in three ways, namely, through *confarreatio* (a religious marriage ceremony), through *coemptio* (sale), or through *usus* (cohabitation). Since *manus* could only be acquired by marriage, he pointed accordingly to certain ways that marriage was entered into in the times prior to his. In all three ways it was usual, if not essential, to have the formal *deductio in domum mariti*, i.e., placing the woman in the man's custody, for constituting marriage in its complete legal effect.[14]

There was also a marriage without *manus*. Such a union was divested of all formalities; it was contracted simply by means of consent. It was known as "free marriage." This latter type became the only type in the later Roman Empire.[15] Despite the fact that marriage was not considered a contract in Roman Law, nevertheless, to bring it into existence there was required the consent, made manifest at times by many persons.

Roman jurists laid it down as a general principle that the consent of the parties was the essential element in marriage. Ulpian (+ 228) insisted that it was consent, and not sexual relations, that constituted marriage.[16] The consent of the *paterfamilias* was essential for the validity of the marriage. The parties' consent was regarded in time by the jurists as a requisite element. Before the fifth century, one cannot say with certainty that such was the case with the *filia familias*. Her consent could be regarded as given tacitly if she did not oppose the union, and as long as the man was not of a lower station in life or debased in his morality. Provided that she took

[13] Gaius, I, 110. *Manus* was the full power that a husband had over his wife. By this means, she broke all cognatic ties with her family and joined the agnatic family of her husband, taking on the legal position of a daughter to him, if he happened to be a *paterfamilias*. All her property and power of dealing with it went over to the husband or the *paterfamilias* in whose power the husband was. If she was not *in manu*, she remained in her own family and was subject to her own *paterfamilias*.

[14] Joyce, *Christian Marriage*, p. 41.

[15] Corbett, *Roman Law of Marriage* (Oxford: Clarendon Press, 1930), pp. 90-94.

[16] "Nuptias enim non concubitus, sed consensus facit."—D. (50.17) 30; (50.1) 15.

part in all the ceremonies, the very fact of her presence proved sufficient for sealing her marital status.[17]

Inasmuch as the required form, if it may be termed thus, looked simply to the placing of the wife in the husband's control,[18] as long as he accepted her upon her *deductio in domum mariti* when she had gone willingly with him, the requisite consent seemed duly manifested. Joyce (1864-1943) was of the opinion that the *deductio* simply afforded proof of the marriage, but did not itself effect the marriage. The consent of the betrothal was considered as passing automatically into a consent to an actual, present union.[19]

Since the earliest Christians were Jews, their customs in all spheres, with reference also to marriage, tended to have an effect and to wield an influence in the early Church's marriage laws. The early Fathers of the Church occupied themselves with the question of whether or not the relationship between the Blessed Mother and St. Joseph was a true marriage. In the course of their discussions, of necessity they spoke of Jewish marriage customs and showed how some of these customs continued to exist even in their own day.

Although the betrothment itself usually meant nothing more than a customary declaration that a marriage was in the process of being arranged, the solemn rite for the Jews meant that all the juridic effects of a marriage followed. Once the prenuptial agreement was arranged, it became binding on both parties, who then and there were regarded as man and wife in all religious as well as legal aspects, with the lone exception of cohabitation. Thus in two places where the words occur in the Old Testament, the betrothed woman is called a wife.[20] The New Testament gives us a perfect example when it speaks of the Blessed Mother and St. Joseph. The angel termed her "wife" (*coniugem tuam*) [21] even though the Evangelists declared that she was espoused to St. Joseph (*desponsata*),[22] who in turn was designated as her husband.[23]

[17] Corbett, *op. cit.*, pp. 53-55.

[18] Buckland, *Textbook of Roman Law,* p. 112.

[19] *Christian Marriage,* p. 42, footnote 1.

[20] II Kings, III:13; Deut., XXII:24.

[21] Matt., I:20.

[22] Matt., I:18.

[23] Matt., I:19; Luke, I:27.

Rabbinical Law declared bethrothals to be equivalent to actual marriage.[24] As to the requirement of consent, very little was known. The giving of the girl's consent was implied, it seems, in the father's consent. Rab, the Babylonian, who lived toward the end of the second and the beginning of the third century after Christ,[25] acknowledged as severely punishable the act of anyone who married his betrothed partner without her consent.[26]

After the espousal, the nuptials did not take place until after a period of waiting had run its course. This was the custom despite the fact that an actual, inchoate marriage had already taken place at the espousal. The nuptials were merely a celebration which ended with the solemn escorting of the betrothed woman to the bedchamber of the man. It is interesting to note that no further expression of marital consent was deemed necessary; the consent given in the espousals was considered marital consent. For all intents and purposes the couple were considered man and wife, in an inchoate, i.e., unconsummated marriage. This helped the early Fathers of the Church to explain the espousals of the Blessed Mother and St. Joseph as a true marriage, and later served as a foundation for the opinion that the early Church considered *desponsatio,* for all intents and purposes, a true marriage.

The Roman and Jewish systems were not the only systems with which the Church had to reckon. From the fifth century onward, the Church came in contact with the Germanic peoples from the north. Their customs were widely different. Whereas normally the betrothal is a promise of a future marriage, among the Germanic tribes it was no mere promise of a future contract, but at least the

[24] Neufeld, *Ancient Hebrew Marriage Laws* (New York: Longmans, 1944), pp. 84, 142-143. However, Freisen (*op. cit.,* p. 97) claimed that the betrothal did not constitute marriage; that it did not make married people of them till the *copula carnalis* took place.

[25] Freisen, *op. cit.,* p. 92. The reference is probably to Abba Arika (usually called Rab), who died in 247. He was a Babylonian Rabbi who founded the Jewish Academy of Sura (on the Euphrates in Syria). He was recognized as among the greatest of the haggadists of the Babylonian schools.

[26] *The Babylonian Talmud, Kidduschim* (London: Sancino Press, 1936), Kid. 13 a.

initial stage of the contract, the nuptials serving simply as a ratification of the same.[27]

One might say that the Germanic conception of a betrothal held a middle ground between the mere promise of the Romans and the actual, inchoate marriage as recognized by the Jews; if anything, the resemblance favored the latter more than the former. In the beginning not much attention was paid to the girl's will in the matter; she had to obey her *mundoaldus*.[28] However, with the advent of Christianity, greater respect was paid to the girl's wishes; her consent was required.[29]

In the Lombard Kingdom in Northern Italy (568-774), it was customary previous to the actual nuptials for the couple to make a formal declaration of their consent to the union before the local assembly. At this ceremony an *orator* or *Fürsprecher* played an important part; it was his office to ask and receive the consent of the parties to the marriage. As time went on, it became customary to relegate this to the marriage itself, with friends and relatives taking the part of the local assembly.[30] The presence of witnesses was required by law, either at the betrothal, or at the nuptials, or at both, to give them a public character; clandestine marriages were frowned upon.[31]

The betrothal was essential for a marriage with *mundium*, the only *matrimonium legitimum*. Of itself, however, it was not sufficient

[27] Joyce, *Christian Marriage*, pp. 48-50.

[28] This was similar to the *patria potestas* and the *paterfamilias* system known to the Romans.

[29] *Edictum Rothari, a. 643*, n. 182, 195; *Liutprandi Leges anno septimo decimo* (a. 729), 17—*Leges Longobardorum*—*Monumenta Germaniae Historica, Leges* (5 vols., Vols. I-IV, ed. G. Pertz; Vol. V, edd. G. Pertz, G. Waitz, H. Brunner, Hannoverae, 1835-1899), IV, pp. 41, 42, 154 (*Monumenta Germaniae Historica* will be cited hereafter *MGH*); *Chlothaharici I Regis Constitutio*, n. 7—*MGH, Leges*, I, 2; cf. also the Capitulary of King Pippin in 757—*MGH, Leges*, I, 28.

[30] Von Hörmann, *Quasi-Affinität* (2 vols., Innsbruck, 1897-1906), II, 194; Friedberg, *Das Recht der Eheschliessung* (Leipzig, 1865), p. 25; Joyce, *Christian Marriage*, p. 49.

[31] *Lex Visigothorum Recessvindo rege edita a. 654*, III, 1,3 and III, 4,2—*MGH, Legum Sectio I*, Vol. I, *Lex Visigothorum* (ed. K. Zeumer, Hannoverae, 1902), p. 122; *Pippini Capitulare Vernense, a. 755*—*MGH, Leges*, I, 26.

to constitute marriage. There was needed besides a handing over of the bride to the groom. This *deductio* was necessary in every marriage, even in a *matrimonium non legitimum* (one recognized by law, but remaining without full legal effects), for it really sealed the marriage contract. After this *deductio* the couple remained chaste for three days and thereafter went to the church for Mass, Communion and the nuptial blessing.[32] Later it became customary to exchange consent *ante valvas ecclesiae*; in time, the priest began to take part in this ceremony. The couple then entered the church for Mass, Communion and the nuptial blessing.

The State legislated against clandestine marriages because of the divers evils that flowed therefrom. One finds even civil legislation prescribing that no one should marry without the knowledge of the priest of the place and his own relatives. At first the priest acted as an investigator whose office it was to give a *"nihil obstat"* to the marriage, and then the nuptial blessing subsequent to the marriage. As time went on his office grew in importance.

Article II. Church Customs and Laws on Marriage

In its infancy, the Church had no ecclesiastically prescribed form for marriage. It simply accepted the customs and laws of the peoples with which it came into contact, keeping what was not contrary to its doctrine on faith and morals, and developing some customs of its own. The faithful were ordered to observe the civil laws of their native countries.[33] Never was any form of marriage prescribed for validity.

[32] Vestiges of this remained as late as the eleventh century. Cf. *Anselmi Lucensis Collectio Canonum,* lib. X, c. 2—(ed. Thaner, Oeniponte, 1906), p. 483.

[33] Tertullian, *Ad Uxorem,* II, c. 9: ". . . rite et iure nubunt."—Migne, *Patrologiae Cursus Completus, Series Latina* (221 vol., Parisiis, 1844-1855), I, 1302 (hereafter cited *MPL*); *Corpus Scriptorum Ecclesiasticorum Latinorum* (71 vols., incomplete, Vindobonae, 1866-), LXX, 123 (hereafter cited *CSEL*). Pope Nicholas I in his *Responsa ad Bulgaros* (cf. *MPL,* CXIX, 979; Jaffé, *Regesta Pontificum Romanorum ab condita Ecclesia ad annum post Christum natum MCXCVIII* [2. ed., 2 vols., correctam et auctam auspiciis Gulielmi Wattenbach curaverunt F. Kaltenbrunner ad annum 590, P. Ewald ab anno 590 ad annum 882, S. Loewenfeld ab anno 882 ad annum 1198, Lipsiae, 1885-1888], JE, n. 2312 [hereafter cited as JK, JE, or JL]; *MGH, Epistulae,* Vol. VI [Karolini Aevi IV], pars prior [curante Ernesto Dümmler, Hannoverae,

The early Fathers of the Church treated of marriages mostly in conjunction with their doctrine regarding the true marriage between the Blessed Mother and St. Joseph and in connection with their teaching on the espousals of virgins to Christ. Since betrothals as incidental to marriage were customary among the Romans and necessary among the Jews and Germanic peoples, the early Christians found no difficulty in accepting this practice. Besides, they had the example of the Blessed Mother, who herself had been espoused. As in all the customs mentioned above, there was a period of waiting between the betrothal and the nuptials. Augustine (354-430) mentioned this in his sermons.[34]

It seems that from very early days a sacred rite was attached to the celebration of the nuptials, only subsequent to which followed the cohabitation of the wedded pair. St. Ignatius (+ 107) in his letter to St. Polycarp wrote: "For those of both sexes who contemplate marriage it is proper to enter the union with the sanction of the bishop."[35] Tertullian (ca. 160-ca. 230) spoke of a marriage ceremony that was employed perhaps as a refinement of the *confarreatio* ceremony, wherein pagan sacrifices were supplanted with the holy sacrifice of the Mass.[36]

The celebrated text regarding the formation of marriage comes from the famous *Responsa ad Bulgaros* of Pope Nicholas I (858-867).[37] In his reply to a series of questions proposed by the Bulgarian Christians, the Pope delineated the customs connected with the celebrating of marriages as they were observed at Rome. He wrote that the customs were accepted by the Church in very ancient

1902]; pars II, fasc. I [curante Ernesto Perels, Berolini, 1925], pars II, fasc. I, pp. 569-570) refers to the Roman Laws as *venerandae*—". . . nec inter eos venerandae Romanae leges matrimonium contrahi permittunt."

[34] E.g., *MPL*, XXXIV, 452; *CSEL*, XXVIII, 376.

[35] *Epistola ad Polycarpum*, V, 3—Migne, *Patrologiae Cursus Completus, Series Graeca* (161 vols., Parisiis, 1857-1866), V, 867 (hereafter cited *MPG*). Translation from *The Epistles of St. Clement of Rome and St. Ignatius of Antioch* (translation by James A. Kleist), Ancient Christian Writers, The Works of the Fathers in Translation, n. 1 (Westminster: Newman, 1946), p. 98.

[36] *Ad Uxorem*, II, c. 9—*MPL*, I, 1302; *CSEL*, LXX, 123.

[37] JE, n. 2312; *MPL*, CXIX, 979-980; *MGH, Epistulae*, VI, pars II, fasc. I, pp. 569-570.

times, and that it still held them. The Roman Pontiff then divided the entire process into four stages. There was first a betrothal, which was then followed by the rite of the *desponsatio,* at which a ring was placed on the woman's finger. Thirdly, there followed the celebration of the Mass either immediately (*mox*) or at some convenient time (*aut apto tempore*). Lastly there was the crowning of the couple as they were leaving the church. This decretal had a great influence in the development of the Church's law; it meant that the Church had accepted the classic Roman Law on the formation of marriage.[38] This, said the Pope, was the custom at Rome. However, one may say that it seems to have been the custom also in the Frankish and Lombard Kingdoms.[39]

If there was one matter that the Church stressed as essential from the very beginning, it was consent. It adopted the old Roman principle: *Consensus, non concubitus, facit nuptias.* Tertullian, speaking of betrothal, treated it as a foretaste of marriage, for *"mens per voluntatem exprimitur."* [40] It is not the deflowering of a virgin but rather the conjugal pact that constitutes marriage.[41] St. John Chrysostom (354-407), according to Pope Nicholas I, in his Homily 32, on St. Matthew, taught that *"matrimonium non facit coitus, sed voluntas."* [42]

In the same context, Pope Nicholas I made it clear that it is consent alone that brings marriage into existence. Even if all the ceremonies mentioned by him had been omitted, as long as matrimonial consent was present, there existed a marriage. Pope Hadrian II (867-872), successor of Nicholas I, in a reply to a question proposed to him in the year 872, answered that, inasmuch as a marriage was entered into *utriusque partis assensu,* it must be considered a true marriage and was not to be dissolved.[43]

It was for this reason that the Church had trouble with clan-

[38] Von Hörmann, *Quasi-Affinität,* II, 217.

[39] Von Hörmann, *op. cit.,* II, 187, footnote.

[40] *De Oratione,* c. 22—*MPL,* I, 1190; *CSEL,* XX, 196.

[41] St. Ambrose, *De Institutione Virginis,* VI, 41—*MPL,* XVI, 315.

[42] *Responsa ad Bulgaros*—*MPL,* CXIX, 980; *MGH, Epistulae,* VI, pars II, fasc. 1, pp. 560-570.

[43] JE, n. 2948; *MPL,* CXXII, 1318.

destine marriages. True, it was prescribed that marriages should take place publicly; still, if they were entered into secretly, they were considered as true marriages.

The priest is mentioned as taking part in the nuptials from the very beginning.[44] His presence was prescribed either for a confirming of the agreement (marriage) already existing, or for the blessing of it.[45] Despite the fact that his presence was either assumed or even called for, nowhere was it prescribed for the validity of the marriage. In fact, marriages contracted apart from his presence were deemed valid as long as consent had been manifested.[46]

Any history of the development of the formation of marriage in the early Church would not be complete without a mention of the meaning of the *desponsatio* ceremony and the *copula* theory. In the early Church, the *desponsatio* had a great significance. It seems that the *desponsatio* was looked upon as a real marriage, the nuptial ceremony being performed simply *"ad honestandam mulierem."* Two canonists of the Eastern Church stated that in the Mosaic Law *sponsalia* constituted a true marriage.[47]

The Fathers used the term *sponsa* for wife, i.e., at least for one who had not as yet begun physical relationship with her husband.[48] Further evidence is found in conciliar legislation and papal decretals concerning the sacredness and apparent indissolubility of the *desponsatio.*[49] In view of all these decisions it is easy to see how Von

[44] *Epistola Sti. Ignatii ad Polycarpum—MPG,* V, 867; Tertullian, *De Pudicitia,* c. 4—*MPL,* II, 987; *CSEL,* XX, 225.

[45] Possidius, *Vita Sti. Augustini Episcopi—MPL,* XXXII, 56.

[46] JE, n. 2948; *MPL,* CXXII, 1318.

[47] Matthaeus Blastares, *Syntagma Alphabeticum,* c. XV—*MPG,* CXLIV, 1186; Theodorus Balsamon, *In Concilium in Trullo,* c. 98—*MPG,* CXXXVII, 854.

[48] Ambrose, *De Institutione Virginis—MPL,* XVI, 315; Tertullian, *De Virginibus Velandis—MPL,* II, 897; Cyprian, *Epistola ad Pomponium—MPL,* IV, 368; *CSEL,* III, pars 2, p. 475; Augustine, *De Nuptiis et Concupiscentiis—MPL,* XLIV, 420; *CSEL,* XLII, p. 224.

[49] *Concilium Ancyranum* (314), c. 11—Bruns, I, 68; Hardouin, I, 276; Mansi, II, 525; St. Eusebius (+ 309)—JK, n. 169; Mansi, II, 425; Siricius (384-399), in his letter to Himerius, Bishop of Tarragona—JK, n. 255; *MPL,* XIII, 1136; Mansi, III, 655; St. Gelasius (492-496)—JK, n. 692; Nicholas I in his reply to Addo, Archbishop of Vienne (860-875)—JE, n. 2697; *MPL,* CXIX, 796; *MGH, Epistulae,* VI, pars II, fasc. 1, p. 619.

Hörmann (1865-1946) at the beginning of this century pointed to them as proof that the early Christians combined the rites of the betrothal and marriage, so that the ceremony was no longer simply a promise of a future marriage, but the actual marriage itself.[50] This opinion has probability, but a definitive answer cannot be given.

As for the *copula* theory, its origin is hidden in obscurity.[51] A staunch defense of it can be found in *"De Nuptiis Stephani et filiae Regimundi comitis"* composed by Hincmar of Rheims (+ 882). In this work, the Archbishop contended that consummation is essential to marriage, and that without it there is no union of the partners.[52] Von Hörmann thought that Hincmar held the consent to be sufficient for the marriage, but also that the *copula* was necessary if the marriage was likewise to be a sacrament.[53]

There is no difficulty in seeing the possibility of error on Hincmar's part. He based his doctrine on what he thought had been the tradition of the Church. His argument was taken from what he thought emanated from St. Augustine[54] and St. Leo I (440-461). However, although the words he quoted from St. Augustine had been ascribed to the latter during the Middle Ages, they cannot be found in any of his works.[55] In regard to St. Leo I, Hincmar simply offered a mistaken interpretation of a decretal sent by that Pope to Bishop Rusticus of Narbonne.[56]

In summary, one may say that "the variety of marriage customs current among Christian nations prevented the Church from singling out any one rite as essential. She did not want to multiply sins; hence, she moved slowly." [57]

[50] *Quasi-Affinität,* II, 1-223.

[51] Esmein, *Le Mariage in Droit Canonique* (2 vols., Paris, 1891), I, 99.

[52] *MPL,* CXXVI, 137.

[53] *Quasi-Affinität,* II, p. 423, n. 2.

[54] *MPL,* CXXVI, 137.

[55] Joyce, *Christian Marriage,* p. 56.

[56] JK, n. 544; *MPL,* LIV, 1204; Joyce, *op. cit.,* p. 56.

[57] Pollock and Maitland, *History of English Law,* II, 370.

CHAPTER II

THE FORM OF MARRIAGE FROM THE DECREE OF GRATIAN (CA. 1140) TO THE COUNCIL OF TRENT (1545-1563)

ARTICLE I. THE DISPUTE BETWEEN THE SCHOOLS OF BOLOGNA AND PARIS.

WHEN Gratian (+ca. 1157) set out to make a collection of the existing canons, he found a maze of seemingly contrary, and at times contradictory, texts and decretals. In fact, the name he gave to his collection—*Concordia Discordantium Canonum*—is well descriptive of its contents. It is to be expected that he encountered the same difficulty in regard to the canons on the formation of marriage.

At the time he made his collection, there were four possibilities, or theories, if one may use that term, that he had to keep in mind. Naturally he had to remember that the Church, from the very beginning, held to the Roman concept that consent, and not sexual relations, made the marriage. Secondly, there was the theory that consent was not sufficient; that a *copula carnalis* was necessary to conclude the marriage, since only then would the union of Christ and His Church be symbolized and the sacrament be present. Thirdly, he needed to advert to the great importance that the *desponsatio* held in the Church. It was believed that the consent given at the *desponsatio* became in time the marital consent. Finally, he had to recall that the requirement that each couple receive the nuptial blessing before they began to cohabit was still being observed by some and neglected by others.

Because of these various possibilities, it was inevitable that a dispute would arise when Gratian presented his solution for the problem. Two schools of thought arose as to what really constituted marriage in its full existence, viz., the School of Bologna, which followed Gratian, and the School of Paris, which followed Hugh of St. Victor (+ 1141) and Peter Lombard's treatment of marriage in his

Book of Sentences (1150-1152). The former School held for the *copula* theory; the latter held for the consent theory, championing the existence of a true marriage between the Blessed Virgin Mary and St. Joseph. When this dispute was settled, it was decided once and for all what was essential in the formation of marriage.

A. *The Decree of Gratian and the School of Bologna*

In question 2 of the 27th Cause, Gratian offered his doctrine on the formation of marriage. In the first section of this question [1] he cited texts that seem to substantiate the theory that consent alone brings the marriage into existence; that such consent is present in the *desponsatio*; and that the *sponsus* and *sponsa* are true *coniuges*. In the following section of the same question [2] he presents the contrary thesis, namely, that a *copula carnalis* was necessary for the constituting of the marriage,[3] and that the *desponsati* are not true *coniuges*. In his *Dictum* to c. 29, there is found the weakest point of his whole solution, for there he proceeded contrary to tradition by maintaining that the Blessed Virgin and St. Joseph were not man and wife.[4]

The solution he reached was that through the *desponsatio* (es-

[1] Cc. 1-15, C. XXVII, q. 2.

[2] Cc. 16-34, C. XXVII, q. 2.

[3] He cited a text from St. Augustine (c. 16) and one from Pope Leo I (c. 17). According to Friedberg, *Corpus Iuris Canonici* (2. ed., 2 vols. in 3, Lipsiae, 1879-1881), I, pars 2, col. 1066, footnotes 123 ff. to c. xvi, the one ascribed to St. Augustine is spurious, and the one ascribed to Pope Leo I is not reproduced as it is found in the original; a *non* was inserted to change the meaning of the original, viz., Gratian has: "Cum societas nuptiarum ita a principio sit instituta, ut praeter communionem sexuum *non* habeant in se nuptiae Christi et ecclesiae sacramentum . . .," while the other reading, as found in MSS of Pope Leo's writings, and as found in Burchard and Ivo, has instead of *"non habeant,"* the word *"haberet."* However, Friedberg added immediately that the text in Gratian is also found in Ivo's *Panormia*, VI, 23: ". . . in Pan. tamen VI, 23 sunt ut ap. Grat." The Correctors in the edition of 1582 allowed it to remain "ut respondeat verbis Gratiani, qui manifeste utitur hoc loco depravato, itemque Magistri, et glossae, et posteriorum doctorum, nihil est in textu mutatum." Friedberg also allowed it to remain.

[4] "Unde apparet eos non fuisse coniuges."

pousals) marriage was indeed begun, but was completed only through a union of the sexes. Hence, between the spouses there is only an inchoate or incipient marriage. Summarizing his theory one must say that marriage was brought into existence only with the *copula*. The consent, which was necessary, was simply a *conditio sine qua non*; the *copula*, however, was essential. The consent effected an incipient marriage (*matrimonium initiatum*), but only the *copula* made it a complete and perfect marriage (*matrimonium ratum*).

In treating of clandestine marriages in *Causa XXX, q. 5,* he showed that they were forbidden. However, if they did take place, they were indeed to be judged as illegal, but nonetheless as true marriages, valid and indissoluble.

The Bolognese School of canonists adhered strictly to the teaching of Gratian; what is more, they went even further. Whereas in c. 50, C. XXVII, q. 2, Gratian seemed not to allow the breaking of a solemn espousal blessed by the Church, the School did not accept this as an exception to the rule that a *copula* after a second espousal nullified the first espousal if it had not been accompanied with a *copula*.[5] Besides, they enumerated eight reasons in consequence of which an unconsummated "*desponsatio*" could be dissolved.[6]

B. *Peter Lombard and the School of Paris*

The other view prevalent at the time also found many defenders. St. Peter Damian (+ 1072) rejected as absurd the contention that the *copula* made the marriage.[7] However, it was the University at Paris and the French Church that bore the brunt of the defense of the traditional doctrine. It fell to Peter Lombard (ca. 1100-ca. 1160) in his Four Books of Sentences to present the view held by the School of Paris. He it was who introduced the distinction between the *consensus de praesenti* and the *consensus de futuro* to explain the two different kinds of *desponsatio*. It served to eliminate the

[5] *Summa Paucapaleae,* C. XXVII, q. 2—ed. Von Schulte (Giessen: Roth, 1890), p. 114.

[6] E.g., Rufinus, *Summa Decretorum,* C. XXVII, q. 2—ed. H. Singer (Paderborn, 1902), p. 443.

[7] *De tempore celebrandi nuptias—MPL,* CXLV, 660.

arbitrary usage of the latter term in two distinctly different senses. His one big aim was to vindicate the relationship between the Blessed Virgin and St. Joseph as a true marriage.

According to Peter Lombard, the efficient cause of marriage is consent, not any consent, but one that is expressed in words of the present, and not in words of the future tense. If the consent were *de futuro,* or merely internal and not externalized in any manner, marriage would not be effected.[8] It should be apparent that consent brings marriage into existence even if no *copula carnalis* either preceded or followed the exchange of consent. Using this distinction, he was able to explain the existence of a true marriage between the Blessed Virgin and St. Joseph and also the fact that *sponsi* could leave each other, exchange consent with someone else or choose to enter a monastery as long as the first *desponsatio* had remained only *de futuro.* If it was *de praesenti* this could not be done.

As for clandestine marriages, they were considered prohibited and sinful if there was not a sufficient reason for contracting them thus. However, they were valid.[9]

C. *Settling of the Dispute*

A solution for this problem which evoked such a diversity of opinion, which in turn led also to a diversity of practice, was reached toward the end of the twelfth and the beginning of the thirteenth century, largely through the course of action adopted by Pope Alexander III (1159-1181). The latter, as Rolando Bandinelli, prior to his elevation to the papacy, wrote a *Summa Decretorum,* in which he followed the Bolognese School; as Pope, on the other hand, he leaned more toward the School of Paris. He decided in favor of

[8] *Lib. IV Sententiarum,* Dist. xxvii, c. 3—*Libri Sententiarum Quatuor* (2. ed., 2 vols., cura et studiis PP. Collegii S. Bonaventurae, ad Claras Aquas [Florentiae], 1916), II, 917; cf. also *MPL,* CXCIV, 910. In the same vein also St. Thomas Aquinas, *Super Libris Magistri Sententiarum Libri Quatuor,* lib. IV, Dist. xxvii, art. 2.—*Opera Omnia* (25 vols., Misurgia: New York, 1948-1950) XXII, 403-408.

[9] *Lib. IV Sententiarum,* Dist. xxviii, q. 2.—*MPL, loc. cit.*; ed. PP. Coll. S. Bonav., II, 926.

the theory that consent alone was sufficient if it was a consent *de praesenti.*[10]

If one sought briefly to summarize the doctrine of Alexander III, one could say that he held for the sufficiency of a consent *de praesenti* in the constituting of marriage; consummation made the marriage indissoluble. He put an end to the dispute, once and for all; the Church's doctrine on the efficient cause of marriage was definitely established. The succeeding popes issued decretals totally in harmony with this doctrine. Nevertheless, it took some time before a uniformity in practice was reached. Innocent III (1198-1216) reprimanded the diocese of Modena for not disposing of the old custom and for not keeping the law of Rome.[11]

Article II. Clandestine Marriages Before the Council of Trent

A matter which was a source of much trouble and grief to the Church in the Middle Ages now merits attention—the matter of clandestine marriages. Although the Church had not prescribed any form of marriage that had to be observed under pain of nullity, it seems that the Church had little, if any, trouble with clandestine marriages in its early history. The complete lack of conciliar legislation and papal decretals on this matter seems to bear evidence to this contention. Even Pope Nicholas I stated that it would not be a sin for poor people if they did not observe the ceremony of marriage as described by him.[12] It hardly seems incongruous to assume that, had there been any difficulty in this regard, the popes would have seized their opportunities to prohibit clandestine unions.

That many persons in time must have contracted marriages secretly, i.e., without seeking the Church's blessing, is quite evident from the complaint of Bishop Jonas of Orleans (+ 844),[13] and from

[10] C. 14, X, *de sponsalibus et matrimonio,* IV, 1; c. 3, X, *de sponsa duorum,* IV, 4; c. 2, X, *de conversione coniugatorum,* III, 32.

[11] C. 5, X, *de sponsa duorum,* IV, 4.

[12] *Responsa ad Bulgaros—MPL,* CXIX, 980; *MGH, Epistulae* VI, pars II, fasc. 1, pp. 569-570.

[13] *De Institutione Laicali,* II, c. 2—*MPL,* CVI, 171.

the compiler of the Pseudo-Isidorian Decretals.[14] Once the trouble began, the Church had no peace in this regard till the reform at the Council of Trent.

A marriage could be considered clandestine if:

(1) it was contracted apart from the presence of witnesses who, if the occasion arose, could testify to its celebration;

(2) the solemnities mentioned by Pope Nicholas I in the *Responsa ad Bulgaros* and incorporated in C. XXX, q. 5 of the *Drecretum Gratiani* were omitted;

(3) later, i.e., after the IV General Council of the Lateran (1215), the banns, then a prescribed formality, were omitted.[15]

Despite the prohibitions from the ecclesiastical and civil laws, such marriages had to stand as valid unions. They ran the risk of being judged as concubinage until the contrary could be proved. It is interesting to note that the two schools of thought on the formation of marriage, even though they engaged in acrimonious disputes on the main point at issue, nevertheless agreed that clandestine marriages were valid.[16] No evidence is found that the popes ever declared marriages invalid on the ground of clandestinity. Finally, conciliar legislation forbidding such marriages in the strongest terms never questioned their validity.[17]

[14] Hinschius, *Decretales Pseudo-Isidorianae et Capitula Angilramni* (Lipsiae, 1863), 87.

[15] *Glossa ordinaria* sub v. *clandestina,* ad c. 4, X, *de clandestina desponsatione,* IV, 3. Cf. also Hostiensis, *Summa Aurea* (Venetiis, 1570), p. 334, where a fourth type was added, namely, a marriage contracted without the permission of the bishop, if, for some reason, the person was forbidden by the Church to marry.

[16] *Dictum* post c. 8, C. XXX, q. 5; *Summa Paucapaleae,* C. XXX, q. 5, ed. Von Schulte, p. 123; St. Thomas Aquinas, *Super Libris Magistri Sententiarum* Liber IV, Dist. xxviii, art. iv: "Nam de essentia matrimonii sunt personae legitimae ad contrahendum quasi materia, et consensus per verba de praesenti expressus quasi forma. Alia sunt de solemnitate sacramenti; unde cum desunt in matrimonio clandestino, veritatem matrimonii non tollunt, licet contrahentes peccent nisi habeant excusationem legitimam."

[17] *IV Concilium Lateranense* (1215)—Mansi, XXII, 1038; *Concilium Lan-*

Why did it not declare all such marriages invalid and avoid all the confusion and difficulty stemming from such marriages? Joyce, in his *Christian Marriage,* p. 116, gives the following answer:

> The answer is that it was widely believed that she lacked the power to take such a step. The greater number of theologians held that the matter and form of each sacrament had been determined by Christ Himself; that the Church had authority only as regards their administration but could not make any law affecting the validity of the sacred sign itself. . . . From this it seemed to follow that if two persons, whose union was not hindered by a diriment impediment, chose to give each other the mutual pledge which was commonly held to furnish the matter and form of the Sacrament of Matrimony, not even the Church herself could prevent the sacrament from efficaciously being conferred. All that could be done was to forbid such marriages under the pain of mortal sin and impose the greatest ecclesiastical censures on all who should violate the command.

gensiense (Langeais) (1278)—Mansi, XXIV, 627; *Praecepta Antiqua Dioecesis Rotomagensis* (Rouen) (1235)—Mansi, XXIII, 383.

CHAPTER III

THE DISCIPLINE FROM THE DECREE *TAMETSI* OF THE COUNCIL OF TRENT TO THE DECREE *NE TEMERE* (1907)

WHEN the Fathers of the Council of Trent came together in the year 1545, they were faced with what seemed a superhuman task of clarifying and explaining the dogmas of the Church, and with what seemed even more insurmountable, a sorely needed disciplinary reform. One of the matters that cried for reform was the marriage discipline, especially the grave evil of clandestine marriages which had been plaguing the Church for about five hundred years, necessitating legislation by particular and even general councils as well as iterative condemnation in the decretals of the Roman Pontiffs. It was here that for the first time a universally prescribed form of marriage was proposed and adopted.

ARTICLE 1. THE FORM OF MARRIAGE ACCORDING TO THE DECREE *Tametsi*

Despite the fact that it was clearly evident that some type of reform had to take place in regard to clandestine marriages, many of the Fathers at the Council rebelled at the idea of invalidating clandestine marriages. When the first draft of the marriage discipline was proposed, there were many objections. The usual reasons given were, first, that such marriages had always been recognized as valid in the eyes of the Church; [1] secondly, that if the proposal were accepted, then the Church would be overstepping its bounds by tampering with the matter and form of a sacrament, a power not accorded by its Divine Founder, and, thirdly, that the Church could not forestall the reception of a sacrament as long as a couple other-

[1] Conc. Trident., sess. XXIV *de ref. matrim.*, c. 1: "Tametsi dubitandum non est clandestina matrimonia libero contrahentium consensu facta, rata et vera esse matrimonia quamdiu ecclesia ea irrita non fecit. . . ."—Schulte-Richter, *Canones et Decreta Concilii Tridentini* (Lipsiae, 1863), pp. 216-217 (hereafter cited Schulte).

wise capable of entering marriage would exchange consent in terms of the present, for that was all that was required by the natural law for the contract of marriage.

The arguments against these objections were well explained by Laymann (1574-1635),[2] who used the analogy of the State invalidating *ipso iure,* for the common good, contracts of minors, profligates, etc., by rendering these persons *inhabiles* (incapable) and the contracts null if they lacked certain solemnities. If this was so, then the Church, because of the fact that marriage is a sacrament and consequently falls under its jurisdiction, could aso, for the good of souls, render those who attempted to contract marriage secretly, i. e., without the prescribed solemnity, incapable of contracting marriage. He thereby answered the difficulty of the Church's apparent changing of the matter and form in the sacrament of matrimony. He conceded that the Church cannot directly (*per se*) change or invalidate the matter or the form of a sacrament as instituted by Christ. However, he added, it can do so indirectly (*per accidens*). It does this by invalidating the natural contract of marriage if it is entered into clandestinely. Such a contract thenceforth would not be *"legitimus"* and *"ex institutione Christi in legitima viri ac foeminae coniunctione seu contractu sacramentum fundatur."*

After three proposed texts proved unsatisfactory, a fourth one was proposed and finally adopted on November 11, 1563, even though a large number of dissident votes were cast. The approved text became the universal marriage discipline under the well-known name of *Tametsi,* taken from the first word of the text of the law.

A. *The Essential Points of the Decree* Tametsi

Despite the fact that the Council of Trent instituted a universally prescribed form of marriage, nevertheless this form did not bind everywhere in the world. The Fathers of the Council enjoined each ordinary, as soon as he possibly could, to promulgate this as the Law of the Council of Trent in every parish of his diocese, and

[2] *Theologia Moralis in quinque Libros Distributa—editio nova ab auctore recognita et primum in Italia excussa* (Venetiis, 1630), lib. V, tract X, pars II, c. 4 (hereafter cited Laymann).

that this should be done as often as possible in the first year, and afterwards as often as he deemed it expedient. Further, the Council prescribed that only after thirty days from the first day of publication in a parish was this law to take effect there.[3]

The territoriality of this law depended on its promulgation and explanation in the parish in question. If the ordinary did not promulgate it in his diocese; or, if he promulgated it in Latin without explaining it, it would not bind in his diocese. Promulgation and explanation of the decree *Tametsi* as the law of the Council of Trent, but only in some of the parishes of the diocese and not in the others, would make the law obligatory only within the boundaries of the parishes within which it was promulgated. It was for this reason that there were many places throughout the world where this law did not bind because of its non-promulgation. In those places the former discipline of the Church obtained.

Just as the decree *Tametsi* was not universally binding in its territorial aspect, so too it was not universally obligatory in its personal aspect. Inasmuch as it was a purely ecclesiastical law, it could bind only baptized persons, whether Catholics or heretics, who because of their baptism became subject to the laws of the Church. The heretics were not exempt from this form, for they were not to benefit through their defection from the Faith. Because of this fact, many invalid marriages were contracted by heretics.[4] Since it was baptism that made one subject to this law, non-baptism left one free of this obligation. Hence, infidels, even though they lived in a territory where the law was promulgated, were not bound by this law. They had to follow the prescripts of the civil law, if any, or follow the prescripts of the natural law.

Besides, it was necessary to have a domicile in the territory where the law obliged, for marriage had to be contracted before one's proper pastor, or a priest delegated by the pastor or the ordinary. If the baptized party had a domicile where the law obliged,

[3] Conc. Trident., sess. XXIV *de ref. matrim.*, c. 1—Schulte, p. 216.

[4] This was so until the Benedictine Declaration of Pope Benedict XIV on November 14, 1741, by which heretics were freed from the obligation of observing the decree *Tamesti.* Cf. Denzinger, *Enchiridion Symbolorum et Definitionum* (ed. decima emendata et aucta a Clemente Bannwart, Friburgi Brisgoviae, 1908), nn. 1452-1457.

he could not, to circumvent the law, go to a place where the law did not oblige, in order to contract marriage there. However, a person bound by the decree *Tametsi,* when wishing to contract marriage with a person not bound thereby, was freed of this obligation because of the well-known principle in pre-Code jurisprudence: the party free of the obligation of observing the form communicated this immunity to the other party.[5]

To conciliate the divergent opinions and to avoid giving the impression that they were changing the matter and form of the sacrament of matrimony, the Fathers of the Council of Trent made clandestinity a diriment impediment to marriage. They decreed that anyone who would in the future attempt to contract marriage in any other way than in the presence of the pastor, or of another priest delegated by the pastor or the ordinary, and of two or three witnesses would be completely incapable of contracting such a marriage, and all such marriages would be null.[6] To contract marriage validly, then, wherever the decree *Tametsi* obliged, the parties had to do so in the presence of the proper pastor, who did not necessarily have to be a priest,[7] or in the presence of some authorized priest and of at least two witnesses. If this form was not observed, the marriage was termed clandestine and, as such, invalid, because of the diriment impediment of clandestinity.

B. *Provisions When the Form Could Not Be Observed*

Because of the general wording of the law, seemingly not admitting any exceptions, a natural question arose quite soon after its adoption at the Council of Trent. What would happen in the event that no priest was present to witness the marriage? Would it mean that the people in those circumstances would be incapable

[5] ". . . pars immunis a forma servanda communicat cum altera parte suam immunitatem."—Benedictus XIV, *De Synodo Dioecesana* (2 vols., secunda Parmensis editio, Parmae, 1744), lib. 6, c. 6, n. 1 (hereafter cited *De Synodo*).

[6] Schulte, p. 217.

[7] At the time, a parochial benefice could be conferred upon a cleric, i. e., one who had already received at least Tonsure. Under the present discipline (c. 453, § 1), it is necessary that one have received the Sacred Order of Priesthood before one can be appointed pastor.

of entering marriage? Such an unhappy eventuality would not affect those who were not held to the prescribed form.[8] For these people what would normally be a clandestine marriage would be a valid marriage under any circumstances. It would be illicit if no excusing reason was present. The difficulty would arise when one had to deal with persons held to the form of marriage. It was the development of the discipline in answer to this difficulty that led to the present-day institute of the extraordinary form of marriage.

In a work that appeared shortly after the Council of Trent, Dominic Soto (1494-1560), in commenting on the opinions of Peter Lombard in the latter's *Book of Sentences,* asked himself whether clandestine marriages would ever be licit. His reply[9] mentioned four cases which to him seemed to permit one to contract clandestinely: first, after a union had been contracted *in facie ecclesiae* but with an occult impediment, the validation could take place secretly; secondly, in case of urgent necessity, when witnesses could not be had, e. g., in an invasion or in a case of patent fornication, the couple could with view to saving their life, contract marriage immediately to pose as husband and wife; thirdly, if a girl were to lose her patrimony through the machinations of her guardian; finally, if later there would be no opportunity of marriage. To this list Tanner (1571-1632) added a fifth case, namely, that the marriage could not without grave damage be contracted openly.[10] One must keep in mind that Soto died before the decree *Tametsi* was approved, even though the edition of his work here cited was not published till after his death.

[8] Cf. S. C. S. Off. (Sutchuen), 15 ian. 1784—*Collectanea Sacrae Congregationis de Propaganda Fide* (Romae: Typographia Polyglotta S. C. de Prop. Fide, 1893), n. 1394 (hereafter cited *Collectanea S. C. de Prop. Fide,* ed. 1893); *Collectanea Sacrae Congregationis de Propaganda Fide* (2 vols., Romae, 1907), n. 566 (hereafter cited *Collectanea S. C. de Prop. Fide,* ed. 1907); *Codicis Iuris Canonici Fontes,* cura Emi Petri Card. Gasparri editi (9 vols., Romae: Typis Polyglottis Vaticanis, 1923-1939. Vols. VII-IX, ed. cura et studio Emi Iustiniani Card. Serédi), n. 846 (hereafter cited *Fontes*).

[9] *Commentarium in Quartum Sententiarum* (2 vols., Venetiis, 1584), lib. IV, dist. 28, q. 1, art. II.

[10] Apud Schmalzgrueber (1663-1735), *Ius Ecclesiasticum Universum* (5 vols. in 12, Romae, 1843-1845), lib. IV, tit. III, c. 2, n. 104 (hereafter cited as Schmalzgrueber).

This opinion allowing clandestine marriages under such circumstances never found much favor, and was reprobated by subsequent authors, usually indirectly, but at times even directly.[11] The classic explanation of the nature of the form prescribed by the Council of Trent was given by Sanchez (1550-1610).[12] He categorically stated that, no matter what the necessity, a marriage contracted without the presence of an authorized priest and at least two witnesses would be invalid. His reason was the following: by stating that marriage cannot take place in any other way (*aliter*), the Council of Trent made this the form of marriage, and since a thing cannot exist without its form, neither can marriage. The Council was very specific when it rendered altogether incapable of marriage (*omnino inhabiles*) those who contracted otherwise, and there was no necessity that could supply for the invalidity of the matter or the form in a sacrament. He went further in saying that the divine law was also involved because of the precept that no one is allowed to know carnally one who is not his or hers, and in such cases the parties could not be each other's because of the impediment. The use of *epikeia* was not allowed in such a case, for the law was not merely a *lex praecipiens aut prohibens,* but a *lex inhabilitans,* requiring a substantial solemnity in the action. As to the cessation of ecclesiastical laws in grave necessity, that could indeed have obtained but for the presence also of the divine law. This explanation was accepted by many of the authors who came after Sanchez. They perhaps changed the wording, but their meaning remained substantially the same.[13]

[11] *Diana Coordinatus seu Omnium Resolutionum Moralium eius ipsissimis verbis ad propria loca et materias, per v.p. Martinum de Alcolea fideliter dispositarum tomi 10* (10 vols. in 5, Venetiis, 1728), Tom. II, tract 6 (*de matrim.*), res. 73 (hereafter cited as Diana); Verde (+ 1706), *Institutionum Canonicarum Libri Quatuor* (2 vols., Neapoli, 1735), lib. II, tit. 12 (*de sacr. matrim.*), c. 23, n. 4040 (hereafter cited as Verde); Pontius (1569-1629), *De Sacramento Matrimonii Tractatus* (Venetiis, 1756), lib. V, c. 6, n. 243 (hereafter cited as Pontius).

[12] *Disputationum de sancto matrimonii sacramento tomi tres* (3 vols., Antuerpiae, 1626), lib. III, disp. XVII, cc. 3-5 (hereafter cited as Sanchez).

[13] Pontius, lib. V, c. 6, n. 3; Perez (1578-1660), *De Sancto Matrimonii Sacramento-Opus Morale-Theologicum* (Lugduni, 1646), disp. XXXIX, sectt. 2-6 (hereafter cited as Perez); Reiffenstuel (1642-1703), *Ius Canonicum Uni-*

It was not long before the Sacred Congregation of the Council, which had been instituted for the purpose of interpreting the laws of the august Council of Trent, was being besieged with problems in regard to the procedure to be followed when an authorized witness was unavailable. It began to issue replies and thus established norms of action in such eventualities. Inasmuch as replies from the Holy See to the difficulties presented to it showed a definite development, it will be helpful for the sake of clarity to show this unfolding of the mind of the Holy See in regard to, first, the inability of having the pastor or an authorized priest present for the marriage; secondly, the presence of witnesses; thirdly, the annotation of such marriages; and, finally, the obligation of receiving the nuptial blessing.

1. Unavailability of a Priest

With the spread of Protestantism in Europe and with the growth of persecutions not only in Europe but throughout the world, even as far as China and Japan, it was not a rare occurrence to find parishes wherein the decree *Tametsi* had been promulgated to be without resident pastors or any priest at all, either because they had been killed off or exiled, or because they remained in hiding for fear of the heretics and infidels. At times, because of the prescripts of the civil law, a pastor, though present, could not officiate at a marriage ceremony because of fear of reprisals from the civil government. In response to all such eventualities, replies had been forthcoming from the Holy See.

Actual physical absence of a priest. As early as the year 1602, not quite fifty years after the Council of Trent, the Sacred Congregation of the Council was faced with a problem from Belgium as to what was to be done in the case wherein the decree *Tametsi* had been promulgated but no pastor was on hand inasmuch as the parish was vacant, and the diocese lacked both a bishop and a chapter,

versum-iuxta titulos quinque librorum decretalium (5 vols. in 6, Romae, 1831-1834), lib. IV, tit. III, c. 3, n. 133 (hereafter cited as Reiffenstuel); Leurenius (1646-1723), *Ius Canonicum Universum* (3 vols., Venetiis, 1729), Vol. II, quaest. 144 ad lib. 4, tit. III (*de cland. desp.*) (hereafter cited as Leurenius); Schmalzgrueber, lib. IV, tit. III, c. 2, nn. 103-107.

either of which could have delegated another priest to assist at the marriage. If one adhered strictly to the wording of the law, no marriage could then be contracted. The Congregation decreed that the contracting of a marriage undertaken in such circumstances without the presence of the pastor could nevertheless be valid as long as two witnesses were present.[14]

In the year 1625, the Sacred Congregation for the Propagation of the Faith issued two replies to the Bishops in Japan in reference to problems that affected people in that part of the world. On June 13th, it decreed that in regard to marriages that were to be contracted, the decree of the Council of Trent notwithstanding, if in the place in question or in the neighboring place there was no pastor or other priest, secular or religious, delegated by the bishop, the marriages could be contracted solely in the presence of witnesses. Two weeks later, the same Congregation issued a reply to the request that the Holy Father deign to dispense by supplying the defect of the necessary solemnities omitted in the marriages that had already been contracted without the presence of the pastor in Japan after the persecution of 1614, which brought about a great lack of priests. This favor was requested because it would be very difficult to validate all such marriages. The reply was that the law of the Council of Trent did not oblige in Japan (this, even though it had been promulgated there) and that the marriages that had been contracted were and continued to be valid as long as two witnesses were present. On July 2nd of the same year, Pope Urban VIII (1623-1644) approved this decision when stating that it was in accord with the one that had been given by the Congregation of the Council for Holland, Zeeland, and Friesland.[15]

[14] Pallottini, *Collectio omnium conclusionum et resolutionum quae in causis propositis apud Sacram Congregationem Cardinalium S. Concilii Tridentini Interpretum prodierunt ab eius institutione anno MDLXIV ad MDCCCLX distinctis titulis alphabetico ordine per materias digesta* (17 vols., Romae, 1868-1893), Vol. XIII, s.v. *Matrimonium,* c. XV, n. 86 (hereafter cited as Pallottini).

[15] *Collectanea S. C. de Prop. Fide* (ed. 1893), n. 1386, 1387; *Collectanea S. C. de Prop. Fide* (ed. 1907), n. 17. Cf. also S. C. S. Off., *Vic. Ap. Sutchuen,* 15 ian. 1784—*Collectanea S. C. de Prop. Fide* (ed. 1893), n. 1394; (ed. 1907), n. 566; *Fontes,* n. 846, where almost the identical words are used and mention is made that the Holy See has answered often in the same manner when the same question was proposed.

The Congregation of the Council adverted to the reply of Cardinal Bellarmine (1542-1621) as quoted in Rota Decision 308, n. 25, coram Dunozetto,[16] in its reply to the Archbishop of Cologne, when it stated that if there was no Catholic pastor, a marriage would be valid without his presence. It mentioned that at other times it had also decided in this manner, always insisting, however, on the presence of witnesses.[17]

Pope Pius VI declared that the Congregation of the Council had often declared that, if the presence of the pastor could not be had, the purpose of the Council of Trent was satisfied when marriage was contracted in the presence of two witnesses.[18] Even as late as the nineteenth century, the Holy Office stated that the law of the Council of Trent remained suspended as to its effects as often as it could no longer be observed because of insurmountable difficulties, such as the absence of the pastor.[19]

Difficulties also arose in regard to cases when indeed pastors were not absent, but for one reason or another proved unavailable. In this regard the Congregation of the Council decreed that marriage could be contracted without the pastor or a priest if really and truly it was unknown where the pastor or the bishop was, or

[16] *Sacrae Romanae Rotae Decisiones Recentiores* (ed. Pr. Farinacius, Paulus Rubeus, et Joannes Baptista Compagnus, pro annis 1518-1684, 25 vols., Romae, 1618-1703), Pars IV, t. 2, Annotatio ad Dec. 431, n. 35 ff (hereafter cited *S. R. Rotae Decisiones Recentiores*); cf. also the letter of Pope Pius VI (1775-1799) to the Archbishop of Rouen, dated April 22, 1795, where the reply of Bellarmine is quoted. The letter may be found in *Pii VI Pontificis Maximi Acta Quibus Ecclesiae Calamitatibus in Gallia consultum est* (2 vols., Romae: Typis S. C. de Prop. Fide, 1871), II, 112.

[17] S. C. C., *Colonien.*, 27 ian. 1728—*Thesaurus Resolutionum Sacrae Congregationis Concilii* (167 vols., Urbini, 1718-1741; Romae, 1741-1908), IV, 153 (hereafter cited as *Thesaurus Resolutionum*). Cf. also Benedictus XIV, *De Synodo,* lib. XII, c. 5, n. 5, where mention is made of another decision of the same Congregation on March 30, 1669, and reference is made to the authors who agree with this decision.

[18] *Pii VI Pontificis Maximi Acta Quibus Ecclesiae Catholicae Calamitatibus in Gallia consultum est,* II, 12-16.

[19] S. C. S. Off., instr. (ad Praef. Mission. Martinicae, etc.), 6 iulii, 1817—*Collectanea S. C. de Prop Fide* (ed. 1893), n. 1400; (ed. 1907), n. 725; *Fontes,* n. 855.

if it was morally impossible to find him.[20] If it was known where he was, the Holy See in various instances declared that marriages could be contracted apart from his presence: (1) when he was in hiding and it was not safe to approach him; [21] or (2) when the pastor was not free to come to the parties; [22] or (3) when he could not be approached without danger; [23] or (4) when he could not be reached safely or easily; [24] or (5) when, because of persecutions, Christians did not have easy access to him.[25]

Exceptions also obtained outside the cases of danger. The Congregation for the Propagation of the Faith was asked whether marriages could take place without the assistance of the pastor if in a certain place he could not be had because of his very great distance from that locality or his exile from it. The reply of July 7, 1670, pointed to the decree given to the Bishop of Tricarico on January 18, 1663.[26] A similar reply was given to the Vicar Apostolic of Tunkin on March 1, 1784. The reply was not as demanding, however, for it postulated only such a distance in consequence of which the pastor could not conveniently be had. On July 1, 1863, a further step was made. The Holy Office stated that one could forego the presence of the pastor at marriage if it was difficult to get to him and one did not know when he would be available and

[20] S. C. C., *Tricarien.*, 18 ian. 1863—*Collectanea S. C. de Prop. Fide* (ed. 1893), n. 1388, ad 5um; (ed. 1907), n. 149, ad 5um. S. C. C., *Colonien.*, 27 ian. 1728—*Thesaurus Resolutionum,* IV, 153.

[21] S. C. C., *in una Belgii,* 26 sept. 1602—Pallottini, XIII, s.v. *matrimonium,* n. 86; *Tricarien.*, 18 ian. 1663—*Collectanea S. C. de Prop. Fide* (ed. 1893), n. 1388; (ed. 1907), n. 149.

[22] Benedictus XIV, *De Synodo,* lib. XII, c. 5, n. 5; S. C. S. Off., *Quebecen.*, 17 nov. 1835—*Collectanea S. C. de Prop. Fide* (ed. 1893), n. 1402; (ed. 1907), n. 842; *Fontes,* n. 872.

[23] S. C. S. Off. (Sutchuen.), 15 ian. 1784—*Collectanea S. C. de Prop. Fide* (ed. 1893), n. 1394; (ed. 1907), n. 566; *Fontes,* n. 846.

[24] S. C. S. Off., instr. (ad Praef. Mission. Martinicae, etc.), 6 iulii, 1817—*Collectanea S. C. de Prop. Fide* (ed. 1893), n. 1400; (ed. 1907), n. 725; *Fontes,* n. 855.

[25] S. C. de Prop. Fide (C. P. pro Sin.—Vic. Ap. Tunk.), 2 iulii, 1827—*Collectanea S. C. de Prop. Fide* (ed. 1893), n. 1401; (ed. 1907), n. 794.

[26] *Collectanea S. C. de Prop. Fide* (ed. 1893), n. 1389; (ed. 1907), n. 190 and 567.

it was foreseen that he would be away from that place at least a month.[27]

Moral absence of an authorized priest. The Holy See also gave attention to the cases of moral absence of authorized priests, i. e., when they were actually present but when, because of the prohibiting prescripts of the civil law, they could not witness the marriage in question. A celebrated case of this type is seen in the Instruction of the Congregation for the Propagation of the Faith to the Prefect of the Missions on Curaçao in the year 1785.[28] Being a Dutch possession, the island was in the hands of rulers inimical to the Church. There was enacted a law that required a sum of 50 florins to be paid before marriage. Many of the Catholics were poor and could not pay this amount. If the priest, nevertheless, assisted at the marriage, he ran afoul of the law and subjected himself to very grave penalties. As an answer to this dilemma, the Congregation advised that a priest, having apprised himself of the fact that no canonical impediment was present and likewise that the couple was unable to pay the required civil tax, could permit such a couple to contract marriage in the presence simply of two witnesses. *"Ita se gerat Praefectus Missionis in casu necessitatis et magnae contrahentium inopiae."* A warning, however, was issued that the priests should beware of all fraud and should obviate all danger that could result from the reaction of the civil authorities if such a course of action were pursued too often.

Another instance that might be adduced is the decision of the Congregation of the Council on May 27, 1893, in regard to a marriage case presented to it. The facts were the following: a French Baron and a 16 year old girl eloped to Switzerland and contracted marriage there. Because of the civil laws in regard to age, they could not contract marriage in France. Since they had no domicile

[27] ". . . et ignoratur quandonam parochus haberi possit et praevideatur spatio unius mensis a loco abfuturus. . . ." S. C. S. Off., *Vallispraten.*, 1 iulii, 1863—apud Wernz, *Ius Decretalium* (6 vols., Romae, 1898-1914), IV (*Ius Matrimoniale Ecclesiae Catholicae*) (Romae, 1904), footnote on page 267 (hereafter cited as *Ius Matrimoniale*); cf. also *Collectanea S. C. de Prop. Fide* (ed. 1907), n. 1240.

[28] *S. C de Prop. Fide,* instr. (ad Praef. Miss.—Curaçao), a. 1785—*Collectanea S. C. de Prop. Fide* (ed. 1907), n. 571.

in Switzerland and had no delegation from their proper pastor, the validity of the marriage was impugned on the ground that the decree *Tametsi* was not observed. The Defender of the Marriage Bond upheld the validity of the marriage on the ground that, if a couple could not go to their proper pastor, and if there were no other impediments to stand in the way, they could validly contract marriage simply in the presence of at least two witnesses. This was the constant practice of the Holy See. In the case at issue, the couple had the right to marry according to the divine and ecclesiastical law, but were prohibited from exercising that right till the girl became 21 years of age, the required age according to the civil law. In order that the divine and ecclesiastical law be not frustrated and the couple barred from the free exercise of their natural right to contract marriage, they could contract marriage anywhere outside of France, apart from all need of their proper pastor to issue a delegation to the priest who would assist at their marriage. It was the farthest from the mind and purpose of the Council of Trent to hinder the freedom to contract marriage. The Congregation upheld his position and the validity of the marriage was sustained.[29]

Not having the benefit of the replies of the Holy See, as the subsequent authors had, it is no wonder that Sanchez and Perez made no allowance for the contracting of a clandestine marriage even in the case wherein no authorized priest was available. In fact, when Perez adverted to the declaration of Pope Clement VIII (1592-1605) that marriages could take place apart from the presence of the pastor in the towns where there was no pastor, he stated that it did not reflect a general principle, but pointed rather to a dispensation pure and simple.[30]

Despite their intransigence on these points, Sanchez,[31] Perez,[32] and Pontius [33] were ready to acknowledge as valid the marriages of Catholics who were held prisoners in heathen lands, even though they had been held to the form of the decree *Tametsi* before their capture, if they contracted their unions apart from the presence of

[29] *Thesaurus Resolutionum*, CLII, pp. 345-358.

[30] Perez, disp. XXXIX, sec. 6.

[31] Lib. III, disp. XVIII, c. 35.

[32] Disp. XXXIX, sec. 6.

[33] Lib. V, c. 9, n. 7.

the pastor, as long as the pastor could not be had. They felt that the law could not be observed by such Catholics who, if held to its observance, would have to remain celibate and thus be deprived of their right to marry. The contracting of these marriages, however, had to take place in a public manner.

It is remarkable, on the other hand, that sixteenth century authors like Vega, Veracruz and Capua, as mentioned by Sanchez and Perez, held as probable the opinion that recognized as valid a marriage apart from the presence of the pastor when there was no *copia parochi*. Sanchez, Perez, Pontius and Coninck (1571-1633) held for the invalidity of such marriages.[34] But once the Holy See began to reply to such difficulties and the replies became available, then the commentators accommodated their opinions accordingly.

In order to explain how this could be permitted in view of the explanation of Sanchez on the form of marriage and its essential nature, Sylvius (1581-1649) [35] referred to the reply of St. Robert Bellarmine on December 30, 1600, to Octavius, the Bishop of Tricarico. In it, Bellarmine said that the matter was taken up by the Pope and the Congregation of the Council. It was the common opinion that such marriages were valid and that the decree of the Council of Trent did not pertain to them since it could not be observed in such places, and that accordingly it did not extend to those places where there were no pastors.

Reiffenstuel enumerated the three reasons usually given. He rejected the first two and adhered to the third. He rejected the one which, as based on a Rule of Law, contended that no one is obliged to do the impossible,[36] and likewise the other, which was based on the claim of necessity. He conceded that these arguments would

[34] Sanchez (lib. III, disp. XVII, c. 5) reported the opinion of these men as follows: it is probable that the decree of the Council of Trent is to be understood as binding *ubi est copia parochi;* hence, in countries of heretics and in the new world, where there is no *copia parochi* or where he has not been available for a year, marriage probably can be celebrated simply in the presence of witnesses.

[35] *Commentarium in 3. part. Summae S. Thomae* (Antuerpiae, 1667), q. 45, art. V, quaer. IV, as cited in *Acta Pii VII Pontificis Maximi,* II, footnote on page 112.

[36] Reg. 6, R. J., in VI°.

hold if the laws in question were *praecipientes aut prohibentes,* but not when as invalidating (*irritantes*) laws they prescribed a substantial form. The reason, he felt, that satisfactorily accounted for this departure from the Tridentine law was the fact that the Sacred Congregation of the Council, in using *epikeia* and by judging what was just and equitable in such cases, decreed that such cases do not fall under that law, since the Council of Trent in endeavoring to obviate the difficulties arising from clandestine marriages did not wish to go so far as to take away from the people the freedom to marry in places where there were no pastors.[37]

Still another explanation is found in Verde, who offered the explanation given by the Salmanticenses. It is the following: in those places where a pastor could not be had or was not present, there was not a true parish, so that the effect of the promulgation of the decree *Tametsi* no longer obtained, since the disappearance of the parish or the diocese, the very existence of which was postulated for the act of promulgation, carried with it also the dissolution of the promulgation itself.[38]

In enumerating the reasons which served to excuse one from observing the law as to the prescribed form, the commentators listed those which were substantially the same as the ones found in the replies from the Holy See mentioned above. In the same context, however, commentators made mention of the fact that marriages in such eventualities would be valid if they took place in the presence of a Protestant minister or even without him,[39] but they always insisted that at least two witnesses be present [40] and, if possible, a notary.[41]

[37] Lib. IV, tit. III, c. 3; cf. also Schmalzgrueber, lib. IV, tit. III, c. 2, n. 116.

[38] Verde, lib. II, tit. XII, c. 23, n. 4074 in the footnote.

[39] Laymann, lib. V, pars II, c. 4; n. 7; Schmalzgrueber, lib. IV. tit. III, c. 2, n. 116.

[40] Schmalzgrueber, *loc. cit.;* Reiffenstuel, *loc. cit.;* Verde, lib. II, tit. XII, c. 23, nn. 4074-4076.

[41] Fagnanus (1588-1678), *Commentaria in secundum librum Decretalium* (5 vols. in 8, Romae, 1661), *de foro compet.,* c. 5 (*si clericus*); Schmier (1680-1728), *Iurisprudentia Canonico-Civilis seu Ius Canonicum Universum iuxta quinque libros decretalium* (2 vols., Venetiis, 1754), lib. IV, tract. III, c. 5, sect. 4, n. 158 (hereafter cited as Schmier).

Since the usual excusing causes given by the Roman Congregations and the commentators could be taken either in the general sense, as affecting all in the same condition, or in a particular sense, as affecting merely a given singular case, Van Espen (1646-1728) hastened to note that the excusing causes were valid only in the case of a general or inevitable necessity.[42] This was the common opinion of the authors, as is evident from Gasparri (1852-1934) and others.[43] It was on the basis of this opinion that a marriage was declared null by the Rota, Cardinal Lega presiding.[44]

On the other hand, there were others who proposed the opinion that even a particular impossibility would excuse one from this law. Antonius Ballerini (1805-1881) in his annotations to the Moral Theology of John Gury (1801-1866) was its chief protagonist, basing his opinion on the principles of St. Alphonsus. The latter, in reply to a question as to whether in a particular case, when the equitable purpose of the law ceases, the law ceases with it, answered that, if the matter of the law was rendered harmful or very difficult in a particular case, everyone admitted that the law did not oblige. Therefore, argued Ballerini, according to the great Doctor's principles, even in a particular case, necessity will make capable of contracting marriage those whom otherwise the law in general renders incapable (*inhabiles*). Besides, he added, in a *casus*

[42] "Porro quod dictum est, nec necessitatem supplere defectum parochi, id expresse restrinxi ad necessitatem particularem; nam si generalis aliqua et inevitabilis necessitas fuerit, etiam Concilii Decretum cessabit. . . ."—*Opera Omnia Canonica in sex partes distributa—Ius Ecclesiasticum Universum hodiernae disciplinae praesertim Belgii, Galliae, Germaniae et Vicinarum Provinciarum accommodatum* (6 partes in 3 vols., Lovanii, 1732), pars II, sec. I, tit. XII n. 31.

[43] *Tractatus Canonicus de Matrimonio* (3. ed., 2 vols., Parisiis, 1904), n. 1175; Wernz, *Ius Matrimoniale,* footnote on page 267; De Smet, *De Sponsalibus et Matrimonio* (Brugis, 1909), pp. 85-86; De Becker, *De Sponsalibus et Matrimonio Praelectiones Canonicae,* footnote 2 on page 127; Feije, *De Impedimentis et dispensationibus matrimonialibus* (3. ed., Lovanii, 1885), p. 191; Zitelli, *Apparatus Iuris Ecclesiastici* (ed. altera novis curis auctior et emendatior, Romae, 1888), p. 423.

[44] *S. Romanae Rotae Decisiones seu Sententiae* (Romae: Typis Polyglotti Vaticani, 1912-), Vol. II (1910), Decisio XXI (*coram Lega*), pp. 199-207. There it is stated that ". . . eiusmodi impossibilitas aut difficultas debet esse communis. . . ." (hereafter referred to as *Decisiones*).

perplexus (when everything is prepared for a marriage and an impediment is discovered), it is highly probable from the benign interpretation of the will of the Church that an impediment will cease and thereby a particular necessity will render *habilis* one who was *inhabilis*. *A pari*, even in a case of particular impossibility, it is highly probable that the impediment of clandestinity will cease. Since there is a *dubium iuris*, one cannot urge the existence of the impediment with certainty.[45]

Ojetti (1862-1932), while holding the common opinion, and proposing furthermore that the impossibility must have perdured for at least a month, felt that the same perhaps would apply even if there was a case of particular necessity which had perdured for a month.[46] Gasparri found it difficult to contradict Ballerini's argumentation, but asserted that in practice one must not recede from the common doctrine until the Holy See has expressed a liberal mind on the subject.[47]

2. Presence of Witnesses

In all the replies of the Congregations mentioned above, there was always an insistence that there be present at such extraordinary marriages, when an authorized priest could not be had, at least two or three witnesses. The Congregations usually added that the form prescribed by the Council of Trent should be observed as far as possible, i. e., that two or three witnesses be present.[48] This in-

[45] ". . . An cessat, cessante fine adaequato, in casu particulari, S. Doctor Alphonsus (I, n. 199) clarissime respondit: si cessat contrarie, quando scilicet materia legis redderetur in eo casu nociva vel valde difficilis, tunc omnes asserunt legem non obligare. Ergo iuxta generalia principia a S. Alphonso admissa, etiam in casu particulari necessitas eos habiles ad contrahendum reddit quos alioquin lex in genere reddit inhabiles."—Gury-Ballerini, *Compendium Theologiae Moralis* (9. ed., 2 vols., Romae, 1887), II, notes on pages 818-819; cf. also Ballerini-Palmieri, *Opus Theologicum-Morale* (3. ed., 7 vols., Prati, 1898-1901), VI, 819.

[46] *Synopsis Rerum Moralium et Iuris Pontificii* (3. ed., 4 vols., Romae, 1909-1914), I, s.v. *Clandestinitas*, n. 1062.

[47] *De Matrimonio*, n. 1175; cf. also Feije, *De impedimentis et dispensationibus matrimonialibus*, p. 191.

[48] E.g., S. C. C., *Tricaricen.*, 18 ian. 1863—*Collectanea S. C. de Prop. Fide*

sistence derived from the fact that the Council of Trent had demanded their presence to prove the existence of the marriage in question.[49] This stand of the Congregations was so unswerving that the Holy Office in its reply to the Archbishop of Quebec on November 17, 1835, stated that a marriage contracted without two witnesses in a place where the decree *Tametsi* was in force was invalid because according to the decree *Tametsi* witnesses *had to be* present.[50] The decision was based on the premise that parishes were constituted in that territory, and consequently that witnesses were available.

This position of the Holy See was quite reasonable, because, whereas one might at times not have a priest available, one could presumably always find two witnesses. The foregoing of their presence would lead to the assumption that one wished to contract marriage clandestinely. On the other hand, one could envision the case wherein even two witnesses could not be had. What then? The writer could find nothing bearing directly on this eventuality. However, one might say that it was touched on implicitly. In many of the replies, the Congregations insisted that the form prescribed by the decree *Tametsi* be observed *in so far as it could be done.*[51] The reply of the Holy Office to the Prefects of the Missions on Martinique and Guadalupe on July 6, 1817, is interesting in this regard. It stated that the law of the Council of Trent *quoad suum effectum* remained suspended even in those places in which it was published as often as it could no longer be observed because of

(ed. 1893), n. 1388; (ed. 1907), n. 149; *Colonien.,* 27 ian. 1728—*Thesaurus Resolutionum,* IV, 153.

49 ". . . Concilium Tridentinum non alia de causa duorum vel trium testium praesentiam in matrimonio celebrando praescripsit quam ut de matrimonio certo constaret idque a testibus affirmari possit."—Pallottini, XIII, s.v. *Matrimonium,* c. XV, p. 224.

50 *Collectanea S. C. de Prop. Fide* (ed. 1893), n. 1402; (ed. 1907), n. 842; *Fontes,* n. 872.

51 ". . . servata tamen in eo in quo potest forma Concilii."—S. C. C., *Tricaricen.,* 18 ian. 1663—*Collectanea S. C. de Prop. Fide* (ed. 1893), n. 1388; (ed. 1907), n. 149; ". . . sic servata fuerit, quantum potuit forma Concilii." S. C. C., *Colonien.,* 27 ian. 1728—*Thesaurus Resolutionum,* IV, 153.

insurmountable difficulties and dangers.[52] It gave as examples the cases in which no pastors were present or could be reached safely and easily. One might ask also, couldn't the same reasoning apply to the case wherein witnesses were absolutely unavailable? Benedict XIV said that the Fathers of the Council of Trent did not wish to take away the freedom to marry.[53] One could ask whether that would not have been the case when no witnesses were available It may have been this reasoning that led certain authors in the cases wherein witnesses could not be had to be ready to dispense with the need of them. Schmier implied that even when witnesses could not be had the marriage would be valid.[54]

In the celebrated reply to Curaçao, the Congregation for the Propagation of the Faith advised the priest who had permitted a couple to marry without his presence and simply in the presence of two witnesses to tell the couple that it should, as soon as possible after the celebration of the marriage, return and tell him (the pastor) of the contracted marriage, so that he could make the necessary annotation of it, at least a secret one, in his register, with the date and mention of the names of the witnesses who were present.[55]

In order to make certain that such marriages would be contracted properly, the same Congregation issued an instruction to the Vicars Apostolic in China on June 23, 1830. In substance it stated that the parents should choose two witnesses who would go with the bridal pair and relatives to a church where, on bended knees, all would recite in common the acts of faith, hope, charity and contrition. In this manner the couple would dispose itself properly for the contracting of marriage. After this was done, the couple would rise and in the presence of the witnesses express their consent to the marriage in words of the present. Then they could

[52] *Collectanea S. C. de Prop. Fide* (ed. 1893), n. 1400; (ed. 1907), n. 725; *Fontes,* n. 855.

[53] *De Synodo,* lib. XII, c. 5, n. 5.

[54] ". . . quod hactenus de praesentia testium et parochi dictum est, ad omne matrimonium spectat . . . nisi contingat ut parochus et *testes* [italics those of the writer] haberi non possint, velut in locis quibusdam Hollandiae."—*Iurisprudentia Canonico-Civilis,* lib. IV, tract. III, c. 5, sec. 4, n. 158.

[55] *Collectanea S. C. de Prop. Fide* (ed. 1907), n. 571.

give thanks and return to their homes. If this could not be done at a church, it could be done also at home.[56]

The Holy See was always anxious to keep before the minds of the people the sanctity of marriages even when contracted apart from the presence of a priest. It was for this reason that in numerous replies it had strongly admonished the couple to receive, as soon as possible, the nuptial blessing of the pastor. It hastened to warn, however, that, even without it, the marriage would still be valid.[57] On one occasion, the Holy Office supported the opinion which taught that those who decline to seek this blessing are hardly worthy of absolution, inasmuch as they refuse to obey the Church in a very grave matter.[58]

Before concluding this article, one should furthermore consider the opinions of the authors concerning danger of death as a cause excusing parties from observing the prescribed form of marriage. With but few exceptions, such as Dominic Soto and Tanner, the commentators overwhelmingly held that the necessity for people in danger of death to contract marriage in order to legitimate the offspring already born, or to safeguard the good name of the woman, did not suffice to offer an excusing cause from the obligation of the Tridentine law. If that law was neglected, the contracted unions were invalid.[59] In the annotations to a case of nullity decided by the Rota on March 11, 1624, *coram Dunozetto*,[60] the compiler, Paulus

[56] *Collectanea S. C. de Prop. Fide* (ed. 1907), n. 816.

[57] S. C. S. Off., (ad Vic. Ap. Sutchuen.), 15 ian. 1784—*Collectanea S. C. de Prop. Fide* (ed. 1893), n. 1394; (ed. 1907), n. 566; *Fontes*, n. 846; cf. also S. C. de Prop. Fide. instr. (Vic. Ap. Sin.), 23 iun. 1830—*Collectanea S. C. de Prop. Fide* (ed. 1907), n. 816.

[58] Instr. (ad Praef. Mission. Martinicae, etc.), 6 iul. 1817—*Collectanea S. C. de Prop. Fide* (ed. 1893), n. 1400; (ed. 1907), n. 725; *Fontes*, n. 855.

[59] Sanchez, lib. III, disp. XVII, c. 4; *S. R. Rotae Decisiones Recentiores*, Pars IV, tom. 2, Adnotatio ad dec. 431, nn. 35 seqq; Perez, disp. XXXIX, sec. 4; Diana, tom. II, tract. 6, res. 73; Leurenius, lib. IV, tit. 3, q. 144; Pontius, lib. V, c. 6, nn. 2, 3; Pirhing (1606-1679), *Ius Canonicum Novo Methodo Explicatum* (5 vols. in 4, Dilingae, 1674-1678), lib. IV, tit. III, n. 7; Engel (1643?-1674), *Collegium Universi Iuris Canonici* (Beneventi, 1670), lib. IV, tit. III, c. 9; Reiffenstuel, lib. IV, tit. III, c. 3, n. 133; Schmalzgrueber, lib. IV, tit. III, c. 2, nn. 106-107.

[60] *S. R. Rotae Decisiones Recentiores, loc. cit.*

Rubeus, stated that the contracting of marriage was not necessary in such cases since other provision could be made for the salvation of the dying person's soul. In the same context, he mentioned that neither *epikeia* nor good faith offered an excuse. Pontius felt that it would be better for one private person to suffer harm than to open the door to the danger of clandestine marriages.[61] It seems that the reasoning behind this opinion was based on the fact that not even the greatest necessity could free one from an invalidating law or put an end to a diriment impediment in a particular case.[62]

In itself, then, the danger of death was never considered as a reason that allowed one to contract marriage without a pastor or witnesses. This was the opinion that prevailed until the time of Pope Leo XIII, when he made provision for dispensing in such cases. If the union was entered apart from the presence of the pastor, one can find commentators who held it as probable that marriage could be celebrated in the presence of but two witnesses. Sanchez and Perez mentioned Vega, Veracruz and Capua as holding this opinion; however, they along with Pontius and Coninck, whom Perez also mentioned, held for the invalidity of such marriages.

An interesting exception to the general rule in such a case was mentioned by Verde, who acknowledged a clandestine marriage when a dying Catholic king needed to marry in order to legitimate his son and thereby make him his heir, if otherwise the kingdom would have fallen into the hands of heretics. The reason adduced was that in such cases the law would work to the detriment of the Church. The law accordingly ceased since it could only have served an evil purpose.[63]

To summarize, then, the opinions of the commentators, after they had the benefit of the replies from the Holy See concerning the impossibility of observing the prescripts of the decree *Tametsi* from the time of the Council of Trent to the time of the promulgation of the decree *Ne temere,* one might say that an impossibility, whether there was a physical or only a moral impediment—the latter in cases of long-standing great difficulty or grave danger—of

[61] *Op. cit.*, lib. V, c. 6, n. 3.

[62] Perez, disp. XXXIX, sec. 4; Reiffenstuel, lib. IV, tit. III, c. 3, n. 133.

[63] Lib. II, tit. XII, c. 23, n. 4078.

approaching the pastor or an authorized priest for the purpose of contracting marriage according to the law of the Council of Trent, excused a couple from observing this law, provided that this impossibility was general for the respective community, and not merely an isolated incident for the couple in question, and provided, further, that the form prescribed by the Council of Trent be observed in so far as it could be, i. e., that the marriage take place in the presence of at least two witnesses.[64] The opinion allowing the use of this extraordinary form in the case of a particular impossibility, though meriting extrinsic probability, was not to be followed in practice.

Article 2. Dispensation From Impediments In This Period

Thus far there has been considered the historical background of the form in extraordinary cases; now it remains to look into the development of the institute mentioned in Canons 1044-1045, namely, that of dispensation from matrimonial impediments for the benefit of parties in danger of death and in cases of grave necessity, inasmuch as references are made in those canons to Canon 1098. For the purposes of clarity, this article will be divided into two sections, the first tracing the history from the Council of Trent to February 20, 1888, when a grant of faculties was made to the ordinaries through the Congregation of the Holy Office, and the second from the latter date to the decree *Ne temere,* which became law on April 19, 1908.

A. *From the Council of Trent To February 20, 1888*

Inasmuch as the Pope is the supreme legislator, it has always been taught that he has power to dispense from all impediments of the ecclesiastical law. As to the bishops, they had no power over the impediments of the common law by reason of their office, for as subordinate legislators they could not derogate from any of the laws of the supreme legislator, in this case from the law of the Council of Trent. They could point to no concession either by reason of the common law or by reason of immemorial custom or tacit

[64] Oesterle, "Elucubratio Historica circa Declarationem c. 1098," *Ius Pontificium,* VIII (1928), 174-182.

approval on the part of the Popes in regard to the public diriment impediments of the ecclesiastical law.[65] By reason of their office, they consistently had been considered as having the power to dispense from ecclesiastical impedient impediments such as existed in consequence of the sacred seasons, in connection with a ban (*vetitum*) or as a result of private non-reserved vows.[66]

In regard to the diriment impediments of the ecclesiastical law, by reason of long-standing custom, which itself served as the best interpreter of the law, and because of the fact that the popes had tacitly conceded such a power to the bishops, the latter could by reason of their ordinary power dispense their Catholic subjects *for the internal forum only* from diriment matrimonial impediments under the following conditions: (1) that a marriage had been celebrated with all the necessary solemnities in the Catholic Church; (2) that at least one of the spouses was in good faith in consequence of ignorance of law or of fact; (3) that the impediment was occult and of the type from which the Holy Father could and usually did dispense through the Sacred Penitentiary; (4) that the case was so urgent that the Holy Father or his delegate could not be reached easily; and, finally, (5) that scandal would arise were the spouses to be separated.[67]

The power mentioned in the preceding paragraph related to marriages that had already been contracted. As to marriages that were to be contracted, Sanchez [68] proposed the opinion, which was later generally followed, that in such cases the bishop could dispense with the same ordinary power in the internal forum if the impediment was occult, if there was a very grave reason, and if

65 Suarez, *Opera Omnia* (26 vols., editio nova a Carolo Berton), Vols. V and VI (*De Legibus et Legislatore Deo,* Parisiis, 1856), VI, c. 14, nn. 3, 4, 8; Bendictus XIV, *De Synodo,* lib. IX, c. 1, n. 5, and cc. 2, 3; Wernz, *Ius Matrimoniale,* n. 616; Reiffenstuel, *Appendix ad Librum Quartum Decretalium,* c. 1, n. 19; Schmalzgrueber, lib. IV, tit. XVI, c. IV, n. 72.

66 Reiffenstuel, *App. ad Libr. Quart. Decret.,* c. 1, n. 10; Schmalzgrueber, lib. IV, tit. XVI, c. IV, n. 62.

67 Sanchez, lib. II, disp. XL, n. 3; Benedictus XIV, *De Synodo,* lib. IX, c. 2, n. 1; Pontius, lib. VIII. c. 13, n. 6; Perez, disp. XLIV, sect. 6, n. 11; Reiffenstuel, *App. ad Libr. Quart. Decret.,* c. 1, n. 15; Schmalzgrueber, lib. IV, tit. XVI, c. IV, nn. 78-79; Wernz, *Ius Matrimoniale,* n. 618.

68 *Op. cit.,* Lib. II, disp. XL, n. 5.

there was not time to approach the Holy See or a Legate of the Holy See by letter. Although this doctrine did not enjoy the same certainty as the other, it had its adherents and protagonists in large numbers.[69] It was followed in practice and had the tacit approval of the Holy See inasmuch as the latter did not reprobate it.[70]

This power was ordinary and therefore could be delegated even habitually. The Vicar General could not use this power without a special mandate.[71] Since pastors were without ordinary jurisdiction in the external forum, even the jurisdiction of a non-contentious character, they had no power of dispensing from matrimonial impediments, either from the law or through custom.[72]

By reason of faculties from the Holy See a greater power could indeed be enjoyed, as it was by missionaries and certain bishops.

The writer has been unable to find that any provision was made whereby a priest, even though not authorized by law or delegated by the pastor or the bishop to assist at a marriage, was given power to dispense from matrimonial impediments in a marriage that was brought to his attention. In fact, the Holy See in its replies almost always inserted a phrase or a clause in which, while allowing the extraordinary form of marriage, it permitted the marriage to take place provided that no canonical impediment was present.[73]

As to whether impediments ceased in such cases of impossibility, the opinions of the authors were in agreement with the opinions mentioned above with reference to the causes excusing from the observance of the form of marriage.

Although bishops had ordinary power, which could be delegated, of dispensing from occult impediments under the conditions stated above, and this surely obtained for the cases in which the parties

[69] Wernz, (*op. cit.*, n. 619, footnote 83, page 891) asserted that St. Alphonsus followed Sanchez' opinion and that it had become the common opinion of the authors. Cf. also Pontius, lib. VIII, c. 13, n. 6; Perez, disp. XLIV, sec. 6, n. 12; Schmalzgrueber, lib. IV, tit. XVI, c. IV, n. 83.

[70] S. C. S. Off., 23 apr. 1890—*Fontes,* n. 1120.

[71] Reiffenstuel, *op. cit.*, c. 1, n. 34; Wernz, *op. cit.*, n. 618.

[72] Suarez, *De Legibus,* lib. VI, c. XIV, n. 10.

[73] *Collectanea S. C. de Prop. Fide* (ed. 1907), n. 571; Pius VI, *Epistola ad Ep. Lucionensem,* 28 maii 1793: ". . . si nihil aliud obstet. . . ."—*Pii VI Pont. Max. Acta,* II, 12-16.

were constituted in danger of death or grave necessity, no provision was made for the granting of dispensations from the public diriment matrimonial impediments of the ecclesiastical law, or in the external forum, not even in danger of death. This was the situation until the Holy See acted on February 20, 1888.

B. *From February 20, 1888, to the Decree* Ne temere

Realizing that their power was restricted and that in many cases they could not by way of dispensing be of help to those who were in danger of death, the bishops of the world began to appeal to the Holy See for wider faculties in the matter of dispensing from matrimonial impediments. The Supreme Sacred Congregation of the Holy Office in an encyclical letter, dated February 20, 1888,[74] stated that Pope Leo XIII (1878-1903) had asked it to consider the advisability and feasibility of granting faculties to the local ordinaries for dispensing from public diriment impediments their subjects who lived in a civil marriage or in concubinage, when these subjects were in danger of death and there was no time to approach the Holy See, so that they might contract marriage in the Church and provide duly for the needs of their consciences.

After the matter had been seriously considered, the Pope approved the proposal of the Congregation and granted the favor in virtue of which local ordinaries would be able to dispense, either by themselves or through some suitable ecclesiastical personage, sick people who were in grave danger of death, when time did not allow for recourse to the Holy See, from all public impediments of the ecclesiastical law, except for the impediments arising from the Sacred Order of Priesthood and from affinity in the direct line when it derived through licit carnal intercourse.[75]

[74] S. C. S. Off., litt. encycl., 20 febr. 1888—*Fontes*, n. 1109; *Collectanea S. C. de Prop. Fide* (ed. 1907), n. 1685; *Acta Sanctae Sedis* (41 vols., Romae, 1865-1908), XX (1887), 543 (hereafter cited as *ASS*).

[75] S. C. S. Off., litt. encycl., 20 febr. 1888: ". . . Sanctitas Sua benigne annuit pro gratia, qua locorum Ordinarii dispensare valeant sive per se, sive per ecclesiasticam personam sibi benevisam, aegrotos in gravissimo mortis periculo constitutos, quando non suppetat tempus recurrendi ad S. Sedem, super impedimentis quantumvis publicis matrimonium iure ecclesiastico diri-

Suitable provision thus was made in aid of people in danger of death who wanted to achieve a rectification of their illicit relationship. For all the impediments but the two mentioned a dispensation could be granted by the ordinaries or their delegates. One must realize that clandestinity was still listed as a diriment impediment. It appears in virtue of this faculty that an ordinary could dispense even from the observance of the form of marriage as prescribed by the decree *Tametsi,* for the faculty did not exclude this. However, a question arose concerning this matter, for which some specific attention is warranted.

In itself, it was not quite clear from the faculty whether the ordinary could grant subdelegation to one person only, and whether he could subdelegate this faculty habitually. This was important, for at times it could prove difficult, if not impossible, to reach the ordinary. Accordingly, the Holy Office was asked whether ordinaries could, by reason of the faculties granted to them on February 20, 1888, grant habitual subdelegation to pastors and to approved confessors. The Fathers of the Sacred Congregation, having duly considered the matter on January 9, 1899, decided to petition Pope Leo XIII to decree and declare that the ordinaries who enjoyed this faculty could grant a general subdelegation, but only to pastors and only in cases wherein even the ordinary could not be reached in time and wherein there would be danger in delay. The pope acceded to their wishes the very same day.[76]

Clandestinity was a diriment impediment, as was mentioned above. Since the potential granting of a dispensation from it was not excluded in the faculties, one could naturally suppose that it fell within the power of the ordinaries to dispense from it. Nevertheless, a question arose which necessitated action on the part of the Holy See. It was asked whether in virtue of these faculties a pastor when he enjoyed a habitual subdelegation from his ordinary could dispense from the impediment of clandestinity. For example, could he assist at a marriage of non-subjects by dispensing from

mentibus, excepto sacro Presbyteratus Ordine et affinitate lineae rectae ex copula licita proveniente."—*Fontes,* n. 1109; *Collectanea S. C. de Prop. Fide* (ed. 1907), n. 1685; *ASS,* XX (1887), 543.

[76] S. C. S. Off., litt. encycl., 1 mart. 1889—*Fontes,* n. 1113; *Collectanea S. C. de Prop. Fide* (ed. 1907), n. 1698; *ASS,* XXI (1888), 696.

the necessity of the presence of their proper pastor, or even at a marriage of his own subjects by dispensing from the necessity of having at least two witnesses present, in the event that there were not present any persons who could act as witnesses? The reply was in the affirmative and the Pope's approval confirmed the decision.[77]

[77] S. C. S. Off., 13 dec. 1899—*Fontes,* n. 1231; *Collectanea S. C. de Prop. Fide* (ed. 1907), n. 2072; *ASS,* XXXII (1899-1900), 500-501.

CHAPTER IV

THE LAW ON THE FORM OF MARRIAGE AFTER THE DECREE *NE TEMERE*

DESPITE the development after the Council of Trent, despite also the favorable replies from the Congregations and the wide faculties given to the ordinaries and their delegates, there was still great need and much room for reform in the Church Law on the form of marriage. Clandestine marriages, which the Church had abhorred for centuries, and which it tried to abolish, were still being contracted, both culpably and inculpably. The decree *Tametsi* had not been published everywhere, so there existed a varying discipline within the Church. Where it had been published, there could remain a doubt as to who was to be considered the proper pastor. It was no wonder, then, that the Holy See was besieged with pleas from the bishops of the world that some revision be made. Pope Pius X (1903-1914) referred the matter to the Sacred Congregation of the Council for its mature judgment and pertinent suggestions. After hearing its proposals as well as those of the Commission of Cardinals to whom was entrusted the monumental task of preparing the Code of Canon Law, the pope ordered that the revised discipline as to the form of marriage be promulgated on August 2, 1907, and that it take effect on the following Easter Sunday, April 19, 1908. This was the law which, from the opening words of the decree, came to be known as the *Ne temere*.[1]

ARTICLE 1. THE FORM OF MARRIAGE ACCORDING TO THE DECREE *Ne temere*

In Article III of the decree *Ne temere* there is stated the law on the ordinary form of marriage; it is substantially the same that is now to be found in the Code of Canon Law. Valid were only those marriages which were contracted in the presence of the pastor, of the local ordinary, or of a priest delegated by either of these, and of

[1] S. C. C., decr. *"Ne temere,"* 2 aug. 1907—*Fontes*, n. 4340; *ASS*, XL (1907), 525-530.

at least two witnesses. The pastor and the ordinary assisted validly at marriages from the day they had taken possession of their benefices, and exclusively within the limits of their territory, provided that they still retained jurisdiction therein; the delegated priest, only within the limits of the mandate. For the first time due provision was made for marriages in extraordinary cases.

In Articles VII and VIII, the decree made provision for such extraordinary cases: in Article VII for the case of danger of death; in Article VIII for other cases of grave necessity. The centuries-old practice of the Church thus became molded as the common law of the Church.

A. *The Form of Marriage With Persons Constituted in Danger of Death*

Article VII reads as follows: when danger of death is imminent and the pastor, the local ordinary, or a priest delegated by either of these cannot be had, then, in order that provision may be made for relief of conscience and, if the case demands it, for the legitimation of the offspring, marriage can be contracted validly and licitly in the presence of any priest and two witnesses.[2]

It should be noted that the decree spoke simply of the danger, and not of the instant, of death (*periculum mortis,* and not *articulus mortis*). Ojetti felt that any sickness that proved dangerous to life offered a sufficient reason for the use of this exceptional norm; in fact, if extreme unction could be administered, this form could be used.[3]

With reference to the words *nequit haberi* (cannot be had), all that was necessary was a probable judgment that the pastor, the local ordinary or a priest delegated by either of these was unable to come to the house of the sick person. This judgment was to

[2] S. C. C., decr. *"Ne temere,"* 2 aug. 1907, art. VII: "Imminente mortis periculo, ubi parochus vel loci Ordinarius vel sacerdos ab alterutro delegatus haberi nequeat, ad consulendum conscientiae et (si casus ferat) legitimationi prolis, matrimonium contrahi valide ac licite potest coram quolibet sacerdote et duobus testibus."—*Fontes,* n. 4340; *ASS,* XL (1907), 529.

[3] *Synopsis,* I, s.v. *Clandestinitas,* n. 1124; Gennari, *Breve Commento della Nuova Legge sugli Sponsali e sul Matrimonio* (2. ed., Romae, 1908), p. 30.

be gained with due reliance on prudence, and not necessarily with the aid of mathematical certification. Extraordinary means were not called for.[4]

B. *The Form of Marriage in Other Cases of Grave Necessity*

Article VIII made the following provision: If it happen that in some locality there cannot be had the pastor, the local ordinary or a priest delegated by either of them as the one before whom marriage can be celebrated, and this condition of things has already lasted for a month, then the marriage can be contracted validly and licitly by the couple expressing their formal consent to the union in the presence of two witnesses.[5]

A few months after the decree *Ne temere* had become the law for the universal Church, the Congregation of the Council found the following doubt presented to it: "Whether, and if so, in what way, could provision be made for the case wherein a civil ceremony cannot take place before the Catholic ceremony, and there is urgent need of contracting marriage for the salvation of the soul and, nevertheless, pastors are forbidden by the civil law to assist at the marriages of the faithful except when a civil ceremony has first taken place. The answer given was: "Non esse interloquendum," or, in other words, the Congregation did not think the question should be answered.[6]

Although it was the intent of the Holy See to clarify the law on the form of marriage, there were still many questions unanswered in regard to the cases of urgent necessity to which Article VIII of the decree *Ne temere* adverted. Ojetti noted that the decree did not touch the question whether a general or a particular impos-

[4] Ojetti, *loc. cit.;* Gennari, *op. cit.*, p. 31.

[5] S. C. C., decr. "*Ne temere,*" 2 aug. 1907, art. VIII: "Si contingat ut in aliqua regione parochus locive Ordinarius aut sacerdos ab eis delegatus, coram quo matrimonium celebrari queat, haberi non possit, eaque rerum conditio a mense iam perseveret, matrimonium valide et licite iniri potest emisso a sponsis formali consensu coram duobus testibus."—*Fontes,* n. 4340; *ASS,* XL (1907), 529.

[6] S. C. C., *Romana et aliarum,* 27 iul. 1908—*Fontes,* n. 4350; *Thesaurus Resolutionum,* CLXVII (1908), 449-493.

sibility was postulated, or whether the absence of the priest was to be measured in a physical or a moral sense.[7]

One of the difficulties, however, did receive an answer from the Holy See. The latter was asked what was meant by the term *regio,* or, in other words, how far distant from an authorized priest the parties needed to be before they might contract marriage in the presence simply of two witnesses. The Congregation of the Sacraments formulated a general reply by answering that the marriage could always be celebrated thus when, after a month had elapsed, a competent priest could not be approached or had without serious inconvenience.[8]

Still many problems remained unsolved. Was the serious inconvenience mentioned in this reply to be restricted simply to terms of distance in the matter of approaching the priest? Or could it also exist as the postulated hindrance, even in a moral sense?

Ojetti, writing prior to this reply, based his opinion on the wording of Article VIII, which, so it seemed to him, studiously avoided the phrase *absens sit* for *haberi non possit;* he likewise looked to the spirit and the character of the legislation. In consequence, he held that any impossibility of having a priest sufficed to make operative the exceptional norm expressed in the Article.[9] Writing after the reply, Wernz (1842-1914) felt constrained to accept the opinion of Ojetti and De Smet in this matter, inasmuch as their opinion was definitely not improbable, within the tenor of the reply from the Sacred Congregation.[10]

Another aspect of the same problem which required the attention of the authors was whether the impossibility had to be a common one, i. e., for all or nearly all in the territory, or simply a particular one, i. e., one that was such for this one couple. Ojetti made the problem very specific, using the very example that had been brought to the attention of the Sacred Congregation of the Council on July 27, 1908. He felt that the postulated impossibility

[7] *Synopsis,* I, s.v. *Clandestinitas,* n. 1132.

[8] S. C. de Sacramentis, *Romana et aliarum,* 13 mart. 1910—*Fontes,* n. 2101; *Acta Apostolicae Sedis* (Romae, 1909-), II (1910), 193-196 (hereafter cited as *AAS*).

[9] *Synopsis,* I, s.v. *Clandestinitas,* n. 1134.

[10] Cf. Oesterle, *Ius Pontificium,* IX (1929), 142.

existed when the pastor was barred from assisting at the marriage by reason of the civil law. He based his reason both on the analysis implied in the decree *Ne temere* and on the tenor of the law. In support of his interpretation he cited the instruction sent at a much earlier time to the Prefect of Missions on the Island of Curaçao.[11] He regarded the refusal of the Congregation of the Council to settle the doubt merely as proof that it did not want to issue a general norm which could appear to advocate the violation of civil laws; it was preferable to have bishops recur in particular cases.[12]

De Smet (1868-1927), while crediting Ojetti's opinion with probability, tried to find a middle course between the latter's opinion and the one calling for the existence of a general impossibility. He felt that probably an *impossibilitas aliqua media* would suffice, i. e., one that affected not all the people in a certain territory or only an individual case, but one that in a certain locality affected certain classes of persons; in the latter event, one might regard it as the equivalent of a regional impossibility. It seemed to him that this opinion was in conformity with Article VIII of the decree *Ne temere,* inasmuch as the two prior schemata that would have required a common necessity were rejected in the final analysis by the Congregation of the Council when it adopted the final draft.[13] Once the probability of these opinions was admitted, there existed accordingly a *dubium iuris* with reference to the existence of a diriment impediment, in which situation the Church was known to supply for the deficiency, that might have actually obtained.[14]

Cronin [15] noted that it had been the common opinion of theologians prior to the promulgation of the decree *Ne temere* that the impossibility had to be common in a certain locality and not merely particular, i. e., for the parties in question. However, since the

[11] *Vide supra,* p. 33.

[12] Ojetti, *Synopsis,* I, s.v. *Clandestinitas,* n. 1135; De Smet, *De Sponsalibus et Matrimonio,* pp. 85-86.

[13] *De Sponsalibus et Matrimonio,* pp. 85-86; cf. also *ASS,* XL (1907), 565, 574.

[14] De Smet, *loc. cit.*

[15] *The New Matrimonial Legislation* (2. ed., revised and corrected. London: Washbourne, 1909), p. 219.

decree *Ne temere* makes no distinction in this regard, "in both cases the marriage would be valid."

De Becker (1857-1936), on the other hand, rejected the opinion regarding the sufficiency of a particular impossibility as proposed by Ojetti and De Smet. He claimed that this opinion lacked even extrinsic probability.[16] According to Oesterle, the reply of 1908 did not favor moral impossibility as a sufficient excusing factor because, even though subsequent to it there had been replies that allowed this in particular cases, these replies were never published. In fact, one could presume that what was thus allowed was not to be considered a general norm, since in the reply given on November 26, 1909, the Congregation for the Propagation of the Faith appended the phrase *in casu,* and in its reply of July 27, 1908, the Congregation of the Council gave faculties to the ordinaries of China to dispense in such cases. Surely, if the decree *Ne temere* really provided for such contingencies, the Congregation could have replied: *"Provisum* in Article VIII of the Decree *Ne temere,"* as they are accustomed to do, and all doubt would have been settled.[17]

Bearing in mind this troublesome divergence of opinion, certain ordinaries, were faced with the very practical problem of what to do in their territories, where pastors were forbidden to assist at marriages unless a civil marriage had preceded and, even though a civil marriage could not take place beforehand, a marriage had to be contracted in order to forestall certain evils and make provision for the good of souls. Despite the fact that in 1908 a similar problem had been presented to the Congregation and no guiding answer had been forthcoming, these bishops appealed to the Sacred Congregation of the Sacraments, asking the very same question, namely, whether, and if so, in what way, could provision be made in such circumstances.

On January 28, 1916, the aforementioned Congregation, meeting in a plenary session, decided that recourse should be made in each case, except in the case of danger of death, when any priest

[16] *De Sponsalibus et Matrimonio Praelectiones Canonicae,* etc., appendix, p. 52.

[17] *Ius Pontificium,* IX (1929), 141-144.

could dispense from the impediment of clandestinity, and thus permit the marriage to take place in the presence of two witnesses alone. Pope Benedict XV (1914-1922) confirmed this decision and decreed that it be made public.[18]

One would think that this reply should have settled the matter; but, such was not to be the case. Authors once again began disputing and taking sides as to whether the recourse in question was necessary *ad validitatem*, or merely *ad liceitatem*. Cappello was of the opinion that the reply did not settle the theoretical question, but simply indicated a norm of action. An invalidating law must be drawn up with an invalidating clause either expressly or equivalently. Such a clause or such a phrase was not to be found in the reply. In practice, therefore, as long as time was available, the recourse was to be made; but, once the marriage was contracted, *standum est pro valore*, even when the recourse had not been made.[19]

Those who supported the opinion which held that recourse was required for validity in every case appealed to the general wording of the reply, viz., that *one* should have recourse, and not simply that *they* (the petitioners in the case presented) should have recourse.[20] The fact that the Pope called for the publication of the reply seemed to prove that the reply was meant as an answer not merely in a particular case but rather as a general one for everybody. Their chief argument, however, derived from the reply of the Sacred Congregation of the Sacraments to the Bishop of Paderborn on March 9, 1916, protocol number 792/16, which was never officially published, but which is found in many manuals.[21] It seems that many foreign workers came to Paderborn during the war (1914-1918) and contracted marriage there apart from the presence of a priest. The priest could not assist at their marriages because of the civil laws. No recourse to the Holy See had been undertaken.

[18] S. C. de Sacramentis, 31 ian. 1916: ". . . recurratur in singulis casibus."—*Fontes*, n. 2114; *AAS*, VIII (1916), 36-37.

[19] *De Sacramentis* (3 vols. in 5, Vol. III [*De Matrimonio*], Taurinorum Augustae: Marietti, 1923), III *(De Matrimonio)*, n. 694.

[20] The wording is *recurratur* and not *recurrant*.

[21] E.g., Linneborn, *Grundriss des Eherechts nach dem Codex Iuris Canonici* (2. und 3. Auflage, Paderborn, 1922), footnote 3, page 331; Leitner, *Lehrbuch des katholischen Eherechts* (3. ed., Paderborn, 1920), p. 208.

The bishop referred the matter to the Holy See for adjudication and received the following reply: the ordinary should not account it as undignified to have recourse in every case according to the decree of January 31, 1916, as issued by this Sacred Congregation. As to the past, the ordinary was given the faculty of sanating the marriages about which the aforementioned letter spoke, but he had to make sure in each case of the continuance of the consent of the putative spouses, and he was to do whatever else the law required.[22]

The reply itself received varying interpretations. Leitner (1862-1929) believed that if dispensations from the impediment of clandestinity had been given without recourse, and in good faith, outside the danger of death, then all such marriages would have to be sanated. It was his opinion that the Holy See did not regard these marriages as invalid, because it said, in the words of his translation of *"Ordinarius ne dedignetur recurrere,"* that the ordinary should have the goodness or courtesy to recur to the Holy See in accordance with the decree of January 31, 1916.[23] Knecht (1866-1932) claimed that the dispensations were given simply *ad cautelam.*[24]

Vermeersch (1858-1936)-Creusen held that even outside the danger of death one can validly in such circumstances contract marriage before two witnesses until such time that the Holy See authentically declares otherwise. The reasons they proposed were: (1) this opinion had the authority of many authors in support of it, so that there was at least a *dubium iuris,* a positive and probable doubt regarding the impact of the law, and so it did not bind; and

[22] "Ordinarius recurrere non dedignetur in singulis casibus iuxta decretum editum ab hac S. Congregatione die 31 ianuarii, 1916. Quod spectat ad praeteritum, eidem Ordinario tribuitur facultas sanandi in radice matrimonia, de quibus in praedictis litteris, constito tamen sibi prius in singulis casibus de perseverantia consensus putatorum coniugum ceterisque de iure servandis."

[23] Leitner, *op. cit.*, p. 209; Oesterle *(Ius Pontificium,* IX [1929], p. 145) disagreed with this interpretation that the Holy See did not consider these marriages that had been contracted as invalid. He believed that if the Congregation did not consider these marriages as invalid, it would not have termed the people in question *putativi coniuges.*

[24] *Handbuch des katholischen Eherechts* (Freiburg im Breisgau: Herder, 1928), p. 647. Oesterle *(loc. cit.)* maintained that this cannot be found either in the text or in the context.

(2) there was no reply in which the Holy See stated directly that the marriages thus contracted were invalid.[25]

Vidal (1867-1938) and Vlaming (+ 1935) held invalid all such marriages which took place without the prescribed recourse.[26] The former went even further in stating that, after the reply of January 31, 1916, which was made public at the order of the Pope, and therefore should refer to all similar cases, he could not understand how the opinion which held that marriages could take place without the prescribed recourse had retained any probability. De Smet didn't go quite so far in the fourth edition of his work. He there expressed the opinion that after this reply one could not contract marriage before two witnesses alone in grave necessity unless recourse was had in each case. However, he was not without sympathetic understanding for the stand taken by Cappello, Vermeersch, Creusen, and others, inasmuch as the law seemed doubtful, and also inasmuch as the private reply given to the Bishop of Paderborn had not been promulgated as binding law.[27]

As all these authors have written also after the Code, whose law is substantially the same as that of the decree *Ne temere,* one can readily see that also after the Code's promulgation the problem of recourse remained as an unsettled question. Most of the authors felt that the reply of the Pontifical Commission for the Interpretation of the Canons of the Code, dated June 25, 1931, settled the matter satisfactorily.[28]

[25] *Epitome Iuris Canonici* (2. ed., 3 vols., Brugis, 1923-1925), II, n. 405; cf. also Vermeersch, *Theologia Moralis* (4 vols., Romae et Brugis, 1922-1924), III, n. 797.

[26] Wernz-Vidal, *Ius Canonicum ad Codicis Normam Exactum* (7 vols. in 8, Vol. V. [*Ius Matrimoniale*] 2. ed., Romae, Apud Aedes Universitatis Gregorianae, 1928), p. 644, footnote n. 68; Vlaming, *Praelectiones Iuris Matrimonialis* (3 ed., 2 vols., Bussum, 1919-1921), II, n. 590.

[27] *Tractatus Canonico-Moralis De Sponsalibus et Matrimonio* (4. ed., a Codice altera, Brugis: Beyaert, 1927, pp. 111-112 (hereinafter cited as *De Sponsalibus et Matrimonio*).

[28] "Whether the physical absence of the pastor or Ordinary mentioned in the reply of March 10, 1928, includes also a case where the pastor or Ordinary, although materially present in the place, is unable by reason of grave inconvenience to assist at the marriage, asking and receiving the consent of the contracting parties?"—The reply was in the affirmative.—*AAS, XXIII* (1931), 388.

In regard to the other condition required in Article VIII, there was unanimity among the authors regarding the required lapse of a full month in which an authorized priest could not be had before this extraordinary form of marriage could be invoked. Once the month had elapsed, even if the priest was expected momentarily, a marriage celebrated without his presence stood as valid, and even licit if necessity demanded it.[29]

Article 2. The Faculty of Dispensation From Diriment Impediments From the Decree *Ne temere* to the Code of Canon Law (1918)

It has been noted in the previous chapter that it was the common law teaching for many centuries that ordinaries could, under certain conditions, dispense in the forum of conscience from certain occult diriment impediments, certainly so when it was a question of convalidation, and most probably so when it was a question of a marriage still to be contracted. In the encyclical letters of 1888 and 1889, faculties were given to local ordinaries. These faculties could be habitually subdelegated to the pastors, and implied the power of dispensing in danger of death from public diriment impediments of the ecclesiastical law with a view to providing relief of conscience for the parties and legitimation for their children, if there were any. The faculty was to be used by the bishop when there was no time to refer the matter to the Holy See, and by the pastor when there was no time to reach the bishop. The faculty availed for all impediments but two, namely, the impediments arising from the Sacred Order of Priesthood and the impediment of affinity in the direct line when it derived through a *copula licita.*

These faculties had not been revoked, and therefore could be enjoyed even after the promulgation of the decree *Ne temere.* According to Article VII of the decree *Ne temere,* in the event that there could not be had for assistance at the marriage, either the pastor or the ordinary, or a priest delegated by either of these,

[29] Ojetti, *Synopsis,* I, s.v. *Clandestinitas,* nn. 1132-1133; De Becker, *De Sponsalibus et Matrimonio,* appendix, p. 52; Gennari, *Breve Commento della Nuova Legge sugli Sponsali e sul Matrimonio,* p. 32.

then any priest could assist at that marriage if a danger of death existed for either of the parties. However, even this provision could prove worthless if he found that there existed a diriment impediment between the parties. Accordingly, the Ordinary of Parma and others appealed to the Sacred Congregation of the Sacraments to grant a priest so assisting the same faculties that were granted to the bishops and pastors in 1888 and 1889. On May 7, 1909, the Congregation considered the matter in a general session, and on May 9th Pope Pius X approved its proposal to grant the priest mentioned in Article VII the faculty as requested.[30]

The encyclical letter of the Holy Office by which the faculties had been originally granted to the ordinaries remarked that the Supreme Sacred Congregation was asked by the Pope to consider the matter of granting faculties in the cases of danger of death when people who were living in a civil union or in concubinage wished to rectify their relationship and to make provision for the relief of their consciences. On the other hand, the grant of these faculties did not include the words "living in a civil union or in concubinage." A natural question arose: "was the faculty to be restricted solely to the latter case?" In answer to a query as to whether the priest mentioned in Article VII of the decree *Ne temere* and to whom faculties to dispense had been granted on May 14, 1909, was to be restricted in their use solely for the case of those living in a civil union or in concubinage, or whether he could use them even in the case wherein the parties were not living in such sinful relationships, but there existed some other reason for providing relief for the consciences of the parties and, if the case demanded it, for the legitimation of the offspring, the Congregation of the Sacraments answered in the negative to the first part, and in the affirmative to the second part.[31]

[30] " . . . quemlibet sacerdotem, qui ad normam art. VII decreti *Ne temere,* coram duobus testibus matrimonio adsistere valide ac licite potest, in iisdem rerum adiunctis dispensare quoque posse super impedimentis omnibus etiam publicis matrimonium iure ecclesiastico dirimentibus, excepto, sacro Presbyteratus Ordine et affinitate lineae rectae ex copula licita." S. C. de Sacramentis. *Parmen. et aliarum,* 14 maii 1909—*Fontes,* n. 2097; *AAS,* I (1909) 468-469.

[31] S. C. de Sacramentis, *Venetiarum,* 16 aug. 1909—*Fontes,* n. 2099; *AAS,* I (1909), 656.

On July 29, 1910, a reply was given to the final doubt to be resolved by this Congregation in this regard before the Code. It was decreed that within the scope of the phrase *quemlibet sacerdotem* (any priest), pointing to the priest who according to Article VII of the decree *Ne temere* assisted at a marriage when the danger of death was present and to one to whom faculties to dispense had been granted on May 14, 1909, was to be included also the pastor, even though he had not been given habitual subdelegation by his ordinary to dispense in such cases.[32]

[32] S. C. de Sacramentis, *Romana et aliarum,* 29 iul. 1910—*Fontes,* n. 2102; *AAS,* II (1910), 650.

Part Two
Canonical Commentary

INTRODUCTION

THE Code of Canon Law has, as has been seen in the historical conspectus, adopted with but slight modifications the discipline of the decree *Ne temere.* It sets forth two forms for the contracting of marriage, one the ordinary form, as indicated in Canons 1094-1097, and the other the extraordinary form, as delineated in Canon 1098. The latter form is used when the ordinary form is impossible of observance. It is interesting to note that both forms are substantial, juridic forms, each legally valid. The form delineated in Canon 1098 is not to be considered as a mere exception to the ordinary form; it is also a juridic form as valid and as legal as the ordinary form. This is plainly evident, first, from the fact that Canon 1098 is listed under Chapter VI of the Code treating of marriage, entitled *De Forma Celebrationis Matrimonii.* Secondly, Canon 1099 lists those who are bound to observe the law as to the form of marriage and states plainly that those mentioned are bound to the *form* mentioned above.[1] It does not list the canons for the ordinary form nor does it exclude the canon depicting the extraordinary form. Accordingly, one may say that those who are obliged to observe the ordinary form of marriage must, if the said ordinary form cannot be observed, contract marriage according to the extraordinary form and that the extraordinary form is binding on all those who in the absence of abnormal circumstances are bound to the ordinary form of marriage.

In the succeeding chapters, the writer proposes to treat of (1) the unavailability of a qualified witness for the marriage; (2) the postulated conditions for the use of the extraordinary form; (3) the necessity of having witnesses; (4) the postulated conditions for the licit use of the extraordinary form; (5) the power of dispensing enjoyed by a priest assisting at a marriage according to this form.

[1] Ad statutam superius formam servandam tenentur . . .

CHAPTER V

THE UNAVAILABILITY OF A QUALIFIED WITNESS FOR THE MARRIAGE

According to the natural law, the sole consent of the contracting parties to a marriage, externalized in words or signs, would suffice to bring the contract of marriage into existence. As long as there would be no impediment to stand in its way, marriage could be contracted in this manner. However, the Church, as a public authority and as custodian of the sacraments, prescribes certain formalities to be observed under pain of nullity in the exchange of matrimonial consent. True, it has no power over the natural value and validity of acts of the human mind and will. Still it can, and at times does, render such acts juridically inefficacious if certain prescribed formalities are not observed.[1] Accordingly, the Code states that marriage is brought into existence by the legitimately manifested consent of the parties who are capable in law of contracting marriage.[2] Unless this consent is legitimately manifested, it has no juridic effect and marriage is not contracted.

In order that consent be legitimately manifested, certain formalities must be observed. In ordinary cases, the consent must be expressed not only in the presence of two ordinary witnesses but also in the presence of an authorized or qualified witness, who assists in the name of the Church. Just as in ordinary civil matters the State may require the presence of a public notary for the validity of certain contracts, so also the Church may require the presence of its qualified witness for the marriage to be valid.[3] It is in this witness that the Church places its trust that a marriage has really taken place.[4]

[1] Wernz-Vidal, *Ius Matrimoniale* (ed. 3., a Philippo Aguirre recognita, 1946), n. 531 (hereafter this edition is used exclusively).

[2] Canon 1081, § 1.

[3] Gasparri, n. 932.

[4] Benedictus XIV, *De Synodo*, lib. XIII, c. XXIII, n. 6.

Although the Church requires the presence of a priest at the celebration of marriage, one must not forget that it is not the priest but rather the parties themselves who are the ministers of the sacrament. This can readily be seen from the fact that the marriage contract is *ipso facto* a sacrament among the baptized.[5] The importance of this doctrine becomes more evident when one realizes that if marriage is contracted apart from the presence of a priest, as long as the marriage is valid, the sacrament of matrimony is received. Nowhere in the Code is there any mention that in such an eventuality the sacrament would not be received. This would certainly be the case if the priest were the minister of the sacrament.

The wording of Canon 1098 is quite definite. The conditional clause beginning with *si* pertains equally to both sections of part 1 of the canon. It is only when the condition is verified that the extraordinary form may be used. The clause has the force of an invalidating law, since to use this form when the condition is not verified would render the marriage invalid. One may argue analogously from Canon 39, where it is stated that conditions are considered essential for the validity of rescripts if they begin with words like *si, dummodo,* and the like. The ordinary form is to be used at all times except when a qualified witness cannot be had. It will be necessary, then, first to treat of the nature of the valid assistance of a qualified witness at a marriage, and only subsequently of the nature of the impossibility of having such a qualified witness, which would permit one to use the extraordinary form of marriage.

Article 1. The Valid Assistance of a Qualified Witness At a Marriage

The Code of Canon Law in Canon 1094 lists the following as qualified witnesses to assist at marriages: pastors, local ordinaries, and priest delegates of either. Each of these within certain specified limits may validly assist at marriages. The persons mentioned in the first two classifications do so in virtue of the offices they hold and their jurisdiction may be termed ordinary; [6] the third classi-

[5] Canon 1012, § 2.

[6] Canon 197, § 1.

fication lists those who have no power to assist at a marriage except that which they receive from either the pastor or the local ordinary. Prescinding for the moment from the conditions under which these persons may validly act, one must ascertain which ecclesiastical persons fall under the classifications just enumerated.

A. *Qualified Witnesses in Law*

1. Pastors

Since there are no restricting clauses, anyone who is a pastor in the strict sense of the term (Canon 451, § 1) and anyone who has by law powers equivalent to those of a pastor (Canon 451, § 2) may fall under this classification.

PASTORS IN THE STRICT SENSE

Canon 451, § 1, defines a pastor in the strict sense as a priest or a moral person on whom a parish is conferred legally with the care of souls to be exercised under the authority of the local ordinary. A pastor can be a physical person or a moral personality. In the former case, he must be a priest.[7] This is a change from the pre-Code discipline, under which a parish could be conferred on a cleric who would subsequently become ordained. If it were to be conferred today on a cleric who had not yet been ordained a priest, the canonical provision would be invalid.[8] If the parish is given to a moral personality, e. g., to a religious house or to a capitular church and the like, then the vested care of souls pertains to the moral personality, but the effected care is entrusted to an actual vicar (*vicarius actualis*). He it is who has the exclusive care of souls with all the duties and rights of a pastor. The moral personality cannot claim any right to assist at any marriage; that right belongs to the *vicarius actualis* appointed by it.[9]

[7] Canons 451, § 1; 453, § 1; 154.

[8] Canon 453, § 1.

[9] Canons 471, §§ 1, 4; 452, § 2.

PASTORS IN THE WIDE SENSE

Under this group come all those who although they are not pastors, nevertheless have parochial obligations and rights equivalent to those of pastors and in law come under the name of pastors.[10]

1. *Quasi-pastors.* These are priests who are entrusted with the care of a quasi-parish, which is a territorial division of a prefecture or vicariate apostolic.[11] The relationship of a quasi-parish to a vicariate or prefecture apostolic is equivalent to the relationship of a parish to a diocese. The quasi-pastor has a church and has the care of the faithful in the quasi-parish to which he is assigned.[12] For purposes of clarity it is necessary to note here that, even in the vicariates or prefectures apostolic where quasi-parishes have not yet been erected, the missionaries, as far as marriages are concerned, are to be regarded as assistants of the vicars or prefects apostolic. The vicar or prefect may entrust them with the care of souls for the entire vicariate or prefecture or for a determined part of the same. Although they may have all the parochial powers delegated to them by the vicar or prefect apostolic, they are not pastors nor are they equivalent to pastors in law. In order that they may assist at marriages, they must have a general delegation from the vicar or prefect apostolic. This delegation may extend to the entire vicariate or prefecture or any determined part of it.[13]

2. *Parochial Vicars with full parochial powers.*[14]

(a) The actual vicar (*vicarius actualis*) who has the actual care of souls in a parish, the title to which is vested in a moral personality.[15]

(b) The administrator of a vacant parish (*vicarius oeconomus*). As soon as possible after a parish becomes vacant, the bishop is to appoint an administrator, who by law will have all the rights and duties of a pastor till a pastor is appointed to the parish.[16] Before

[10] Canon 452, § 2.

[11] Canons 216, § 3; 452, § 2, 1°.

[12] S. C. de Prop. Fide, instr. 25 iul. 1920—*AAS,* XII (1920), 331.

[13] S. C. de Prop. Fide, instr. 25 iul. 1920—*AAS,* XII (1920), 331 ff.

[14] Canon 451, § 2, 2°.

[15] Canon 471, §§ 1-4.

[16] Canons 472; 473, § 1.

an administrator is named by the ordinary, the care of souls devolves upon the assistant, if there is one in the parish; if there are more than one, on the senior assistant; if all have equal seniority, on the one who first came to the parish.[17] This would have little effect on the status of the assistants in the parish in regard to witnessing marriages except in cases where they have no general delegation from the local ordinary; if such should be the case, the administrator would receive this power *de iure*. If there is no assistant in the parish, the care of souls falls to the neighboring pastor; if it is a church that is entrusted to religious, it falls to the superior of the house.

(c) The substitute or supplying priest (*vicarius substitutus*) has full parochial powers unless the ordinary or the pastor himself has made certain restrictions in his power.[18] The vicar substitute supplies for a pastor whose legitimate absence from the parish is to be protracted beyond a week,[19] or is designated by the bishop to take care of a parish while an appeal is being made to a higher court or to the Holy See by the pastor against the sentence depriving him of his parish.[20] In the former case he is named by the pastor and receives approval from the ordinary. If the pastor is a religious, the substitute needs the approval not only of the ordinary but also that of the religious superior.[21] Should the departure of the pastor be unexpected and sudden, and his absence to last beyond a week, he is to inform the bishop immediately and indicate the priest who is substituting for him. The latter has by law all the rights and duties of a pastor immediately upon his selection and retains them while in such capacity unless the bishop should provide otherwise.[22]

As to the power of a priest supplying for the pastor whose absence is protracted beyond a week, the Pontifical Commission for the Interpretation of the Code has issued certain authentic interpretations. The vicar substitute may assist at a marriage *only after*

[17] Canon 472, 2°.

[18] Canon 471.

[19] Canon 465, § 4.

[20] Canons 1465, § 1; 1923, § 2; 2146, § 3; 2156, § 2; 2161, § 2.

[21] Canon 465, § 4.

[22] Canon 465, § 5.

he has received approval from the ordinary.[23] If he is a religious, he may assist at marriages after such approval even if he has not as yet received the approval of his religious superior.[24] If he was chosen by the pastor who had to depart suddenly and unexpectedly, he may assist at marriages from the moment of his selection and may continue to do so until the ordinary, whose approval in the meantime is anticipated, should decide otherwise.[25]

The Code speaks of approval by the ordinary. It does not state what type of approval is necessary. It cannot be said from the wording of the Code that explicit approval is necessary in each particular case. It would seem, according to Cappello, that a general approval given to the priests of a certain religious house in the diocese to fill such needs would suffice.[26] The power of approval by the ordinary is an ordinary power which is attached to his office. He can delegate the superior of a religious house in the diocese to select one of his own priests to act as vicar substitute for any parish in the diocese, upon the request of a departing pastor. Thus such a priest would *ipso facto* have the approval of the ordinary. If an assistant is left in charge of a parish by his pastor, he would be considered a *vicarius substitutus,* the approval of the ordinary being implicit in the fact of his designation as an assistant at that parish.[27]

If the absence of the pastor is not to last at least a week, even though provision is made for a priest to supply during his absence, this priest is not a substitute in the sense of the Code and has no power by reason of his office to assist at marriages. The

[23] Pontificia Commissio Interpretationis, 14 iul. 1922 ad IIum—*AAS,* XIV (1922), 527 (hereafter cited as P.C.I.); cf. also, Bouscaren, *The Canon Law Digest* (2 vols. and Supplement through 1948, Milwaukee, Wisc.: The Bruce Publishing Co., 1934, 1943, 1949), I, 539 (hereafter cited as *Digest*).

[24] *Ibidem,* ad IIIum.

[25] *Ibidem,* ad IVum.

[26] *Periodica de Re Morali, Canonica, Liturgica,* XIX (1930), 3* (hereafter cited *Periodica*).

[27] Toso. "Consilia et Responsa," *Ius Pontificium,* X (1930), 341-342; Carberry, *The Juridical Form of Marriage,* The Catholic University of America Canon Law Studies, n. 84 (Washington, D. C.: The Catholic University of America Press, 1934), p. 53.

Code is specific in demanding an absence that is expected to be longer than a week.

(d) Vicar Adjutant (*vicarius adiutor*) who is given by the ordinary to a pastor who by reason of age, weakness and the like is unable to fulfill his parochial obligations. If the pastor is totally incapacitated, the adjutant will take the place of the pastor in all things, except in regard to the *missa pro populo*. As a rule, the question of whether he can assist at marriages will be determined in his letters of appointment.[28]

(e) Assistants who have full parochial power. As a rule the *vicarius cooperator* does not have full parochial power.[29] He is given to a pastor who, because of the great number of souls committed to his care or for other reasons, cannot satisfactorily acquit himself of his parochial duties. He may be appointed to assist the pastor in the care of souls in the entire parish or simply in a certain part of it. In regard to assistance at marriages, canonists are agreed that by reason simply of his office he is without right and power in this matter, for otherwise Canon 1096, § 1, allowing a general delegation to be given to him, would be superfluous and meaningless. Furthermore, the Code Commission in its reply of December 28, 1927, stated that assistants with general delegation could subdelegate another priest to assist at a marriage at which they could assist. This reply would also be meaningless if an assistant had the power to assist at marriages in virtue of his office.[30] The problem received an answer in a private reply by the Eminent President of the Code Commission on September 13, 1923, which declared that assistants did not have ordinary power to assist at marriages.[31] A final answer, settling the whole matter, was given by the Code Commission on January 31, 1942. It was declared that an assistant cannot in virtue simply of his office assist validly at marriages.[32]

In the decree *Ne temere*, a priest to whom the care of souls had

[28] Canon 475.

[29] Canon 476, § 6, states that his power can derive through a commission of it from the ordinary or the pastor.

[30] *AAS*, XX (1928), 61, 62; cf. also Bouscaren, *Digest*, I, 541.

[31] Cf. *Apollinaris*, VII (1934), 77; Bouscaren, *Digest*, II, 333.

[32] *AAS*, XXXIV (1942), 50; Bouscaren, *Digest*, 332.

been entrusted by the ordinary in a definite territory in which parishes had not been canonically erected was to be considered the equivalent of a pastor.[33]

The Sacred Congregation of the Council on March 10, 1908, in a private reply to the ordinary of Trent stated that if *curatores animarum,* even though they were not pastors in the strict sense of the term, nevertheless had full parochial power immediately delegated from the bishop, they were to be considered equivalent to pastors as to the capability of assisting at marriages.[34] Gasparri believed that this can happen only in the case where an assistant is given full parochial power over part of a parish which is situated at a great distance from the parish church.[35] In such a case he would *de iure* have the power of assisting at marriages.[36]

3. *Personal Pastors.* According to the common law of the Code, pastors normally are termed territorial or local. The parish is a determined part of the territory of a diocese with a particular church and a determined people to whom is given a *rector* who is to be their pastor.[37] However, in virtue of an apostolic indult, parishes may be erected for a specific group of people living in a certain territory, in view, namely, of the difference in language or nationality. Likewise, there are parishes that may be termed strictly personal, e. g., for a certain family.[38] These groups constitute exceptions to the general rule that normally applies; still, at times, the allowance of such exceptions may be absolutely necessary. One may distinguish three classes of personal pastors, namely, strictly personal pastors; per-

[33] S. C. C., decr. *"Ne temere,"* 2 aug. 1907, Art. II—*Fontes,* n. 4340; *ASS,* XL (1907), 528.

[34] Cf. Linneborn, p. 345, n. 3.

[35] *De Matrimonio,* n. 935, 5°.

[36] Canon 476, § 2, with Canon 451, § 2, 2°. Cf. also S. C. C., *Principis Albertenen. et Saskatoonen.,* 5 mart. 1932, wherein the Congregation declares that one must look only to whether the permanent vicar has full parochial power to determine whether he is equivalent to a pastor. If he has this power, then according to Canon 451, § 2, 2°, he has all the rights and duties of a pastor. This declaration received the approval of the Pope on March 20, 1932. (*AAS,* XXIV [1932], 436-438.)

[37] Canon 216, § 1.

[38] Canon 216, § 4.

sonal pastors who have a specified territory; pastors whose jurisdiction is partly territorial and partly personal.

(a) Strictly personal pastors. Such pastors exercise a care of souls completely independent of the notion of territory. They may be entrusted with the care of souls of a certain family or families (*paroecia familiaris seu gentilitia*) or with the care of souls of the persons under arms (*paroecia castrensis*), as are military chaplains.[39] As to the power to assist at the marriages of their subjects, pastors who have no territory may assist at the marriages of their subjects anywhere in the world.[40]

As for military chaplains, the Code states that one must look to the particular faculties given by the Holy See.[41] The jurisdiction of the military vicar and his chaplains is strictly personal and may be exercised over their proper subjects any place on earth.[42] It embraces parochial power in regard to their own proper subjects.[43] In the list of faculties given to the Military Vicar of the United States by the Holy See, under number 17 of the faculties is listed the faculty pertaining to the valid assistance at marriages on the part of military chaplains. The military chaplains, in virtue of general delegation by the Military Vicar, may assist at marriages of all subjects of the Military Ordinariate placed under the chaplains' charge by the Military Vicar or his delegate.[44] At one time, the chaplain's powers were so personal that he could assist at marriages of only those who were attached to his post. This was changed so that a chaplain may assist at the marriages of *milites peregrini* who come to his military or naval post. His jurisdiction outside his post extends everywhere in regard to those who belong to his post; in regard to others who are subjects of the Military Ordinariate, he may assist at their marriages even at other posts, provided the post

[39] Gasparri, n. 976.

[40] S. C. C., *Romana et aliarum*, 1 febr. 1908 ad VIIum—*Fontes*, n. 4344.

[41] Canon 451, § 3.

[42] S. C. Consist., litt. ad Excmum ac Revmum Delegatum Apost. Amer. Sept., die 1 iulii, 1940, Prot. num 186/39—apud Bouscaren, *Digest*, II, 597.

[43] S. C. Consist., die 8 dec. 1939—*AAS*, XXXI (1939), 710; Bouscaren, *Digest*, II, 587.

[44] S. C. de Sacram., die 9 apr. 1941, Prot. num. 5446/41—apud Bouscaren, *Digest*, II, 597.

in question does not have a Catholic Military Chaplain of its own. Outside the military posts he has no jurisdiction over those who do not belong to his own post.[45]

The Sacred Consistorial Congregation placed the following under the jurisdiction of the Military Vicar and his chaplains:

1. All members of the Armed Forces belonging to the Army, Navy and Air Force who are in the active military service of the Federal Government or of the particular states;

2. The wives, children, relatives and servants of the men in the armed forces who reside in the same house with them;

3. All civilians staying within the limits of the military reservation;

4. All religious and others, even lay persons, who are attached to military hospitals;

5. All priests who are subjects of the Military Vicar, by reason of service with the Armed Forces.[46]

By reason of their territory, the local pastor and the diocesan ordinary have cumulative jurisdiction along with the military vicar and his chaplains over the subjects of the Military Ordinariate. The jurisdiction of the military vicar and his chaplains is not exclusively theirs; they share it with the local ordinary and the local pastor.[47] Furthermore, this jurisdiction extends merely to the Catholic parties listed among those who have been placed under the care of the Military Ordinariate. Therefore, if it is a case wherein neither party is subject to the Military Ordinariate or wherein only the person who is under the Military Ordinariate is a non-Catholic, the chaplain may not assist validly at such a marriage in virtue of his faculties. It would be necessary for him to be designated as an assistant in the parish within which the military reservation is situated and then receive general delegation to assist at marriages, or he would need special delegation for each particular marriage of this type.

[45] Marbach, "The Recent Instruction of the Sacred Consistorial Congregation Regarding Military Ordinariates"—*Jurist,* XII (1952), 149-150.

[46] Litt. ad Excmum ac Revmum Delegatum Apost. Amer. Sept. die 1 iulii, 1940 (Prot. num. 186/39)—Bouscaren, *Digest,* II, 587; *Jurist,* XII (1952), 146.

[47] S. C. Consist., instr. 24 apr. 1951 sub num. 2.—*AAS,* XLIII (1951), 563.

One might mention under the classification of strictly personal pastors the chaplains of orphanages, sanatoria, homes for the aged, universities and the like, whose institution has been taken completely away from the jurisdiction of the local pastor, the chaplain having full parochial power.[48] The jurisdiction of these chaplains to assist at marriages is not as wide as that of the strictly personal pastors mentioned above. They may assist at marriages of only those persons whose care has been entrusted to them and only in the place wherein they exercise their jurisdiction.[49]

(b) Personal pastors exercising jurisdiction in a certain territory. These pastors exercise jurisdiction over certain determined persons in a determined territory which is not strictly a territorial parish.[50] Such are, for example, parishes constituted in a large city for the faithful of another rite, or for the faithful of a different nationality or language group. It is a question of fact whether their jurisdiction is merely personal or whether they are given certain territorial boundaries within which to exercise their jurisdiction. In the United States, the so-called national parishes have become not merely personal but also territorial.[51] In the United States at least, unless the contrary be evident, the pastors of national parishes hold their territory cumulatively with the pastors of one or more territorial parishes. It is in view of this fact that pastors of these national parishes may assist validly within the limits of their respective parishes at all marriages of all Catholics, even those who are not their parishioners.[52]

In his Apostolic Constitution *Exsul Familia* of August 1, 1952,

[48] Canon 464, § 2.

[49] S. C. C., *Romana et aliarum*, 1 febr. 1908—*Fontes*, n. 4344.

[50] Coronata, *De Sacramentis Tractatus Canonicus* (3 vols., Vol. III [*De Matrimonio et de Sacramentalibus*], Taurini-Romae: Marietti, 1946), III, n. 565 (hereafter cited as *De Matrimonio*).

[51] Ciesluk, *National Parishes in the United States*, The Catholic University of America Canon Law Studies, n. 190 (Washington, D. C.: The Catholic University of America Press, 1944), p. 124. The author also mentions that there have been various objections to this view on the ground that such parishes are strictly personal and cannot be otherwise since they have no definite territory and the law requires that there be only one pastor in a given territory. Cf. *Periodica*, XVI (1927), 261*.

[52] S. C. C., *Romana et aliarum*, 1 febr. 1908 ad VIIIum—*Fontes*, n. 4344.

Pope Pius XII has made provision for the spiritual care of immigrants, displaced persons, and the like.[53] In article 32 of the constitution, local ordinaries were urged to seek indults from the Sacred Consistorial Congregation for the purpose of erecting parishes for immigrants, displaced persons and foreigners of a certain nationality or linguistic group, wherever such parishes were not already in existence. Wherever the erection of such parishes does not seem feasible in the judgment of the local ordinary, the latter is to follow the rules laid down in articles 34-40 of said constitution.

The constitution states that the local ordinaries are to entrust the care of souls of these foreigners, immigrants, etc. to priests who are of the secular clergy or belong to a religious order, who are of the same nationality or speak the same language and who have a special mandate for such work from the Sacred Consistorial Congregation. The care of *advenae* and *peregrini*[54] who are of the same nationality or language group should also be entrusted to such priests. The persons, the care of whose souls has been entrusted to such priests, would then become subjects of these priests.

Priests to whom such care has been entrusted are the equivalent of pastors in the care of souls. Their jurisdiction is personal, to be exercised solely over persons the care of whose souls has been entrusted to them. This jurisdiction they hold cumulatively with the local territorial pastor.

In regard to marriages, such a priest, to whom the care of foreigners has been entrusted, assists validly at a marriage only within the limits of the territory entrusted to him and only in a case in which at least one of the contracting parties is his subject.[55]

As for pastors of parishes constituted for the faithful of an Oriental rite, it must be said that they may assist, by reason of

[53] *AAS*, XLIV (1952), 649-704.

[54] Article 40 of the constitution *Exsul Familia* lists as belonging to this classification: (1) all foreigners, including those who may have migrated from the colonies of that country, who are staying in a foreign country, no matter what the period of time may be, no matter what the reason, even if it be for the purpose of studying; (2) their descendants in the first degree of the direct line, even in the cases where they may have already become citizens in said country.

[55] Pius XII, const. "*Exsul Familia,*" 1 aug. 1952, art. 39; S. C. Consist., 7 oct. 1953, II, a.

their office, only at marriages in which at least one of the two contracting parties is a member of his own Oriental rite,[56] or, if neither of the contracting parties is of his particular rite, at least one of the parties is considered by law his parishioner and he that party's proper pastor.[57] This situation takes place in two cases, namely, in a territory in which a hierarchy of the rite to which the party belongs has been constituted there is no pastor of this rite. In this eventuality, the party's hierarch names a pastor of another rite, with the permission of this pastor's ordinary, to care for the spiritual welfare of the people of the rite in question.[58] The second case is the one when locally there has not been constituted a hierarchy of the rite to which the party belongs. In this eventuality, the ordinary of the place becomes the proper ordinary of the party, and the pastor of the place can become his proper pastor; if there is more than one ordinary, e.g., of two different rites, then the proper ordinary is the one designated by the Holy See.[59]

(c) Pastors whose jurisdiction is partly personal and partly territorial. This situation develops when a pastor having a definite territory within which to exercise his jurisdiction has been given the care of certain determined persons or groups of persons who live outside his own proper territory.[60] These pastors validly assist at all marriages within the limits of their territory and likewise at the marriages of the parties entrusted to their care, but dwelling outside the territory, no matter where they may be. Outside his territory, it is solely at the marriages of these parties that he may assist validly.[61]

2. The Local Ordinary

In Canon 198, the Code of Canon Law very specifically enumerates the ecclesiastical personages who are to be considered local ordinaries and therefore in virtue of Canon 1094 are empowered

[56] Pius XII, litt. apost. "*Crebrae allatae sunt,*" 22 febr. 1949, Canon 86, § 1, 2°.—*AAS,* XLI (1949), 108.

[57] *Ibidem,* Canon 86, § 2.

[58] *Ibidem,* Canon 86, § 3, 2°.

[59] *Ibidem,* Canon 86, § 3, 3°.

[60] Coronata, *De Matrimonio,* n. 536, 3.

[61] S. C. C., *Romana et aliarum,* 1 febr. 1908 ad IXum—*Fontes,* n. 4344.

by law to assist at marriages. They are the following: the Roman Pontiff for the entire world; in their own respective territories, residential bishops, and abbots as well as prelates *nullius* together with their vicars general; administrators, vicars and prefects apostolic and the vicars delegate appointed by the vicars and prefects apostolic,[62] and finally those who by law or approved constitutions succeed the above-mentioned during a vacancy in the office or if the office is otherwise impeded, i.e., the cathedral chapter, acting as a corporate body according to Canon 101,[63] the abbatial or prelatial chapter[64] before the election of a vicar capitular,[65] in mission countries, the pro-vicars and pro-prefects apostolic,[66] and, in countries where cathedral chapters are not constituted, the diocesan board of consultors, whose function it then becomes to designate the administrator of the vacant diocese.[67] Such corporate bodies as such would not assist at a marriage. They would delegate a priest to act in their stead.

3. Priest Delegate

The third group of *testes auctorizabiles* (qualified witnesses) for valid assistance at a marriage according to Canon 1094 is constituted by priests delegated either by the pastor or by the local ordinary. This is a concession from the lawgiver allowing those who have ordinary power to designate another to act as a qualified witness in their stead.[68] The Code uses the words *licentia*[69] and *delegatio*[70] interchangeably to designate the power to assist validly

[62] In a letter of the Sacred Congregation for the Propagation of the Faith dated December 8, 1919, and addressed to Vicars and Prefects Apostolic, the latter were empowered henceforth to name a vicar delegate who would have all the faculties a vicar general has by law. This was a new grant because vicars and prefects apostolic did not have, in virtue of the Code of Canon Law, the power to appoint a vicar general. Cf. *AAS,* XII (1920), 120.

[63] Canon 431.

[64] Canon 324.

[65] Canon 435.

[66] Canon 309, § 2.

[67] Canon 427.

[68] Canon 1095, § 2.

[69] Canon 1095, § 2; 1096, § 1, § 2.

[70] Canon 1094; 1095, § 1.

at a marriage. This assistance is not strictly an act of jurisdiction; still it follows the rules of delegation of jurisdiction.

The canon speaks only of a *delegatus;* it does not, however, mean to exclude the *subdelegatus,* i.e., a properly subdelegated priest. The delegate receives his authorization from one who has ordinary power; the subdelegate, his from one who has either a general delegation *a iure* or a general delegation from one who has ordinary power.

Delegation and subdelegation must follow certain definite rules as enacted in Canon 1096, § 1. If these prescripts are not observed, the delegation or the subdelegation will be invalid, and the consequent assistance at marriage will also be invalid (*secus irrita est*). These rules are the following:

1. The delegation or subdelegation must be expressly given. This excludes any tacit, interpretative, or presumed delegation on the part of the delegate.

2. It must be given to a priest.

3. It must be given to a determined priest, i.e., the delegator must in some way himself determine the priest to whom he is granting delegation. He may do so explicitly or implicitly, directly or indirectly, so long as he is the one who is determining the priest to be delegated.[71] The Code Commission declared a delegation invalid because the pastor did not sufficiently determine the priest to be delegated.[72] He need not know the priest he is delegating as long as he is determining the priest himself.[73]

4. It must be given for a definite, specific marriage. It need not be restricted for one marriage only; it may be given for many at the same time as long as each one is sufficiently determined. The sole exception to this rule is the general delegation which may be given in virtue of Canon 1096, § 1, to a *vicarius cooperator* by the local ordinary or by the pastor himself, to be exercised only in the limits of the parish to which he is assigned. This power of the

[71] Cappello, *De Matrimonio,* n. 674.

[72] P.C.I., 20 maii, 1923, ad VIum—*AAS,* XVI (1923), 115; Bouscaren, *Digest,* I, 541.

[73] Cappello, *De Matrimonio,* n. 674; Carberry, *The Juridical Form of Marriage,* p. 86.

vicarius cooperator, may also be subdelegated by him to another priest for a given marriage.[74]

These are the only requirements in Canon 1096, § 1. However, as will be seen shortly, the pastor and the local ordinary may assist validly at marriages only in the limits of their respective territories. Hence, they cannot grant delegation for assistance at marriages outside these territories, for they cannot grant to another the power they themselves do not possess.[75] Even if the delegation was extorted by force or fear, it would according to the more common opinion, nonetheless be valid because of the lack of an invalidating clause to that effect in the Code.[76] The delegation may be communicated to the delegate in any manner in which people communicate with one another, even by telephone, telegraph, radiotelephone, etc.[77] On the part of the delegate, it is the more common opinion that he must at least implicitly accept the delegation which has been given.[78] If he knows nothing of the delegation that is sought and obtained for him, he cannot validly assist at the marriage.[79] However, if the delegation is given in a diocesan statute or by law, the delegate's acceptance is not required for it can be given even to a priest who is unwilling and refuses it.[80]

B. *The Postulated Conditions for Valid Assistance At a Marriage*

After enumerating those who can act as qualified witnesses at a marriage, the Code in the very same canon limits this capability by postulating certain conditions which must be fulfilled in order that the aforementioned ecclesiastical personages may assist validly at a marriage.

[74] P.C.I., 28 dec. 1927—*AAS,* XX (1928), 61; Bouscaren, *Digest,* I, 541.

[75] "Nemo potest plus iuris transferre in alium quam sibi competere dignoscatur."—Reg. 79, R.J., in VI°.

[76] Wernz-Vidal, *Ius Matrimoniale,* n. 538; Chelodi-Ciprotti, *Ius Canonicum de Matrimonio* (5. ed., Vicenza: Società Anonima, 1947), n. 133 (hereafter cited as Chelodi-Ciprotti).

[77] De Smet, *op. cit.,* p. 95, nota 5; Wernz-Vidal, *op. cit.,* n. 538, 5.

[78] Coronata, *De Matrimonio,* n. 542.

[79] Cappello, *De Matrimonio,* n. 675.

[80] Wernz-Vidal, *Ius Matrimoniale,* n. 538, nota 46; Gasparri, n. 951.

1. Possession of One's Canonical Office

In the case of those who may validly assist at a marriage in virtue of the office they hold, it is necessary that they have taken canonical possession of their respective offices according to the prescripts of the Code.[81] As for vicars general or the vicars delegate of the vicars and prefects apostolic, they may assist at a marriage from the moment that they have entered upon their respective offices by accepting the appointments to them. The ecclesiastics who succeed to the rule of a vacant diocese by law or by approved custom, may exercise this right as soon as the diocese is vacant. The vicar capitular and the administrator of a diocese have this right upon the acceptance of their election to that office by the respective cathedral chapter or board of consultors.

This much is quite evident from the fact that the faculty to assist at a marriage is dependent on the office that is held. If one has not as yet taken canonical possession of the office, he does not enjoy this faculty. If the office is lost, the faculty is lost with it. The legislator himself determines in what manner canonical possession of an office is taken.

As for the delegate, since it is not ordinary power that he possesses, the canonical possession of an office is not necessary. All that is needed is that he have acquired a valid delegation from either the pastor, the local ordinary, or one who has a general delegation to assist at marriages, and that he stay within the limits of his mandate.

2. Absence of Legal Disqualification

Although one may hold a canonical office in virtue of which one may assist at a marriage, the Code circumscribes this right by forbidding him under pain of nullity to exercise this right if by way of sentence he has been excommunicated, suspended from his office, or placed under interdict, or also when he has been declared as such.[82] A declaratory sentence is issued by an ecclesiastical judge or legitimate superior after the guilt of the party who has

[81] Canons 334, § 3; 1444, § 1; 313; 293.

[82] Canon 1095, § 1, 1°.

incurred a *latae sententiae* penalty has been established.[83] A condemnatory sentence refers to penalties that are incurred as *ferendae sententiae* punishments. Once the guilt of the party in reference to a crime punishable by law has been verified, an ecclesiastical judge or a legitimate superior may be compelled by the law itself to inflict the prescribed penalty, but at times he may be allowed by the law to use his own discretion in doing so.[84] The legal disqualification, then, depends on whether a sentence has been passed on the offender. Before sentence has been passd, even though the pastor or the local ordinary may have incurred a *latae sententiae* penalty, he may assist validly at a marriage. There is one exception to this. Anyone who lays violent hands on the person of the Holy Father becomes *ipso facto* a *"vitandus"* [85] and, according to law, the customary procedure for declaring such a one a *"vitandus"* need not be observed in order that the legal disqualifications follow.[86]

The Code speaks of suspension *ab officio*. Since the question here is one of penalties, the law must be interpreted strictly.[87] Furthermore, the very wording of the canon (vel . . . vel . . . vel . . .) indicates that this is an all-inclusive enumeration.[88] Accordingly, it will not include suspensions *a divinis, a beneficio, ab ordine, a iurisdictione*.[89] The latter suspension will not deprive one of the right of assisting at marriages, for such assistance is not strictly an act of jurisdiction.[90] One must remember, however, that a general suspension also includes a suspension *ab officio*.[91] Hence the pastor

[83] Canon 2223, § 4.

[84] Canon 2223, § 2 and § 3.

[85] Canon 2343, § 1, 1°.

[86] Canons 2258, § 2; 2266.

[87] Canon 19.

[88] Gasparri, *De Matrimonio*, n. 973; Carberry, *op. cit.*, p. 67.

[89] Gasparri, *loc. cit.;* Cappello, *De Matrimonio*, n. 662.

[90] One might question the validity of excluding a suspension *a beneficio*, since a benefice (c. 1409) consists of an *office* with the established right to an income therefrom. Surely the greater, i.e., the benefice, should include the lesser, i.e., the office. However, since this is a matter of penalties, the law must be interpreted strictly. Therefore, a suspension *a beneficio* would not disqualify a priest.

[91] Canon 2278, § 2.

who has incurred a general suspension through a condemnatory sentence or has been declared to be under a general suspension, is legally disqualified from assisting at a marriage.

In the event that a declaratory or a condemnatory sentence has been passed on a pastor or a local ordinary, provision will usually be made by the legitimate superior to supply for the offender during the time of his legal incapacity.

In virtue of Canon 1095, § 2, if a pastor or a local ordinary has been legally disqualified, he cannot delegate another to act in his stead. The wording of the canon excludes this, since only those who may validly assist can grant a delegation to another to assist in their place. If despite their disqualification they could do so, they would be giving to another a power which they themselves do not have.[92]

A very pertinent question at this point is whether the delegate falls under the same legal disqualification if he should be excommunicated, suspended *ab officio,* or sustaining an interdict after the intervention of a declaratory or a condemnatory sentence. Commentators are divided. Wouters (1864-1933) [93] and Vlaming (+ 1935) [94] hold that he does not fall under the same disqualification, since the Code does not mention this, and since in the absence of such a restriction one cannot hold that he is disqualified. Vermeersch-Creusen,[95] De Smet [96] and Cappello [97] held that in view of the purpose of the law he also is disqualified. In view of the doubt of law, one must hold that a marriage witnessed by such a delegated priest would have to be held as valid.[98]

92 "Nemo potest plus iuris transferre in alium quam sibi competere dignoscatur"—Reg. 79 R.J. in VI°.

93 *De Forma Promissionis et Celebrationis Matrimonii* (ed. 5a ad Codicem Iuris Canonici accommodata, Bussum in Hollandia, 1919), p. 25.

94 *Praelectiones Iuris Matrimonii* (3. ed.), n. 573.

95 *Epitome,* II, 396.

96 *De Sponsalibus et Matrimonio* (4. ed.), n. 122.

97 *De Matrimonio,* n. 677.

98 Canons 15 and 209.

3. Restriction Within Respective Territory or Delegated Jurisdiction

Within their respective territories the pastor and the local ordinary can validly assist at all marriages, even of those who are not their subjects. Outside their respective territories they cannot, without proper delegation, assist at any marriages, even of their own subjects,[99] unless the pastor's relationship to them is of a strictly personal nature, as was mentioned above. A church or a house of an exempt religious community is to be considered as part of the territory of the parish or diocese within which it is located and, therefore, the pastor or the local ordinary may assist validly at marriages celebrated therein.[100]

The delegate may not exceed the terms of his mandate, otherwise he would be acting invalidly.[101] He may assist at only those marriages for which he has been delegated and only within the limits prescribed by the delegator. The territorial limits may never exceed the territorial limits of the delegator himself.[102]

4. Unconstrained and Active Assistance

The Code demands that, for the marriage to be valid, it is necessary that the qualified witness be not constrained by force or fear in asking and receiving the matrimonial consent of the contracting parties.[103] The purpose of the law is to have marriages not take place *ex inopinato*, i.e., unknown to the pastor, and to have the assisting priest to be completely free, as the dignity and the reverence due to the sacrament demand. There is a change in the present law. No longer is passive assistance at a marriage sufficient; active assistance in the manner of asking and receiving the consent to the marriage from the contracting parties is now necessary for validity, even in cases of mixed marriages.[104] The Pon-

[99] Canon 1095, § 1, 2°.

[100] S. C. de Sacramentis, *Romana et aliarum*, 13 mart. 1910, ad VIIIum—*Fontes*, n. 2101.

[101] Canon 203, § 1.

[102] Canon 1095, § 2.

[103] Canon 1095, § 1, 3°.

[104] This is evident from a reply of the Supreme Sacred Congregation of the Holy Office, dated November 26, 1919, to the Archbishop of Prague. This

tifical Commission for the Interpretation of the Code declared on March 10, 1928, that Canon 1102, § 1, revoked the faculty which was granted in some places by the Holy See of assisting passively at illicit mixed marriages.[105] It is necessary, then, that the assisting priest both ask and receive the matrimonial consent. If he were merely to ask and not receive, or not to ask and yet receive the consent, the marriage would be invalid.[106] All that is required for validity is that the priest manifest his interrogation clearly enough to be actually understood, and that the parties externally manifest their intentions to him.[107] For reasons that are obvious, a priest who is deaf and dumb or is not *sui compos* cannot assist validly at a marriage.[107a]

The active assistance given by a priest at a marriage will suffice for validity provided that he is not constrained by force or grave fear to take part in the marriage. The fear that is spoken of is one that is inflicted *ab extrinseco,* for Canon 1095, § 1, 3°, speaks of a priest being *constrained* to assist; this can mean only extrinsic fear.[108] It must be inflicted for the purpose of having the priest assist at the marriage, and it matters not whether it is inflicted by the parties themselves or by others. Gasparri declared that fear of a punishment threatened by the ordinary when a priest unjustly refuses to assist at a marriage, or a threat made by the parties to report the priest who unjustly refuses to assist at their marriage, will not in-

reply was not published in the *Acta Apostolicae Sedis,* but it may be found in the *Linzer Quartalschrift,* LXXIV (1921), 249. The Holy Office thereby changed its directive which was approved by Pius X on May 23, 1912, and issued on June 21, 1912 (*AAS,* IV [1912], 443-444), wherein passive assistance was allowed in certain countries in mixed marriages in which the non-Catholics refused to make the usual promises.

105 *AAS,* XX (1928), 120; Bouscaren, *Digest,* I, 546.

106 Cappello, *De Matrimonio,* n. 669.

107 Wouters, *op. cit.*, p. 20; Payen, *De Matrimonio in Missionibus ac Potissimum in Sinis Tractatus Practicus et Casus* (2. ed., 3 vols., Zi-ka-wei: Typographia T'ou-Se We, 1935-1936), II, n. 1774 (hereafter cited as Payen); Rossi, *De Matrimonii Celebratione iuxta Codicem Iuris Canonici* (Rome: Pustet, 1924), 81 (hereafter cited as Rossi).

107a Rossi, p. 81; Carberry, p. 76.

108 Payen, *loc. cit.;* Cappello, *De Matrimonio,* n. 668.

validate the marriage in question.[109] One should note that fraud perpetrated by the parties or others to secure the assistance of the priest will not render such assistance invalid, since the Code does not mention it as invalidating the assistance.[110]

Article 2. Unavailability of a Qualified Witness

If a marriage cannot, without serious inconvenience, be contracted according to the ordinary form, then the obligation to observe it ceases.[111] Inasmuch as the form is divisible as to the presence of a qualified priest and as to the presence of ordinary witnesses, there must be observed that part of the form which can be observed.[112] In Canon 1098, the legislator prudently made provision for cases in which a qualified witness would be unavailable to the parties. The matter of witnesses will be taken up in a subsequent chapter.

In the preceding article it was shown who can act as a qualified witness for the Church at a marriage. It was seen that some do so in virtue of the office they hold; others, in virtue of the delegation they have received. Both groups must follow certain prescriptions in order that their assistance at a marriage may be valid. Outside these limitations the rendered assistance is invalid and the marriages thus contracted are null. In the ordinary course of events, when a Catholic, or for that matter one who is bound by the juridic form of marriage,[113] desires to contract marriage, he must invoke the assistance of such a qualified witness. Unless he or she does so, the attempted marriage will have no juridic effects.[114] However, at times this ordinary form is impossible of observance; it is then that the exception, the extraordinary form of Canon 1098, may be allowed. In order to avoid uncertainty and ambiguity, the legislator himself

[109] *De Matrimonio,* n. 979.

[110] Gasparri, *loc. cit.*

[111] Gasparri, n. 988.

[112] Such was the usual reply of the S. C. of the Council whenever it allowed marriages to be contracted without the observance of the form prescribed by the decree *Tametsi.* *Vide supra,* p. 39.

[113] Canon 1099.

[114] Canon 1094.

wisely decreed what type of impossibility would suffice for one to be excused from observing the ordinary form.

The legislator postulated that a pastor, a local ordinary, or a delegated priest, who according to Canons 1095 and 1096 could act as a qualified witness *cannot be had (haberi)* and *cannot be approached (adiri)*. The *nequit haberi* pertains to the priest himself, when it is he himself who is impeded.[115] He cannot be had if he cannot be called either by the party or by others, or also, though he has been called, if he cannot get to the parties in order to ask and receive their consent,[116] e.g., for the reason that he is sick, is confined in prison, or has become insane. Likewise the same can be said if the priest who can be had cannot assist validly because he has become legally disqualified,[117] is sojourning outside the limits of his territory,[118] or lacks the needed delegation and cannot receive any. In all these cases, even though materially he is at hand, he is not to be had in the sense required by the canon, i.e., for assistance in accordance with the requirements of Canons 1095 and 1096.

A qualified witness cannot be approached or gotten to *(adiri)* as long as even one of the parties cannot go to him for the purpose of contracting marriage,[119] e.g., one of the parties is sick or crippled, or there is no qualified witness in the region. This latter impossibility of being unable to get to a qualified witness will be the more likely occurrence in cases of danger of death; the former one the more likely occurrence in cases of a foreseen month's absence.

One must keep in mind that the canon pertains to all possible qualified witnesses. It does not refer simply to one possible qualified witness or to one's proper pastor or local ordinary or to a priest delegated exclusively by them when it deals with an unavailable agent. The wording is quite general; it postulates the unavailability of all possible qualified witnesses as a condition for the valid

115 Coronata, *De Matrimonio,* n. 565.

116 Cappello, *De Matrimonio,* n. 691; Payen, II, n. 1816, footnote 4; Regatillo, *Interpretatio et Iurisprudentia Codicis Iuris Canonici* (Santander: Sal Terrae, 1949), p. 380; Gasparri, n. 1004; Wernz-Vidal, *Ius Matrimoniale,* n. 544, footnote 62.

117 Canon 1095, § 1, 1°.

118 Canon 1095, § 1, 2°.

119 Cappello, *loc. cit.;* Coronata, *loc. cit.;* Gasparri, *loc. cit.*

use of the extraordinary form. If a neighboring qualified witness can, without serious inconvenience, be approached or had in his own territory, the condition is not fulfilled and the canon will be inoperative. Further it must be noted that the conjunction *vel* as used by the legislator in his joining of the words *haberi* and *adiri* must be taken in the conjunctive, and not in the disjunctive, sense. The *vel* has the force not of *aut . . . aut,* but rather of *nec . . . nec. . . .* Both impossibilities must be in evidence, otherwise the extraordinary form cannot be invoked.[120]

The impossibility of having or getting to a qualified witness must be, but also suffices if it is, personal, i.e., it must affect both parties in the matter of having a priest or either party in getting to the priest.[121] The impossibility need no longer be *communal,* i.e., affecting the entire community, as was required under the Tridentine discipline, nor must it be *local,* as postulated by the decree *Ne temere.* In fact, if the impossibility is common and local but not personal, it will not suffice. This is evident, first, from the wording of the text of the canon which does not postulate a communal or local impossibility. It postulates only a serious inconvenience. If the impossibility is not personal, there is no inconvenience.[122] Secondly, it is evident from the common opinion of the commentators who have written since the Code has come into effect.[123]

120 Sipos, "Forma Celebrationis Matrimonii extra Mortis Periculum,"—*Ius Pontificium,* XX (1940), 94; Miceli, "De Forma Celebrationis Matrimonii iuxta c. 1098,"—*Monitor Ecclesiasticus,* LXXV (1950), 235; Schönsteiner, *Grundriss des kirchlichen Eherechts* (2. ed., Wien: Ludwig Auer, 1937), p. 727.

121 Coronata, *loc. cit.;* Payen, II, n. 1816; Gasparri, n. 1006; S. R. Rotae, *Nullitatis Matrimonii,* 29 iul. 1926, coram R.P.D. Josepho Florczak, dec. XXXVI, n. 4—*Decisiones,* XVIII (1926), 289; *Nullitatis Matrimonii,* 7 dec. 1931, coram R.P.D. Andrea Jullien, dec. LV, n. 3—*Decisiones,* XXIII (1931), 473.

122 S. R. Rotae, *Nullitatis Matrimonii,* 29 iul. 1926, coram R.P.D. Josepho Florczak, dec. XXXVI, n. 4—*Decisiones,* XVIII (1926), 289.

123 De Smet, *De Sponsalibus et Matrimonio,* n. 131; Payen, II, n. 1816; Cappello, *loc. cit.;* Coronata, n. 565; Chelodi-Ciprotti, n. 136; Rossi, p. 111; Cerato, *Matrimonium a Codice I.C. integre desumptum* (ed. IV., Patavii, 1929), p. 164 (hereafter cited as Cerato); Chrétien, *De Matrimonio (Praelectiones)* (2. ed., Metis: Typis Imprimerie du Journal "Le Lorrain," 1937), n. 340; Knecht, *Handbuch des katholischen Eherechts,* p. 645; Vlaming, *Praelectiones Iuris Matrimonialis,* II., n. 201.

The impossibility must be actual, i.e., a priest *de facto* cannot be had and cannot be approached; in other words, a priest is *actually* unavailable. This much is clear from the text of the canon. With reference to the unavailability, nothing is said about a prudently foreseen or possible unavailability. The text clearly states that the consequences obtain only if the stated condition is verified. A priest is not unavailable if he is merely thought to be, or also adjudged to be, or even prudently foreseen to be, unavailable. All these would predicate merely a condition which in the judgment of the parties could be subjectively regarded as true, but objectively remained erroneous. Such a practice would be fraught with danger and could lead to frequent clandestine marriages. The Pontifical Commission for the Interpretation of the Canons of the Code in the interpretation given to the canon on November 10, 1925, stated that the *fact* of the absence of a pastor was not sufficient for the use of this canon; it demanded that this condition be foreseen to last for a month.[124] Therefore, the *fact* of absence is essential; it is the starting point for the application of the canon. Logically, it is impossible to have a prudent prevision that a *presumed absence* will last a month. It is the actual impossibility that is postulated by the Rota in its jurisprudence.[125] Therefore, a mere presumption on the part of the parties as to the unavailability of a competent priest, even an otherwise prudent judgment as to his unavailability, will

[124] *AAS*, XVII (1925), 583; Bouscaren, *Digest*, I, 542.

[125] S. R. Rotae, *Nullitatis Matrimonii*, 30 ian. 1926, coram R.P.D. Maximo Massimi, pro-Decano, dec. IV, n. 3: ". . . requiritur in primis *factum* quoddam quod nempe haberi vel adiri nequeat sine gravi incommodo parochus vel loci ordinarius vel sacerdos delegatus qui matrimonio adsistant."—*Decisiones*, XVIII (1926), 18; *Nullitatis Matrimonii*, 7 dec. 1931, coram R.P.D. Andrea Jullien, dec. LV, n. 3: ". . . *Factum* imprimis a lege requiritur, seu *rerum conditio* sunt ipsa verba cit. canonis, ob quam *reapse* et *objective* haberi vel adiri nequeat sine gravi incommodo sacerdos competens. . . . Sed quia falsa nostra existimatio rei veritatem non mutat, si partes, ex vana imaginatione vel errore etiam excusabili, existiment haberi vel adiri non posse sine gravi incommodo sacerdotem competentem, deest factum seu non verificatur conditio rerum requisita a lege et invalidum est matrimonium contractum coram solis testibus. Non sufficit ergo quaelibet subjectiva persuasio, sed requiritur impossibilitas seu gravis difficultas saltem moralis, innixa fundamento reapse existente."—*Decisiones*, XXIII (1931), 472-473. [Italics are the writer's.]

not suffice. An objectively false judgment, even one that is excusable, will not change the facts of a determined case.[126] Accordingly, unless the *fact* of a priest's unavailability is established, the canon may not be used. Prudent prevision refers to and only follows upon an actual absence or impossibility. Prudent judgment is to be made about the *duration* of the absence, and not about the *fact* of the absence. This pertains to both eventualities mentioned in number 1° of the canon.

In view of this requirement, it seems inadmissible to subscribe to the opinion of Payen[127] and Vlaming,[128] whom Payen cited in support of his own opinion, which states that as long as one has prudently judged that a competent priest cannot be had or approached without serious inconvenience a marriage contracted apart from his presence would be valid, even though, *de facto,* this judgment is objectively erroneous. The reason they give is that all that the canon requires is a human conviction as to the unavailability of a qualified priest. Since it is only a human judgment, so they contend, it is not infallible. Both authors seem to fall into the error of applying here with reference to the factual absence of a qualified witness the prudent judgment which is later required in the canon (1°) with reference to a continued state of things. The prudent judgment is postulated by the canon only *after* the *factual* absence has been established, and it is restricted to the expected duration of the said actual absence or unavailability. Vlaming identified the prudent judgment regarding an extant case of danger of death with the prudent judgment regarding the unavailability of a competent

[126] S. R. Rotae, *Nullitatis Matrimonii,* 30 ian. 1926, coram R.P.D. Maximo Massimi, pro-Decano, dec. IV, n. 3: "Hinc, si quis per errorem, licet excusabilem, credat ministrum catholicum . . . haberi vel adiri non posse sine gravi incommodo, coram solis testibus contrahere nequit."—*Decisiones,* XVIII (1926), 18; *Nullitatis Matrimonii,* 7 dec. 1931, coram R.P.D. Andrea Jullien, dec. LV, n. 3; "Sed quia falsa existimatio rei veritatem non mutat, si partes, ex vana imaginatione vel errore etiam excusabili existiment haberi vel adiri non posse sine gravi incommodo sacerdotem competentem, deest factum seu non verificatur conditio rerum requisita a lege . . . non sufficit ergo quaelibet subiectiva persuasio, sed requiritur impossibilitas seu gravis difficultas saltem moralis, innixa fundamento *reapse existente.*"—*Decisiones,* XXIII (1931), 473.

[127] *Op. cit.,* II, n. 1816.

[128] *Praelectiones Iuris Matrimonialis,* II, n. 589.

priest. In the case of a danger of death, a prudent judgment is all that can be expected; still, this must follow upon the fact of a factual unavailability of a qualified witness. Even in danger of death, if it is taken for granted that a priest is unavailable and *de facto* he is available and could assist at the marriage, a marriage contracted without his assistance would be invalid. As for the unavailability of a competent witness, it is a case that differs widely from the case of a danger of death. The judgment, even though innocently erroneous, will not change the fact of a priest's availability. If the judgment is erroneous, the marriage will be invalid.[129]

In postulating only a serious inconvenience as an excusing cause, the legislator demonstrated that he did not demand an absolute or physical impossibility. Such would be the case, for example, if there were no priest in the region, as would happen on a deserted island, or if there were no means of reaching him, as would happen in a village in the mountains that is blocked all winter by snowdrifts. In such cases the natural right of a person to marry would supersede the obligation of the ecclesiastical law, and the latter would cease to bind. The Church itself acknowledges this. All that the legislator demands is that there be a moral or relative impossibility of having a priest assist at one's marriage, i.e., for these persons and in these circumstances. If it is only with great difficulty that a person can get to a priest or vice versa, the requirement in this canon will have been fulfilled. In determining what would constitute a serious difficulty, the legislator indicated that such a difficulty would obtain if the parties could not approach the priest, or the priest the parties, except with serious inconvenience. He does not demand a most serious inconvenience (*gravissimum incommodum*).[130]

What constitutes a serious inconvenience? This is a difficult question, one to which a definitive, all-inclusive answer can hardly be given. Because of the various circumstances and various combination of circumstances that could produce an inconvenience serious enough to excuse one, it is impossible to formulate a general norm. Gasparri very prudently noted that an inconvenience which is light for one

[129] S. R. R., *locc. citt.*
[130] Payen, II, n. 1817.

may be serious for another.[131] One must judge each case individually, taking into consideration the parties and the priest, their capabilities, the circumstances of time and place, the means at their disposal, etc.

It can be said that a grave inconvenience is present if, in getting to a qualified witness, notable moral or material harm would befall the parties, the priest, or the common good.[132] The material harm could arise from natural or free causes. In the former category one may list the following: the danger of contagion, of floods, of oppressive heat (for people who are weak), of heavy storms, and the like. These usually obtain in cases wherein people are constituted in danger of death. Among those deriving from free causes, one may point to serious riots, persecutions of Christians, danger from marauding bands, etc. As for moral harm, authors list the case wherein a penitent reveals in a confession on his deathbed that, despite the fact that everyone believes he is married, he had never contracted marriage with the woman with whom he has been living in concubinage. It is held that the penitent need not grant permission to the confessor to seek delegation to assist at his marriage from a competent priest who is physically absent. The reasons given are that the good name which must be spared might be endangered if delegation were to be sought from the pastor or the ordinary and that at times there would be danger of violating the sacramental seal.[133] One might question the validity of this argument, in a case in which the sacramental seal would not be involved. Unless it should be that the pastor or the local ordinary are very good friends of the penitent, and it would be most difficult for the penitent to have them know of the situation, the reason would seem not to be a valid one. The pastor may be trusted with the secret as much as the other witnesses whose presence the canon requires. The pastor is trusted with the revalidation of any and all invalid relationships.

[131] *De Matrimonio*, n. 1006: ". . . incommodum enim quod mihi grave est, tibi potest esse leve."

[132] Gasparri, *ibid.;* P.C.I., 3 maii, 1945—*AAS*, XXXVII (1945), 149; Bouscaren, *Digest, Supplement through 1948*, p. 157.

[133] Payen, II, n. 1817; Cappello, *De Matrimonio*, 691; Chelodi-Ciprotti, n. 136, b; Vlaming, *Praelectiones Iuris Matrimonialis*, II, n. 587; Wernz-Vidal, *Ius Matrimoniale*, n. 544.

In danger of death, the priest may in virtue of Canon 1044 dispense the parties from the form of marriage.

Circumstances could be such that they would cause serious harm to the common good if one were to observe the ordinary form of marriage. It could very well happen that the priest is the only one in the territory and that his assistance at the marriage would cause the loss of his ministrations, e.g., during an epidemic when people are dying, or run the risk of his imprisonment or of the prohibition to exercise his priestly functions. The same situation could obtain in the case of a doctor or a nurse who could, as far as they themselves are concerned, get to a priest, but who seem barred from making that approach in view of the fact that their ministrations are essential to so many sick people, especially if they are the only ones in the region. The serious harm to the common good would excuse them from observing the ordinary form of marriage if the other conditions postulated in Canon 1098 are present.

Serious inconvenience would also be present when there are not available the ordinary means of getting to a priest, or of having a priest come to the parties. As an ordinary means of contacting a priest in order to have him come, or to have him delegate someone, there exists the possible use of a messenger or of an ordinary letter,[134] or even the ready employment of special delivery or air mail service.[135] The parties are not obliged to make use of extraordinary means that indeed may be at their disposal. The commentators are of the opinion that the use of the telephone, telegraph, cablegram and the like is not mandatory, inasmuch as such a means of communication is in the jurisprudence of the Holy See considered as an extraordinary means.[136] They base their arguments on two replies from the Holy See which exclude the use of the telephone and the

[134] Chrétien, *De Matrimonio (Praelectiones),* n. 340; Ubach, *Compendium Theologiae Moralis* (2 vols., Friburgi Brisgoviae: Herder, 1926-1927), II, n. 855; Sipos, *Ius Pontificium,* XX (1940), 95; Payen, II, n. 1817; Wernz-Vidal, *op. cit.,* n. 544.

[135] Heylen, *Tractatus de Matrimonio* (ed. 9., Mechliniae: Dessain, 1945), p. 269.

[136] Regatillo, *Interpretatio et Iurisprudentia Codicis Iuris Canonici,* p. 380; Aertyns-Damen, *Theologia Moralis* (2 vols., 14. ed., 6. post Codicem, Torino: Marietti, 1944), II, n. 842; Heylen, *loc. cit.;* Wernz-Vidal, *loc. cit.*

telegraph as means of contacting the Holy See for dispensations or for receiving notification of the same.[137] It has always been the practice of the Roman Curia to consider these as extraordinary means. It has been felt that these are unsafe means because of the danger of having the *gratia* exposed to nullity and because of the fact that information is had by people (operators) who have no right to the same. There are authors, however, as Chrétien,[138] Bender,[139] Sipos,[140] who do not consider the use of the telephone and the telegraph as something extraordinary, since today their use is quite frequent and the telephone has become an ordinary means of communication. They feel that there is no danger to be feared in their use if one considers merely the securing of a delegation or a contacting of the pastor or the ordinary. This opinion seems the better one to the writer, since the purpose underlying the replies from Rome would not be verified in such a case. Besides, the canon does not mention extraordinary means; it merely postulates the presence of a serious inconvenience. If the use of a telephone or of the telegraph is not a serious inconvenience to the parties in question, how can the requisite condition of the canon be verified? However, one must remember that their use is still considered as something extraordinary by the Holy See [141] and according to the

137 The first was from the Secretariate of State to the Bishop of Strasbourg on January 5, 1892. It read as follows: "Ad nonnulla evitanda incommoda quae hisce temporibus evenerunt, Emus Cardinalis a secretis Status mihi in mandatis dedit, nomine Sanctitatis Suae ut Amplitudini Tuae, sicut et aliis Ordinariis in Germania significarem quod, si quae gratiae seu dispensationes a sacris Congregationibus Romanis et ab aliis Ecclesiasticis Institutis impetrandae sint: eaedem non per telegraphum, sed in scriptis, petatur."—*ASS,* XXIV 1891-1892), 447. The second was a reply from the Holy Office, dated August 14, 1892, which read: "Se sia valida una dispensa matrimoniale eseguita dall' Ordinario dietro l'avisso telegrafico, prima di avere ricevuto il documento autenico della grazia concessa. *R. Negative,* nisi notitia telegrafica transmissa fuerit ex officio auctoritate S. Sedis. SSmus adprobavit.—*ASS,* XXIX (1896-1897), 642.

138 *Op. cit.,* n. 340.

139 Vlaming, *Praelectiones Iuris Matrimonii* (ed. 4., a L. Bender, Bussum in Hollandia: Paulus Brand, 1950), p. 429 (hereafter cited as Vlaming-Bender).

140 *Ius Pontificium,* XX (1940), 95.

141 P.C.I., 12 nov. 1922, ad Vum—*AAS,* XIV (1922), 662; Bouscaren, *Digest,* I, 502.

common opinion of the authors. Accordingly, if the only means available to the parties of reaching the pastor are the telephone and the telegraph, it is to be considered a grave inconvenience and consequently, until the Holy See declares otherwise, one may proceed as if he were unavailable. One might say that a *dubium iuris* exists and therefore the law does not bind.[142]

The distance to be traveled may constitute a grave inconvenience. Once again all the circumstances will have to be considered. Most certainly the parties or the priest are not expected to undergo a great expense or to make a dangerous trip to get to one another. A short railroad trip can hardly be classed as a serious inconvenience. Payen believes that a round trip that would require in all three days would be a serious inconvenience.[143] Under ordinary circumstances the distances between parishes would not be classed as something extraordinary, for otherwise the people would even be excused from attending Mass on Sundays and holydays. The use of the aeroplane is not to be considered mandatory at all. As for the use of the automobile, many authors [144] hold that its use is to be considered as an extraordinary means and therefore to be disregarded. However, as Cappello observes,[145] one must consider the circumstances of each place to determine whether its use is something ordinary or extraordinary. This appears true especially in the United States, where the automobile has become practically a common necessity. Its use would hardly constitute a serious inconvenience for the greater number of people, especially if they have one or easily can get the use of one. In such a case, the serious inconvenience would hardly be classed as *personal* to the parties, as indeed it must be if it is to serve as an excuse from the law. Each case would have to be judged individually for a determining of whether a serious inconvenience is present.

What distance would excuse the parties or the priest if an automobile or the like is unavailable? Once again it would be necessary

[142] Canon 15.

[143] *De Matrimonio,* II, n. 1817, 4), 4°, a.

[144] E.g., Vlaming, *Praelectiones Iuris Matrimonii,* II, n. 586; Aertnys-Damen, *loc. cit.*

[145] *De Matrimonio,* n. 237.

to consider the circumstances of the case, the pecuniary condition of the parties, the condition of the roads, the weather, the safety in taking such a trip, etc. One is not expected to take a trip that is not safe or one that would necessitate a risk to one's life or health. In all these problems one must be guided by the cardinal principle: "What is serious for me may be light for you," and that the inconvenience must be a personal one, since a common one will not invariably suffice. If the parties or the priest can without serious inconvenience do whatever is to be done, they are obliged to do it, for otherwise the inconvenience would not be a personal one and the essential condition of the canon would not be verified.

A question that proposes itself now is whether the canon is applicable in a case where a qualified witness is indeed available in that he is not physically absent, but at the same time refuses to assist at the marriage. There is no doubt that the exceptive provision of the canon will not apply if the competent witness refuses to assist because of some impediment, or because of a lack of certainty regarding the free state of the parties. This canon must be understood in conjunction with the other canons on marriage; it is not to be taken alone. The priest must always accommodate his action to the ruling of Canon 1019, which prescribes that a priest is not to assist at a marriage until he has attained moral certainty that there is nothing to stand in the way of its valid and lawful celebration. Until he has that certainty, he is not allowed to assist at such a marriage. A refusal on this account is completely in accord with the law. Were this type of refusal to constitute him as "absent" for the parties or as causing them a serious inconvenience, it would destroy the very safeguards instituted by the legislator. The subjective persuasion of the parties as to their free state in regard to marriage is not sufficient; it must be demonstrated.[146] For a priest to act in any other way would make the law ridiculous, for on the one hand the law forbids his assistance, and on the other it would allow the parties to contract apart from his presence.

If the only possible qualified witness is manifestly unjust in his refusal to assist at a marriage, would that constitute him as absent and thereby allow the parties to invoke the provisions of Canon

[146] E.g., Canon 1069, § 2.

1098? An example might illustrate the point at issue. The parties are not bound by an impediment either of the divine or the ecclesiastical laws. They have fulfilled all the requirements of the civil and ecclesiastical law in preparation for the contracting of marriage. There is absolutely no doubt about their free state. The only reason the priest may have is his dislike for the parties. Must the couple be kept from contracting marriage or, granted that all the other conditions as postulated in Canon 1098 are present, may they contract marriage apart from his presence?

It seems that this type of "absence" is not comprehended by the legislator in Canon 1098. Such an action would indeed be a rare occurrence for which the legislator would not seek to make provision by way of an enacted law.[147] The canon does not distinguish between a priest who is willing and a priest who is unwilling to assist. Finally, it is only by stretching the meaning of the words of the canon—but as furnishing an exceptive norm it must be interpreted strictly—that one can consider such a priest as one who is absent, or as one who cannot be had or approached. Accordingly, the provisions of Canon 1098 would not apply to such a case.

Still, some provision must be made for the parties under such circumstances when they rightfully wish to marry. There is no express provision in the law for such a case. However, in virtue of Canon 20, it seems that Canon 1098 could be invoked as a norm of action in this case. One can say that Canon 1098 exists as a law enacted in a given similar case, i.e., when a priest cannot be had. Secondly, the general principles of law when applied with the equity that is proper to Canon Law seem to demand such a course of action. It has been a commonly accepted rule in ecclesiastical jurisprudence that in any equal conflict between the ecclesiastical law and the natural law, the latter prevails. Such would be the case with the natural right of marrying. Hence, if all the other conditions postulated in Canon 1098 are verified, the parties may contract marriage according to the norm of Canon 1098. This they may do, not primarily in virtue of Canon 1098, but rather in virtue of Canon 20.

[147] For laws are to be adapted to events which frequently occur rather than to such as rarely happen. In fact what happens only once or twice, as Theophrastus says, legislators omit."—D. (1.3) 5, 6.

The situation is quite different where the priest is available but, in view of some grave harm which threatens either him, the parties or the common good, is either unable or unwilling to assist. This would usually happen when the civil laws conflict with the laws of the Church. There were instances, e.g., in Mexico, when priests were forbidden to assist at marriages under the penalty of death. In other countries, a non-observance of the civil laws by the priest in assisting at marriages could lead to heavy fines or even imprisonment. The parties may be free to contract marriage as far as the Church is concerned, but are forbidden to do so because of some impediment of the civil law which the Church does not recognize. This can happen, e.g., when the civil law forbids miscegenation; when it demands that a man have completed his military training before it allows him to marry; when it refuses to grant a marriage license to the parties because one or both parties are legally bound by former ecclesiastically invalid marriages; when medical certificates are required before the issuance of a marriage license and a medical certificate is refused. In such a case the parties have a natural right to marry, but the priest cannot assist at their marriage for fear of grave harm. Could one consider that a priest in such circumstances could not be had or approached *sine gravi incommodo*, or, in other words, would Canon 1098 apply to such a case?

This problem has had a long history in the matrimonial discipline of the Church beginning with the famous reply to Curaçao in 1785 and ending with the replies of the Pontifical Commission for the Interpretation of the Canons of the Code in 1931 and of the Congregation of the Sacraments in 1935.[148]

With the publication of the Code of Canon Law, this matter had not been settled. The commentators who took sides on the interpretations of the decree *Ne temere* continued in the same vein of thought. Those who claimed that this case fell within the purview of the law as it was found in the Code, offered the following arguments:

[148] P.C.I., 25 iul. 1931—*AAS*, XXIII (1931), 388; S. C. de Sacramentis, ad Epum. Metensem, 24 apr. 1935—*Periodica*, XXVII (1935), 45.

(1) The words of the canon are very general and are not to be restricted;
(2) The decrees of the Congregation of the Sacraments, dated January 31, 1916, and to the Bishop of Paderborn, March 9, 1916, did not settle the theoretical question, but merely gave a norm of action. There was no invalidating clause in either reply;
(3) If time is had, recourse should be made to the Holy See; however, if it is not, one must hold for the validity of the marriage according to Canon 1014;
(4) There is a doubt of law and therefore Canon 15 applies;
(5) Nowhere has the Holy See declared such marriages invalid; until it does so authentically, such marriages cannot be held invalid.

The proponents of the other view fall back on the practice of the Roman Curia under the discipline of the decree *Ne temere.* Since the Code practically restates Article VIII of that decree, it is really not a new law, and hence must be interpreted as the earlier law in virtue of Canon 6, 2°. The legislator, therefore, implicitly accepted the replies of the Congregation of the Sacraments, which was the official interpreter of the decree *Ne temere.* It was their contention that recourse to the Holy See, which was demanded by the Congregation, was still in effect. They claimed a further victory in the private reply of the same Congregation to the ordinary of the diocese of Metz. This reply was dated May 25, 1920. It showed that the Sacred Congregation still demanded recourse to itself in such cases.[149] It was but a private reply, and consequently did not have a universal binding force. It pertained merely to the problem at Metz. On June 16, 1922, the ordinary of the Diocese of Bruges was allowed by the Congregation of the Sacraments to permit a marriage in the presence of witnesses alone.[150] The course of action pursued by the Congregation seemed to indicate that the canon did not pertain to the case in point. Since the replies were

[149] "Ordinarius provideat per opportuna media ad hoc ut opifices exterarum nationum in sua dioecesi commorantes sibi comparare valeant documenta pro explendis nuptiis etiam coram civili magistratu: quatenus vero id obtineri nequeat, recurrendum est ad S. Congregationem in singulis casibus."—apud De Smet, *De Sponsalibus et Matrimonio,* p. 110, footnote 3.

[150] Cf. De Smet, *op. cit.,* p. 110, footnote 1.

merely of a private nature, the commentators continued to hold the opinions they espoused previously. Finally, the problem seemed settled by an authentic interpretation of the Code Commission in the year 1928. It was asked whether Canon 1098 was so to be understood that it referred only to the physical absence of a pastor or local ordinary. The reply was in the affirmative.[151]

Canonists immediately began to interpret this reply in the sense that only a physical absence of a qualified witness from the place where the marriage was to be celebrated would allow Canon 1098 to be invoked. A moral absence—when a priest was indeed present, but refused to assist at the marriage because of some grave harm threatening him for such contemplated assistance did not suffice.[152] This reply also disallowed the use of the concession in the canon in cases wherein a pastor refused to assist at a marriage because he felt that by so doing he could forestall a misalliance, e.g., a mixed marriage, or because there was a great disparity in the ages of the parties, or in view of the extreme youth of the parties, and the like.

The reply did not settle the controversy. Canonists began to reason that the reply could have two meanings, viz., physical absence from the place of the marriage and, also, a presence indeed in the place, but a physical absence from the act of the celebration of the marriage. Hence the controversy continued,[153] and necessitated a further reply from the Pontifical Code Commission. It was asked whether the physical absence of the pastor or the ordinary mentioned in the reply of 1928 includes also a case wherein the pastor or the ordinary, although materially present in the place, is unable by reason of grave inconvenience to assist at the marriage asking and receiving the consent of the parties. The reply was in

[151] P.C.I., 10 mart. 1928: "An Canon 1098 ita intelligendus sit ut referatur tantum ad physicam parochi vel ordinarii loci absentiam. *R. Affirmative.*—*AAS,* XX (1928), 120; Bouscaren, *Digest,* I, 542.

[152] Maroto, "Animadversiones ad responsa ad proposita dubia 10 martii, 1928"—*Apollinaris,* I (1928), 334-339; De Becker, "De Recta Canonis 1098 Codicis Iuris Canonici Interpretatione," *Ephemerides Theologicae Lovanienses,* IX (1932), 284-291.

[153] *Periodica,* XXI (1932), 42-45.

the affirmative.[154] Cardinal Gasparri, the eminent president of the Code Commission, in the new (1932) edition of his treatise on the matrimonial discipline of the Code, stated that by the grave inconvenience mentioned in this reply the Code Commission had in mind especially the inconvenience arising from civil laws which forbid or prohibit certain marriages.[154a] Many commentators understood the reply in that sense.[155]

However, there were those who could not see how the reply referred to the moral absence of a qualified witness. For them it was just a wider interpretation of the term physical absence. A qualified witness could be physically absent if, even when he was materially present in a place, he could assist at a marriage by asking and receiving the matrimonial consent of the parties because of some *physical* impediment, e.g., the danger of contracting sickness or a disease; very bad weather, especially at night; a serious riot inducing danger to one's life or bodily integrity. All these had to be considered as physical and not as moral impediments to his presence. These were what the Code Commission referred to in its reply of July 25, 1931.[156] This group continued to teach that it was unwarranted to apply this response to the case wherein a priest was impeded by the civil law from assisting at a marriage. There was no room for an exception. All such cases, except in danger of death, would have to be referred to the Holy See in accordance with the policy adopted by the Congregation of the Sacraments prior to and subsequent to the publication of the Code. In danger of death, provision was made for relief through the faculty of dispensing as enjoyed by the persons mentioned in Canons 1043 and 1044.

[154] P.C.I., 25 iul. 1931: "An *ad physicam parochi vel Ordinarii absentiam*, de qua in interpretatione diei 10 Martii 1928 ad canonem 1098, referendus sit etiam casus, quo parochus vel Ordinarius, licet materialiter praesens in loco, ob grave tamen incommodum celebrationi matrimonii adsistere nequeat requirens et excipiens contrahentium consensum. *R. Affirmative.—AAS,* XXIII (1931), 388; Bouscaren, *Digest,* I, 542.

[154a] De Matrimonio, n. 1017 *in fine.*

[155] Jelicic, "Consultationes," *Ius Pontificium,* XV (1935), 126; *Ius Pontificium,* XI (1931), 255-256; *Periodica,* XXI (1932), 43-45.

[156] Maroto, *Apollinaris,* IV (1931), 381; De Becker, *Ephemerides Theologicae Lovanienses,* IX (1932), 289.

At first glance, the reply of 1931 seems to be in apparent conflict with the repy of 1928. The latter postulates the physical absence of a qualified witness; the former seems to allow the use of Canon 1098 in the case of the moral absence of a priest. This is a serious problem. Either the replies are in complete accord, or they are at variance. If they are at variance, then the first is either declarative and the second extensive, or the first is restrictive and the second extensive. There is no reason to suspect that such is the case. One is not to presume that legislation in such an important matter would be changed in such a short time. It must be presumed, then, that the replies are in harmony.

Gasparri maintained that in the first reply (March 10, 1928), the Code Commission had in mind the fact that the moral presence of a priest at a marriage would not suffice for the validity of the marriage; that a physical, active participation in asking and receiving the consent of the parties was necessary. In the second reply (July 25, 1931), it had in mind the case wherein some serious inconvenience (*grave incommodum*) arose from the civil laws.[157] If one keeps in mind that the Code Commission had in mind two distinct, separate cases, then one can harmonize the two replies.

The reply of 1928 gives no indication that the physical absence there spoken of was related to the question of the asking and the receiving the matrimonial consent. Still, according to Gasparri, that is exactly what was implied. An example may help to illustrate the point. A priest wishing to forestall a marriage at which he is constrained to assist is present at its celebration but takes no active part, since he neither asks for nor receives the consent of the parties. He is indeed present in the material sense of the term but in reality is morally absent. The Code Commission replied that only his physical absence would allow the use of Canon 1098. This is in keeping with the other canons of the Code. If it allowed the use of Canon 1098 in the cases of a moral absence in this sense, then it would contradict Canon 1095, § 1, 3°; active participation by a priest would be of no consequence, because, in the event that he was only materially present but took no active part, the marriage would still be valid, *servatis servandis ad normam canonis 1098.*

[157] *De Matrimonio,* n. 1017.

He would be considered absent. Therefore, according to the Code Commission the physical presence but the moral absence in the sense described would not fall within the purview of Canon 1098.

In the 1931 reply a completely different situation is contemplated. The qualified witness is at hand and, were it not for the prohibition by the civil law, could physically be present and actively assist. However, to do so would cause him, the parties, or the common good a serious inconvenience. Therefore, he cannot assist at the marriage. He may be materially present in the place where the marriage is being contracted, even in the next room. However, he is actually absent, in the physical, material sense of the term from the celebration of the marriage, even though he may be considered as morally present. In such a case Canon 1098 could be invoked according to the reply of the Code Commission.

A closer inspection of the text of the canon will show that this type of case does fall within the comprehension of the canon. It is quite general, requiring an unavailability of a qualified witness in consequence of some serious inconvenience. There is no specification of the type of inconvenience in the canon itself. Knowing the great controversy that had been raging at the time, the legislator could have specified the inconvenience had he so intended. Since he had not, the presumption is that he did not want to. A further presumption favoring the inclusion of this type of case under Canon 1098 can be gleaned from the fact that to the wording of Article VIII of the decree *Ne temere* has been added the phrase *"sine gravi incommodo."* Truly, a prohibition by the civil law constitutes a serious inconvenience. *Ergo.*

In view of Gasparri's explanation as to the mind of the Pontifical Commission for the Interpretation of the Canons of the Code and in view of the private reply to the Bishop of Metz,[158] it is safe to conclude that the prohibition by the civil law, when threatening serious harm, e.g., fines, imprisonment, etc., constitutes a serious inconvenience which makes a qualified witness unavailable, and thus allows the use of the extraordinary form of marriage. Recourse to the Holy See is no longer necessary.

[158] S. C. de Sacramentis, ad Epum Metensem, 24 apr. 1935—*Periodica,* XXVII (1935), 45.

Since the replies of 1928 and 1931 were merely declarative interpretations of the law, explaining the words of the law which in themselves were certain and clear but whose meaning had been called into doubt through a misinterpretation by the authors, they have a retroactive effect which reveals whatever binding force they had since the Code of Canon Law has come into effect.[159]

In practice, then, if all the conditions postulated by the canon are verified, one need not fear to use the concession granted by the canon in cases in which a priest is forbidden by the civil law to assist at a marriage. The law makes provision for such cases, and it should be made use of. There are authors who recommend that instead of using Canon 1098 the ordinary should allow the use of the marriage of conscience,[160] or delegate some unknown priest who is passing through the territory and need not fear reprisals from the civil law. What purpose this would serve is hard for the writer to see. The danger of harm from the civil law will still threaten the priest for assisting at a marriage of conscience, even though it is highly secret. It will also threaten the parties for entering a civilly forbidden or even a civilly bigamous marriage. As for the selecting of an unknown priest, one runs the risk of incurring the anger of the civil authorities against all priests and against the Church in general. The Code had these eventualities in mind. The fact that no mention is made of them in the canon leads one to the conclusion that they may not be looked upon as conditions for the valid use of the extraordinary form.

In its latest interpretation given to this canon, the Code Commission has declared that the *grave incommodum* (serious inconvenience) mentioned in Canon 1098 is not merely that which threatens the pastor or the ordinary, but also that which threatens either or both of the contracting parties.[161] It seems that the serious in-

[159] Jelicic, "Consultationes," *Ius Pontificium,* XV (1935), 126.

[160] Canons 1104-1107.

[161] P.C.I., 3 maii 1945: "Utrum grave incommodum de quo in canone 1098 sit tantum illud quod immineat parocho vel Ordinario vel sacerdoti delegato qui matrimonio assistat, an etiam illud quod immineat utrique vel alterutri matrimonium contrahenti." *R. Negative* ad primam partem; *affirmative* ad secundam.—*AAS,* XXXVII (1945), 149; Bouscaren, *Digest,* Supplement through 1948, p. 157.

convenience that threatens the parties must be of the type whose source is unjust, e.g., an unjust civil law, and not one whose source is not unjust, e.g., the loss of a job because the firm does not keep married parties, or the loss of a pension because the party contracts marriage. Such a loss seems not to offer any excuse from the observance of the ordinary form of marriage. The example of the loss of a pension was presented to the Holy See but it was declared by the Congregation of the Sacraments after World War I that the practice of the Congregation should be followed namely that the loss of a pension was not a sufficient cause for permitting the celebration of marriage without the civil rite (this question was proposed by the Bishops of Italy).[162]

In view of this latest response, it seems that, even if a priest is willing to assist at the marriage of a couple, the parties may insist that they be allowed to use the concession of Canon 1098. An example may illustrate the point at issue. A couple may be unable to fulfill the requirements of the civil law in regard to marriage, requirements which in their case are unjust. They may be unable to obtain a license because of the fact that one or the other is still bound by a civil marriage which is invalid in the eyes of the Church but still binding in the eyes of the civil law. The legal obtaining of a divorce may be beyond the means of the parties. A priest may be willing to risk the danger of harm from the civil law. Must the parties do so likewise? To have the priest assist at their marriage may involve them with the civil law because of an attempted civilly bigamous marriage. In such a case, they may ask the priest or the bishop to allow them to contract marriage according to the extraordinary form. The serious harm that threatens them would be the type of harm that would make a priest unavailable for the parties in such circumstances.[163]

162 "Non esse recendendum a praxi S. Congregationis, ideoque amissionem pensionis non esse causam sufficientem permittendi celebrationem matrimonii absque ritu civili."—Apud Gasparri, *De Matrimonio,* n. 1295. Cf. also Vermeersch, *Theologia Moralis,* III, n. 689, who says that the extraordinary form is not to be used even if it means the loss of certain benefits which are *indebita* (unwarranted).

163 Aguirre, "Annotationes," *Periodica,* XXXIV (1945), 284.

CHAPTER VI

THE SECOND POSTULATED CONDITION: DANGER OF DEATH OR ABSENCE FORESEEN TO LAST A MONTH

In itself, the impossibility of having a qualified witness at a marriage as described above would not suffice to allow one to contract marriage according to the extraordinary form. Not every case in which a qualified witness would be unavailable would permit one to forego his presence and to contract marriage solely in the presence of two witnesses. Although the concession granted in Canon 1098 is indeed a great one, nevertheless the Code of Canon Law very wisely and very prudently circumscribed its use to only two eventualities, namely, in cases in which the contracting parties are constituted in danger of death, and in cases in which the impossibility of having a qualified witness is prudently foreseen to last a month. Each of these cases will be discussed separately.

Article 1. Danger of Death

Under the Tridentine matrimonial discipline, danger of death was not acknowledged as a cause excusing one from observing the prescribed form of marriage.[1] In time, however, the Holy See began to acknowledge danger of death as a cause for allowing marriage to be contracted apart from the strict adherence to the established form of the decree *Tametsi*. Faculties to dispense from the observance of the juridical form of marriage, i.e., from the diriment impediment of clandestinity, were given to local ordinaries, who in turn could subdelegate these faculties to other ecclesiastics. It was still necessary that a priest having these faculties be present so that he could dispense in such a case; otherwise, a marriage contracted in the presence of solely two witnesses was invalid.

With the decree *Ne temere*, provision was made for the first time for people constituted in danger of death when the ordinary

[1] *Vide supra*, p. 41.

prescribed form could not be observed. Even with this concession, the law was still difficult of observance, because the decree demanded the presence of a priest, an imminent danger of death, and, as a reason for its use, that thereby provision could be made for the conscience of the parties.[2] The Code of Canon Law adopted the legislation of the decree *Ne temere,* but with certain relaxations, in order to make it as easy as possible for people in such circumstances to contract marriage.

Under the *Ne temere* discipline, it was necessary that the danger of death be imminent; the Code, using very general terms, merely requires that a danger of death be present (*in mortis periculo*). Accordingly, it is not necessary that death be imminent, that one of the parties is at the point of death (i.e., *in articulo mortis*). Any danger of death that would allow Viaticum to be administered would be sufficient.[3] It is not demanded that there be present such conditions as would allow one to administer the sacrament of Extreme Unction,[4] i.e., that the danger come from bodily infirmity or old age.[5]

Danger of death is that condition in which it is seriously probable that a person may either die or live.[6] The danger may arise from a cause which is intrinsic or internal to the individual himself, e.g., from serious sickness, from a difficult case of childbirth, from a serious operation, or from a cause which is extrinsic or external to the person. The latter can affect the individual alone, e.g., a sentence of capital punishment, or it can affect many persons. In the latter category, one can distinguish two distinct sources whence the danger may arise, namely, natural causes or social disturbances. Among the natural causes, one may consider a raging epidemic; expected further earthquake shocks; hurricanes, typhoons, tornadoes,

[2] S. C. C., decr. "*Ne temere,*" 2 aug. 1907, art. VII—*ASS,* XL (1907), 529; *Fontes,* n. 4340.

[3] Payen, II, n. 1815.

[4] This was the example that was given by Ojetti (*Synopsis,* I, s.v. *Clandestinitas,* n. 1124) in commenting on the decree *Ne temere.*

[5] C. 940, § 1.

[6] D'Annibale, *Summula Theologiae Moralis* (5. ed., 3 vols., Romae: 1908), I, n. 38; Cappello, *Tractatus Canonico-Moralis de Censuris* (4. ed., Romae: Marietti, 1950), n. 114 (hereafter cited *De Censuris*).

cyclones, and the like; the eruption of volcanoes; extensive floods; mine disasters; a disaster at sea; a very dangerous trip, and other similar situations.[7] Among the causes traceable to social disturbances one may list airplane bombings, even of open cities,[8] bloody revolutions, riots which are not just temporary outbursts; invasion by a hostile and barbarous enemy, danger from robber bands, etc.[9]

A condition commonly considered as a danger of death is the condition of mobilization for war. It is true that a person in the Armed Forces is never certain when he or she will be sent to the battle-front, where the danger of death would be imminent. Still one must remember that the mere fact that a person is in uniform does not constitute him in danger of death. All agree that at the battle-front the danger of death is imminent.

A natural question arises in regard to soldiers who are ready to go to a battle-area. Are they to be considered in danger of death? It was this consideration that prompted the Bishop of Verdun to inquire of the Sacred Penitentiary whether any soldier who is in the state of mobilization is *ipso facto* in danger of death and, therefore, capable of being absolved by any priest. To this query the Sacred Penitentiary replied: "In the affirmative, according to the rules proposed by approved authors."[10] To a similar query, asking whether such a soldier may be considered (*aequiparatus*) *ipso facto* the same as one in danger of death, the Sacred Penitentiary on May 28, 1915, gave the same answer, citing the former reply.[11]

Since the first reply was being applied to marriage as well (Art. VII of the decree *Ne temere*), the Bishop of Osnabrück inquired

[7] Gasparri, n. 1107; Coronata, *De Matrimonio,* n. 567; Cappello, *Tractatus Canonico-Moralis De Sacramentis,* Vol. I (*De Sacramentis in Genere,* Romae: Marietti, 1947), nn. 421, 432; Vol. III *(De Matrimonio),* n. 231; Oesterle, *Consultationes de Iure Matrimoniali* (Romae: Officium Libri Catholici, 1942), p. 99.

[8] Military Faculties, n. 14 c.

[9] Gasparri, *loc. cit.;* Coronata, *loc. cit.;* Cappello, *loc. cit.*

[10] S. Poenit., ad ep. V., 18 mart. 1912—apud *Archiv für katholisches Kirchenrecht* (Innsbruck, 1857-1861; Mainz, 1862-), XCV (1915), 156-157. Cf. also S. Poenit., 29 maii 1915—*AAS,* VII (1915), 282, where allusion is made to this response.

[11] *AAS,* VII (1915), 282.

of the Sacred Congregation of the Sacraments on November 28, 1914, whether a mobilized soldier is to be considered *ipso facto* in danger of death so that a priest assisting at his marriage in accordance with Article VII of the decree *Ne temere* could dispense from matrimonial impediments in virtue of the grant of powers made on May 9, 1909, by Pope Pius X.[12] If the reply was to be in the negative, the bishop requested a general sanation of the marriages theretofore contracted.[13] The reply, dated December 17, 1914, without answering the question proposed, left it open for discussion, neither forbidding the practice nor declaring the marriages already contracted invalid. Alluding to the replies of May 14, 1909, and of August 16, 1909, it simply indicated a norm of action and granted the Bishop the faculty to sanate whatever marriages may have been invalid.[14] It was safe to conclude, then, that there was danger of death in such circumstances and that, if all the other prescripts of the law were followed, Article VII of the decree *Ne temere* and the accompanying powers granted to a priest assisting according to this Article could be used.[15]

The same reasoning can be applied to the law as we have it today. In faculty n. 14 of the Military Faculties granted to Military Vicars by the Sacred Consistorial Congregation on December 8, 1939,[16] one reads that all soldiers immediately before a battle, or fighting in battle, are in danger of death.[17] A soldier when being sent to the battle-front, or when in a highly strategic position, such as supply depots, airplane fields and the like, which are prime bombing targets, as well as a sailor when assigned to a ship that is to go into dangerous waters, would *ipso facto* be constituted in danger of death.

Today one would no longer class long ocean voyages or airplane trips as inducing a danger of death. These means of travel have been

[12] S. C. de Sacramentis, *Parmen et aliarum,* 14 maii, 1909—*AAS,* I (1909), 468-469; *Fontes,* n. 2097.

[13] *Archiv für katholisches Kirchenrecht,* XCV (1915). 337-338.

[14] *Loc. cit.*

[15] *Archiv für katholisches Kirchenrecht,* XCV (1915), 341.

[16] *AAS,* XXX (1939), 710-713; Bouscaren, *Digest,* II, 607-615.

[17] . . . omnes milites ante proelium vel in proelio dimicantes, prout in mortis pericula constitutos . . .

so perfected that they can be classified as safe.[18] As a general rule, it may be stated that the norms which approved authors have invoked for determining what constitutes a danger of death truly reflect what is contemplated in the phrase *"in mortis periculo."* The Holy See replied in this sense to the Archbishop of Cincinnati on September 12, 1859.[19]

It is not necessary that both parties be constituted in danger of death. As long as the danger threatens either of the parties, this exemption may be invoked because the wording of the canon is quite general.[20] Absolute certainty as to the existence or seriousness of the danger of death is not demanded. This would make the canon practically inoperative, and would raise many doubts whenever it should be used. Such a demand would take away the very concession that is granted. Accordingly, all that is required is a moral certainty that is based on a probable judgment as to the existence or the seriousness of the danger of death according to the circumstances of each particular case.[21] As long as this judgment is prudently based on common occurrences, on what people commonly consider as inducing a danger of death, one need not fear afterwards if an error should have been made in such a judgment and it should develop that a person quickly recovers from what appeared to be a serious sickness.[22] The opinion of a doctor, though it can be very helpful, is not essential in such a case. However, if he should declare that death is imminent, the parties need not wait for a qualified witness, but may proceed immediately to contract marriage in the presence of witnesses alone, on the supposition naturally that a priest is not present or cannot immediately be had.[23] If the danger is not imminent, the parties in expecting a qualified priest who has been summoned will have to wait till the last possible moment, i.e., just before the person is to be taken to the operating

[18] Cappello, *De Sacramentis,* I, n. 421.

[19] *Fontes,* n. 955.

[20] Payen, II, n. 1815; Gasparri, n. 1007; Cappello, *De Matrimonio,* n. 691.

[21] Gasparri, n. 1107; Coronata, *De Matrimonio,* n. 567; Chelodi-Ciprotti, n. 136.

[22] Chelodi-Ciprotti, *loc. cit.;* Gasparri, *loc. cit.;* Cappello, *De Matrimonio,* n. 691.

[23] Gasparri, *loc. cit.*

room, just before he is to leave for the front, just before he lapses into unconsciousness. If there is any prudent doubt whether there will be time or opportunity later, or some reasonable danger that further delay would prevent the marriage, the parties need wait no longer.

The reason or motive for contracting marriage need no longer be considered. The Code of Canon Law does not postulate any particular reason in view of which alone the extraordinary form may be invoked. The mere desire to contract marriage will suffice. Since the clause *ad consulendum concientiae et si casus ferat ad legitimationem prolis,* which was found in Article VII of the decree *Ne temere,* is no longer found in the present discipline concerning the form of marriage, one may safely say that the legislator studiously omitted it. True, these reasons will often exist, but the use of this form for contracting marriages is not to be restricted solely to such cases. Bad faith in postponing the contracting of marriage till such time will not invalidate the marriage, because the canon does not have an invalidating clause in this respect.[24] One may likewise argue analogically from a reply of the Sacred Congregation of the Sacraments, which declared that a marriage contracted in accordance with Article VIII of the decree *Ne temere* would be valid even if the person betook himself, *in fraudem legis,* to a place where there was no priest.[25]

Article 2. The Qualified Witness' Absence Foreseen to Last for a Month

While the Tridentine discipline obtained, the Holy Office declared that if a pastor was away and it was foreseen that he would be away at least a month a couple could contract marriage in the presence simply of two witnesses.[26] It was considered that a month's delay would constitute a grave inconvenience and consequently would excuse from the obligation of observing the law on the form of

[24] Canon 11. Cf. also Gasparri, n. 1009; Vlaming, *Praelectiones Iuris Matrimonii,* II, 200.

[25] S. C. de Sacramentis, 13 mart. 1910, ad III—*Fontes,* n. 2101.

[26] S. C. S. Off., *Vallispraten,* 1 iulii 1863—*vide supra,* pp. 32-33.

marriage. In Article VIII of the decree *Ne temere* a change was introduced. There the law postulated the pastor's absence for a month before one could use the extraordinary form of marriage. The Code of Canon Law in Canon 1098 returned to the commonly admitted practice as it obtained prior to the *Ne temere* discipline, i.e., it simply postulates the foreseeing of an absence that is to last for at least a month.[27]

The legislator realized that, once everything is prepared for a marriage, to expect a couple to wait for a very long time would cause a great inconvenience. Besides, it would infringe on their natural right of marrying. Accordingly, it was decided that a month's delay would be considered an inconvenience grave enough to excuse one from this particular ecclesiastical law. Absolute certainty that a qualified priest will be unavailable for a month is not required. All that is required by the legislator is that it can be prudently foreseen that this condition will last for a month.[28] To demand certainty would make the canon practically inapplicable, and would defeat the very purpose for which it was instituted. As in all normal human relations, so here too, all that one can expect is moral certitude. Moral certitude as to the unavailability for a month of a qualified priest when based on the knowledge of facts that are known to all, or when based on information gathered from a prudent investigation, will suffice.[29]

In the first place, there must be established the fact of the unavailability of a priest who could assist at the marriage in question. The wording of the canon demands this when it requires that the condition, i.e., that a priest cannot be had, will last for a month. Therefore, any false opinion, even though based on an excusable error, on the part of the parties, which is not verified in fact will not suffice. If a priest could be had and it was judged that he could not be had, a marriage contracted without his assistance would be invalid. A false estimate will not change the actual facts of a

[27] Payen, II, n. 1820.

[28] . . . dummodo prudenter praevideatur eam rerum conditionem esse per mensem duraturam.

[29] P.C.I., 10 nov. 1925—*AAS*, XVII (1925). 583.

situation. The very first requisite would be lacking because an actual and not a presumed unavailability is postulated.[30]

Once the unavailability of a qualified priest has been established, before the extraordinary form may be used, it must be prudently foreseen that this condition will last for a month. Since a prudent prevision has to do with the future it will be based on a human judgment. It connotes also a subjective persuasion of the truth of the judgment that is made. Such a judgment, being human, could prove to be erroneous. However, later facts will not affect a marriage contracted in view of this subjective moral certainty as long as the judgment was not entirely without a basis in fact.[31] The prevision must be truly prudent, based, as the Pontifical Commission for the Interpretation of the Code has stated, on facts known to everyone in the locality or on a diligent investigation. It is possible that the unavailability of a priest for a month will be known to everyone in the neighborhood. This can, and usually does, happen in missionary countries, where, because of the shortage of priests, it is a common practice for a missionary to visit his mission stations only at regular intervals, e.g., once every two months. In fact, he may even announce that he will not be back for two months. From past experience people will know that that is exactly what will happen. Or again, everyone knows that during the winter months the parish church has no pastor, that the church is closed and that the priest will not return till the spring. On the other hand, if the fact of the qualified priest's unavailability is not well known, it can be established through an investigation. One may inquire of people in the neighborhood. From information thus gathered and from the circumstances of the case, it may be prudently judged with moral certainty that the priest will be unavail-

[30] S. R. R., *Nullitatis matrimonii,* 7 dec. 1931, coram R.P.D. Andrea Jullien, dec. LV, n. 3—*Decisiones,* XXIII (1931), p. 473; S. R. R., *Nullitatis matrimonii,* 30 ian. 1926, coram R.P.D. Maximo Massimi, pro-Decano, dec. IV, nn. 3, 9—*Decisiones,* XVIII (1926), pp. 18, 20.

[31] S. R. R., *Nullitatis matrimonii,* 20 iul. 1926, coram R.P.D. Iosepho Florczak, dec. XXXVI, n. 5—*Decisiones,* XVIII (1926), p. 289; S. R. R. Nullitatis matrimonii, 7 dec. 1931, coram R.P.D. Andrea Jullien, dec. LV, n. 3—*Decisiones,* XXIII (1931), p. 473; Vlaming, *Praelectiones Iuris Matrimonii.* II, n. 202; Rossi, p. 112; Coronata, *De Matrimonio,* n. 568.

able for at least a month.[32] In making the judgment, one need consider only the usual and ordinary circumstances and occurrences.[33] One is not expected to foresee any possible extraordinary developments or unexpected happenings. If by chance a qualified priest should have unexpectedly appeared or become available during the month, it would not affect the validity of the marriage.[34] Whether the investigation when made proves sufficient will depend in each case on the capabilities of the persons, the means at their disposal, the sources of information available to them, and the like. Extremes in making practically no investigation and also all undue scrupulosity in the conducting of the investigation are to be avoided.[35] The Rota indicated a practical norm to be followed when it quoted from D'Annibale: "If one doubts, he must inquire either himself or through others, not in every possible way, but with a diligence which is not necessarily of the greatest type, because this could go on *ad infinitum* and would lead to scrupulosity, nor of a perfunctory character, but which is evinced as a common ordinary diligence in proportion to the gravity of the matter under consideration." [36]

A question that has to be asked at this point is whether the prudent prevision postulated by the canon must be had by the contracting parties for the valid use of the extraordinary form. Most commentators leave the question unanswered by delineating the obligation of the prudent prevision in the same impersonal passive phrase that is found in the canon. There are commentators, however, e.g., Sipos,[37] Schönsteiner [38] and Rossi,[39] who demand that the contracting parties themselves prudently foresee that the postulated unavailability will last a month. The merit of this interpreta-

[32] S. R. R., *Nullitatis matrimonii,* 7 dec. 1931, coram R.P.D. Andrea Jullien, dec. IV, n. 3—*Decisiones,* XXIII (1931), p. 473.

[33] S. C. C., *Romana et aliarum,* 27 iul. 1908 ad VIum—*Fontes,* n. 4350; Chelodi-Ciprotti, n. 137; Schönsteiner, *Grundriss des kirchlichen Eherechts,* p. 732.

[34] Gasparri, n. 1009; Cappello, *De Matrimonio,* n. 693, b; Rossi, p. 112.

[35] S. R. R., *loc. cit.;* Regatillo, *Interpretatio et Iurisprudentia Codicis Iuris Canonici,* p. 382.

[36] *Summula Theologiae Moralis,* I, n. 132.

[37] *Apollinaris,* XX (1940), 99.

[38] *Op. cit.,* p. 732.

[39] *Op. cit.,* p. 112.

tion can be seriously called into doubt. In the first place, the very text of the canon does not seem to demand this interpretation. The wording is in the passive impersonal (*prudenter praevideatur*). Had the legislator intended that the parties themselves have this prevision, he could have very easily adopted the wording *"dummodo prudenter contrahentes praevideant."* The fact that he did not do so militates against this interpretation. To demand more would be to read into the canon something that is not intended by the legislator.

In the second place, in instituting this law, the legislator had for his purpose not the hindering of the contracting of marriages, but the certifying of them as certain and valid unions.[40] In many instances the parties could be ignorant of the fact that marriage could be contracted according to the extraordinary form. Consequently, they would know nothing of the postulated prudent prevision. Granted that the unavailability of a qualified priest has been established, and granted, likewise, that it is not known after a diligent investigation just when he will be available (although *de facto* the circumstances are such that it may be prudently foreseen that he will be unavailable for at least a month), the parties may decide to contract a true and valid marriage in the best way they can in the presence of two witnesses, e.g., in a civil marriage or even before a minister. How can such a marriage be declared invalid when the prescripts of the canon have been fulfilled? Accordingly, if the foreseen unavailability is of the type that is not merely personal to the parties but common to all in the territory, the prudent prevision on the part of the contracting parties is not required. It is sufficient that the circumstances will merit such a prevision.[41] If the foreseen unavailability is common but not personal to the parties, the canon, as explained above,[41a] will not apply. However, if the unavailability is not common but merely personal, then an investigation would have to be made and the parties themselves would

[40] S. R. R., *Nullitatis matrimonii,* 7 dec. 1931, coram R.P.D. Andrea Jullien, dec. LV, n. 3—*Decisiones,* XXIII (1931), 473.

[41] Payen, II, n. 1819, footnote 3; Vromant, *Ius Missionarium,* Tom. V (*De Matrimonio*) (Louvain: Museum Lessianum, 1931), p. 207; Oesterle, "De Validitate aut Nullitate Matrimoniorum a Captivis ex Bello in Russia Initorum," *Apollinaris,* IX (1936), 451.

[41a] *Vide supra,* p. 86.

have prudently to foresee that the unavailability will last a month.[42]

If the moral certitude in regard to the unavailability of a priest for a month has to be gathered from an investigation, only two possibilities can be envisioned, viz., either the parties know the law or they do not. If they do, they must govern their actions according to the results of the investigation. If they do not know the law, once again two possibilities present themselves. The foreseeable length of time that the qualified priest will be unavailable will be either definite or indefinite. If it is indefinite, but *de facto* the facts are such that it can be prudently foreseen that the unavailability will last at least a month, a marriage contracted will be valid because the prescripts of the canon have been observed. Should the unavailability, on the other hand, be prudently foreseen not to last a month, a marriage contracted will be invalid because the canon has not been observed. Postulated a period of time that is definite, even though the parties know nothing of the law, the validity of the marriage would depend on whether the period of time was at least a month. Ignorance of the law would not excuse them.[43]

In computing the period of a month's duration in regard to the unavailability of a qualified priest, the initial day (*dies a quo*) is the day when everything is prepared for the marriage (*omnia parata sunt ad nuptias*).[44] It is only with that day that grave inconvenience for the parties can be said to begin. Besides, the legislator demands that an investigation be made concerning the free state of the contracting parties.[45] If one were to consider the day the parties decided to marry as the *dies a quo* in the computation, then the concession granted in Canon 1098 would destroy the very safeguard set up by the legislator in demanding such an investigation. Such was definitely not his purpose. As mentioned previously, Canon 1098 contains an exception to the general law as stated in Canon 1094; consequently, it requires a strict interpretation.[46]

[42] Vromant, *De Matrimonio,* p. 207.

[43] Canon 16.

[44] Regatillo, *op. cit.,* p. 383; Ubach, *Compendium Theologiae Moralis,* II, n. 855.

[45] Canons 1019-1034.

[46] Canon 19.

Accordingly, the concession granted herein is granted only when everything is ready for the marriage to take place except for the fact that a qualified priest is unavailable. It matters not how long the priest has been unavailable [47] nor how long the parties have already waited. One must look to the priest's unavailability from the moment that the marriage is about to be contracted.

In computing the period of one month, one must be governed by Canon 34, § 3, inasmuch as the *terminus a quo* is implicitly given (*cum omnia parata sunt ad nuptias*).[48] Therefore the month is to be taken as it is in the calendar.[49] Since the *terminus a quo* does not coincide with the beginning of the day, or at least is not considered to do so, the first day, i.e., the rest of that day does not enter into the computation, and the month will end with the end of the day that marks the same date in the next month.[50] If the next month should lack a corresponding day marking the same date, then the computed month will end with the last day of the next month.[51] An example will serve to illustrate the computation. If on January 31st, everything is ready for the marriage to take place, then, before the couple can avail themselves of the concession in the extraordinary form, it must be prudently foreseen that no qualified priest will be available until after the midnight between the last day of February and the first day of March. The rest of the day of January 31st does not enter into the computation, and the month will end with the last day of February. Hence, if a priest will not be available till after the midnight mentioned above, the couple can contract marriage according to the extraordinary form anytime on January 31st.

In using the phrase *per mensem,* the legislator intends it to be a

[47] Gasparri, n. 1009; Chelodi, n. 137.

[48] The *omnia parata* spoken of here is not to be taken in the sense mentioned below on page 177, i.e., any case of grave necessity. The phrase is to be understood in the sense that everything is ready as far as the church is concerned for the parties to contract marriage. This would eventuate when all proofs concerning the free state of the parties have been adduced. Cf. below, page 142, where it is stated upon whom this obligation rests and what the extent of the obligation is.

[49] Canon 34, § 3, 1°.

[50] Canon 34, § 3, 3°.

[51] Canon 34, § 3, 4°.

continuous and complete month.[52] Furthermore, the canon requires a strict interpretation. Therefore, the month's foreseen unavailability of a qualified priest must be interpreted as a month that is continuous and complete.[53] If it is prudently foreseen, then, that a qualified priest will be available before the month is complete, the canon may not be invoked. A passing through of a possible qualified priest which is so short that the parties could not possibly have known of his availability, will not be considered as breaking the continuity of the month required by the canon.[54]

There are authors, however, who do not demand this mathematical exactness. Even though Cappello holds that the month must be continuous and complete, he is of the opinion that, when an hour or even a day is lacking in the foreseen month's unavailability of a qualified priest, it would not affect the validity of a marriage contracted under such circumstances.[55] Cerato goes even further. He allows the computation of the month to be left to the parties who need not follow the computation as outlined in the Code.[56] He bases his opinion on the moral certitude demanded by the reply of the Code Commission given on November 10, 1925.[57] He reasons that, if moral certitude about the priest's unavailability suffices, mathematical exactness in regard to the period of one month is not required. Chrétien holds that 30 continuous days, morally considered, will suffice.[58]

It is difficult to see how these opinions can be sustained. Were one to allow Cappello's opinion, then a mathematical norm no longer would be had. If one day were lacking, why not a day and an hour? Why not two days? To avoid ambiguity and uncertainty, the legislator instituted a standard norm which must be followed under pain of nullity. The canon requires a strict interpretation; a month is a month and nothing less. Besides, there is

[52] Reiffenstuel, lib. IV, tit. XXXI, n. 94.

[53] Gasparri, n. 1009; Chelodi-Ciprotti, n. 137; Payen, II, n. 1820; Vlaming, *Praelectiones Iuris Matrimonii,* II, 202.

[54] S. C. C., *Romana et aliarum,* 27 iul. 1908, ad VIum—*Fontes,* n. 4350.

[55] *De Matrimonio,* n. 693, 2d.

[56] *Matrimonium Codice Iuris Canonici integre Desumptum,* p. 165.

[57] *AAS,* XVII (1925), 583; Bouscaren, *Digest,* I, 542.

[58] *De Matrimonio (Praelectiones),* p. 342.

no basis in law or in fact for holding this opinion. As for Cerato's opinion, if it were to be allowed, it would destroy the very law itself, because whatever the parties considered a month would suffice. This would substitute a personal opinion for a standard norm. It would be impossible to question the validity or invalidity of such a marriage on this ground. The conclusion he draws from the authentic interpretation given to Canon 1098 by the Pontifical Commission for the Interpretation of the Code on November 10, 1925, is unwarranted. To say that a person is morally certain that a priest will be unavailable for a month is not the same as to say that a person is morally certain that a qualified priest will be unavailable for a period of time which, morally taken, may be termed a month. Finally, Chrétien seems to reach his opinion, as did Ubach,[59] by using paragraph 2 of Canon 34 to compute the period of one month. It was chosen because they probably felt that the *terminus a quo* is neither implicitly nor explicitly given. This is a mistaken interpretation; as was seen above, the *terminus a quo* is implicitly given, namely, everything is ready for the marriage. Besides, Canon 34, § 3, states that a month is to be taken as it is in the calendar. Therefore, it may have only 28, or 29 days as in February, 30 or 31 days depending on the *terminus a quo*. Would Chrétien and Ubach say that 28 days would be insufficient? or that 30 days would suffice if the month has 31 days?

Foreseeing all these problems, the legislator instituted a practical norm—a period of one month. Since no qualifying words are given, it must be computed according to the Code. Following this norm, one can have a definite norm according to which the validity of a marriage can be judged. For these reasons it is the writer's opinion that the month in Canon 1098 must be continuous and complete and computed according to Canon 34, § 3, 1° and 3°. In practice, it may be said that the problem will hardly ever arise unless a person is definitely certain as to the exact time when a qualified witness will be available; otherwise, it will depend on one's prudent judgment.

An interesting point deserves mention here, namely, whether a coalescence of time would avail in the determining of the postulated

[59] *Compendium Theologiae Moralis,* II, n. 855.

period of one month. The writer has in mind a situation wherein a qualified witness is *de facto* unavailable for a period of time which is foreseen to be less than a month. However, before this unavailability will cease, the qualified witness will be unavailable for some other reason. If the two periods equal or surpass a month, may the extraordinary form be used? The Code allows this, so it has been seen, only in cases of actual unavailability. If, therefore, both unavailabilities are of the actual type, e.g., deriving from adverse prescripts of law, or from a physical absence followed by a moral impossibility traceable to a prohibition of the civil law, and like cases, such an eventuality seems to be comprehended within the scope of the canon. On the other hand, if an actual unavailability is foreseen to be of less than a month's duration, one may not add a period of what may only be a *possible future* unavailability in order to make the period equal a month. Possible future unavailabilities are not contemplated by the legislator in this canon.[60]

As to the actual time for contracting the marriage, it must be contracted while the prudent prevision of the qualified witness' unavailability for a period of one month still obtains.[61] If the unavailability was foreseen to last for a month, but *de facto* the marriage was then planned for and contracted on a day whereon one could foresee that the unavailability would no longer last for a month, the marriage would be invalid. For example, on April 1st the parties wished to marry and it was prudently foreseen that a priest would be unavailable till May 5th. The marriage was then planned for and contracted on April 10th. The marriage would be invalid because the period of one month's unavailability would no longer obtain. If one were to allow marriage to be contracted any time during the month, then it could be postponed till the very day before the qualified priest would become available. This would make the law absurd. Accordingly, as long as the unavailability is foreseen to last at least a month more, marriage may be contracted according to the extraordinary form.

[60] König, "Eine interessante Ehenichtigkeitsklage zu c. 1098," *Österreichisches Archiv für Kirchenrecht,* III (1952), 278-282.

[61] Vlaming-Bender, p. 431.

Finally, a marriage would be valid even though the parties deferred the contracting of their marriage till such time when a qualified priest became unavailable.[62] Since the legislator does not distinguish, it is not for us to do so.

[62] Gasparri, n. 1008; Cappello, *De Matrimonio,* n. 693; Vlaming, *Praelectiones Iuris Matrimonii,* II, 589, who cite the reply of the S. C. de Sacramentis, 13 mart. 1910, ad IIIum (*Fontes,* 2011), in this sense.

CHAPTER VII

THE THIRD POSTULATED CONDITION: EXCHANGE OF MATRIMONIAL CONSENT IN THE PRESENCE OF TWO WITNESSES

ARTICLE 1. EXCHANGE OF MATRIMONIAL CONSENT

MARRIAGE is brought into existence by the exchange of consent between two parties who are capable in law of entering marriage.[1] Therefore, consent is the essential element in the celebration of marriage, as it is in the making of any contract. Adopting the principle from Roman Law, the Church has always insisted that it was the consent of the parties that constituted marriage.[2] It is plain to see, then, why the Code states that no human power can supply for the consent of the parties.[3]

A. *Nature of Matrimonial Consent*

In order to avoid the possibility of ambiguity and uncertainty, the legislator immediately states what constitutes the nature of matrimonial consent. It is the mutual giving and acceptance by the two parties in words or signs of each one's rights, perpetually and exclusively, over the other's body for the performance of acts which of themselves are suited for the begetting of children, which rights are being mutually given at the time of their acceptance.[4] To be valid, this matrimonial consent must be:

> 1. true, i.e., not feigned; if a person does not consent internally, marriage is not constituted, because the nature of a contract demands that one intend to bind oneself. However, once consent is externalized, it is presumed that that person also consented internally; [5]

[1] Canon 1081, § 1.

[2] . . . nuptias enim non concubitus sed consensus facit."—D. (35.1) 15.

[3] Canon 1081, § 1.

[4] Canon 1081, § 2.

[5] Canon 1086, § 1: Internus animi consensus semper praesumitur conformis verbis vel signis in celebrando matrimonio adhibitis.

2. free and deliberate. One must realize the nature of the obligation and must at the same time be willing to accept it. Since it has to be a human act, it must proceed from both the intellect and the will; [6]

3. mutual. The contract of marriage is a bilateral and not a unilateral contract. It is essential that both parties bind themselves;

4. elicited by parties who are in law capable of entering marriage. Everyone has a natural right of marrying. However, this right may be limited by the fact that the person may be bound by an impediment of the natural or the positive divine law, or by ecclesiastical or civil law;

5. elicited in regard to a specified, certain person, who is the object of the matrimonial consent;

6. legitimately manifested. The matrimonial consent must be not only internal, but also externally manifested.[7] The authority to which the parties are subject, ecclesiastical or civil, depending on whether the parties are baptized or not, will indicate in what manner this consent is to be manifested.[8]

One may note that, with the exception of the manner in which the consent is to be manifested, all the other qualities are essential and of themselves suffice to effect a marriage contract according to the natural law. Our Divine Saviour enhanced this matrimonial contract and raised it, in the case of baptized parties, to the dignity of a sacrament. The Church did not change the matter and form of the sacrament, which is the matrimonial contract according to the natural law. It merely regulated in what manner this matrimonial consent was to be manifested if it was to be considered valid. As long as the matrimonial consent is naturally valid, between persons capable in law of entering marriage, and is legitimately manifested, the sacrament of matrimony is constituted in its essence and nothing else is required.[9]

[6] Nil volitum nisi praecognitum.

[7] St. Thomas Aquinas, *Super Libris Magistri Sententiarum*, Lib. IV, Dist. XXVII, q. un., art. II: "Efficiens causa matrimonii est consensus, non quilibet, sed per verba expressus, nec de futuro sed de praesenti. . . . Item si consentiat mente et non exprimat verbis vel aliis certis signis, nec talis consensus efficit matrimonium."

[8] Cappello, *De Matrimonio*, n. 575.

[9] Gasparri, *De Matrimonio*, n. 775.

Inasmuch as the contract of marriage is *ipso facto* a sacrament among the baptized, and inasmuch as the parties themselves are the ministers of the sacrament, it may be asked whether the parties must have the intention of administering the sacrament and the intention of receiving the sacrament of matrimony. In the minister of any sacrament there is required the intention of doing what the Church does in such a case.[10] This intention must be an actual or at least a virtual intention.[11] A virtual intention is one which here and now has an influence on the performance of the act, even though it is not adverted to at the moment. An actual intention, i.e., one which here and now is present and is adverted to, is not required; a virtual intention will suffice. A habitual intention, i.e., one which was had once, never revoked, but here and now has no influence on the act that is being performed and is not adverted to, as also an interpretative intention, i.e., one which in fact never existed but would exist if it were proposed to the person, will not suffice.

In regard to marriage, the baptized parties, even though they do not realize that they are the ministers of the sacrament, can bring the sacrament into existence. This is true even in the case where they erroneously think that matrimony is not a sacrament.[12] All that is required in them is an implicit virtual intention of doing what the Church or other Christians do. In other words, they intend to contract marriage as God instituted it and as other Christians contract it. In having at least such an intention they are presumed to have the intention of doing what the Church does.[13] All that is required, then, of the parties as ministers of the sacrament is to intend a true marriage.[14]

Because of the individual character of the sacrament of matri-

[10] Conc. Trident., sess. VII, *de sacramentis in genere,* can. 11: Si quis dixerit, in ministris, dum sacramenta conficiunt et conferunt, non requiri intentionem faciendi quod facit Ecclesia, anathema sit."—Schulte, p. 41.

[11] De Smet, *De Sponsalibus et Matrimonio,* n. 183; Cappello, *De Sacramentis in Genere,* nn. 39 and 40; Coronata, *De Matrimonio,* n. 18.

[12] Canon 1084: Simplex error circa . . . sacramentalem dignitatem, etsi det causam contractui, non vitiat consensum matrimonialem.

[13] De Smet, *op. cit.,* n. 183; Cappello, *De Matrimonio,* n. 32; Coronata, *De Matrimonio,* n. 18.

[14] Cappello, *loc. cit.*

mony, if both parties administer it then both parties also receive it because they are also the subjects of the sacrament. If the parties intend to bring the sacrament into existence and to confer it, they also automatically have the intention of receiving the sacrament. As was just noted, as long as baptized parties intend contracting a true, valid marriage, they also intend implicitly to confer it on the partner and to receive it from him or her. Provided the parties do not *expressly* exclude the reception of the sacrament, it is received by both.[15] All this follows from the fact that among the baptized a true, valid marriage is also a sacrament. If a party excludes the contract of marriage or excludes the sacrament by a positive act of the will, the sacrament is not brought into existence. In intending to enter a true marriage, the parties are presumed to include the notion of a sacramental marriage, and likewise are presumed to have the implicit intention of receiving the sacrament. If a party alleges that he or she excluded the sacrament from the matrimonial contract, one must not be too hasty in concluding that that marriage is invalid. The party has two intentions in such a case, one of contracting marriage and the other of excluding the sacrament. It will depend on which intention prevailed at the time of marriage. If the party was merely in error about the sacramental dignity of marriage or even denied its sacramental nature, and this error remained totally in the intellect, then, in desiring to contract a valid marriage the party in fact contracted indeed a valid but also a sacramental marriage. Schmalzgrueber remarked that, as long as one intends one of two elements which are inseparably connected, one likewise intends the other element.[16] On the other hand, if the wish of the party is formed into a positive intention of excluding the sacrament, then it will depend on which intention prevailed.[17] If in doubt, one must presume that the parties wished to contract a valid marriage and therefore received the sacrament. The contrary must be proved.[18]

15 Cappello, *De Matrimonio,* n. 32.

16 Lib. IV, tit. I, n. 302.

17 Canon 1086, § 2.

18 Canon 1014.

B. *Matrimonial Consent in the Extraordinary Form of Marriage*

The same type of matrimonial consent that is necessary in contracting marriage according to the ordinary form as depicted in Canon 1094 will be required also in the use of the extraordinary form. There is only one type of valid matrimonial consent. The law makes no distinction in this regard between the two forms of marriage. The only distinction that is made rests in what the law considers the legitimate manifestation or externalization of that consent. If the lawgiver does not distinguish, then no distinction should be invoked. A matrimonial consent that would be valid if it were manifested according to the ordinary prescribed form will also suffice and be valid if it is externalized according to the extraordinary form.[19]

In view of the foregoing it is difficult to understand how certain commentators demand something greater of the parties in the matter of consent when marriage is contracted according to the extraordinary form. Oesterle and Miceli would demand that the

[19] S. R. R., *Nullitatis matrimonii,* 7 dec. 1931, coram R.P.D. Andrea Jullien, dec. LV, n. 4: "Cum igitur conditiones, quas Ecclesia in dato casu exigit ut validum sit matrimonium absque praesentia testis qualificati, verificentur, solutio repetenda est ab eo quod partes voluerunt, utrum scilicet consensus fuerit naturaliter sufficiens, necne. Siquidem comparendo coram magistratu civili et alio teste: *aut* utraque vel alterutra pars positive excludit mutuum consensum naturalem, limitans intentionem ad ponendum verum actum civilem, quia nil aliud vult nisi obtemperare praecepto legis civilis, v.g., ad effectus civiles consequendos; unde efficitur ut positivo actu excludatur matrimonium ipsum, quod igitur exsistere nequit (can. 1081, § 1; 1086, § 2);—*aut* nupturientes volunt, quantum in se est, praestare ac manifestare consensum matrimonialem; ita, si non obstat aliquod impedimentum dirimens, validum est matrimonium, non ratione quidem actus civilis positi, sed ratione consensus naturalis praestiti et legitime manifestati coram solis testibus, seu servata forma in casu requisita a lege ecclesiastica. Enimvero cum ex iis quae Ecclesia in hisce adiunctis requirit, nil desit, contrahentium voluntas ipso facto effectum suum consequitur."—*Decisiones,* XXIII (1931), 474; *Nullitas matrimonii,* 23 apr. 1940, coram R.P.D. Alberto Canestri, dec. XXX, n. 2: "Quaerenti autem sitne validum matrimonium contractum coram magistratu civili, aut alio teste qualificato, v.g.. ministro acatholico, ab ignorantibus exceptionem canone 1098 positam, respondendum est solutionem repetendam ab intentione partium in consentiendo; si ipsae quantum in se erat nubere voluerunt, tunc matrimonium valet. . . ."—*Decisiones,* XXXII (1940), 324.

parties know that the extraordinary form of marriage is an ecclesiastically approved form of marriage and that the parties must intend an *ecclesiastical, canonical, Catholic, sacramental* marriage, otherwise it would be invalid.[20] The purpose of these men in trying to preserve the validity of such marriages and to keep abuses from creeping in is indeed very laudable. However, their demands are a bit excessive. As was seen above, all that is required of the parties to act as ministers and recipients of the sacrament of matrimony is that they have the intention of contracting a valid marriage. If this is so for the ordinary form of marriage, it must be so for the extraordinary form as well. To demand more in the latter case would necessitate demanding more in the former case as well. In that case, two baptized non-Catholics who are in error or even deny the sacramental character of marriage would not contract marriage even though they do intend contracting a valid marriage. This will not be admitted by anyone. Further, in no possible way can this demand, i.e., that the parties know of the extraordinary form and intend a sacramental marriage, be read into the canon, and even less that such is demanded under pain of nullity. In the absence of such an invalidating clause, one cannot claim that such knowledge or intention is required for validity.[21] It would be limiting the extraordinary form too much.[22] Rotal jurisprudence has never demanded this of the people in adjudicating cases brought before it. In a decision *coram R.P.D. Andrea Jullien* on December 7, 1931, it stated in its *"in iure"* section that where all the conditions postulated in Canon 1098 are verified, the solution as to the validity of the marriage in question must be sought in what the parties intended, i.e., whether the consent had been sufficient *naturaliter* (in accordance with what is required by the natural law). Either they positively excluded the natural consent by limiting the intention simply to the placing of a civil act in submission to the

[20] Oesterle, *Apollinaris,* IX (1936), 446-462; Miceli, *Monitor Ecclesiasticus,* LXXV (1950), 234-237.

[21] Canon 11. Cf. also Dalpiaz, "De validitate aut nullitate matrimoniorum a captivis ex bello in Russia initorum," *Apollinaris,* X (1937), 272-275.

[22] Eichmann-Mörsdorf, *Lehrbuch des Kirchenrechts auf Grund des Codex Iuris Canonici* (3 vols., Vol. II [*Sachenrecht*], Paderborn: Schöningh, 1950), p. 231.

civil law—in which case they excluded marriage itself by a positive act of the will and hence no marriage could be effected (Canons 1081 and 1086)—or they wished, in so far as it could be done, to manifest a matrimonial consent, and thus, *servatis servandis,* the marriage was valid by reason of the naturally valid matrimonial consent. The fact that the parties erred in thinking that a marriage contracted civilly in such circumstances would be invalid did not in any way affect the validity of their consent for marriage, because "scientia aut opinio nullitatis matrimonii consensum matrimonialem necessario non excludit" (Canon 1085).[23] It will be noted that the Rota demands merely a consent that is valid according to the natural law. It does not demand that the parties know of the extraordinary form of marriage; that they intend using it; that they intend contracting a marriage which is specifically a canonical, ecclesiastical, Catholic or sacramental marriage. By operation of the law, the naturally valid matrimonial consent is recognized by the Church as juridically efficacious.

The arguments proposed by the adherents of the stricter view are easily answered. The first argument is based on the old philosophical principle "nil volitum nisi praecognitum." How can the parties intend a marriage that is valid when they do not know that marriage can thus be contracted. This seems to be a case of *petitio principii,* i.e., an unwarranted assertion that the parties must intend a canonical or ecclesiastical marriage. This is not so, as was duly explained above. A second argument is this: the parties unknowingly would bring a sacrament into existence. It is a fact that a minister has to have at least an implicit intention *faciendi quod facit Ecclesia.* In answer one can deny that the parties are *inscii.* They know they are contracting marriage, that they are placing the contract of marriage. This much at least is necessary even from the natural law. As long as they intend a valid marriage, implicitly they are wishing to accomplish *quod facit Ecclesia.*[24] Once they have willingly placed the matter and form of the sacra-

[23] S. R. R., *Decisiones,* XXIII (1931), 474; cf. also *Nullitatis Matrimonii,* 23 apr. 1940, coram R.P.D. Alberto Canestri, dec. XXX, n. 2—*Decisiones,* XXXII (1940), 324, where the same principles are enunciated again.

[24] Cappello, *De Matrimonio,* n. 32.

ment (the contract of marriage), the sacrament is present *ex intentione Christi.* If they will the one, i.e., the contract of marriage, they must of necessity will the sacrament also, because among the baptized these are inseparable. It is argued, further, that the parties, not even thinking of an indissoluble union, will contract an indissoluble bond, even contrary to their wishes. If they do indeed positively intend a dissoluble marriage, or, in other words, positively intend to exclude the element of indissolubility from their marriage, the marriage would be null *ab initio* not only by reason of canon law (Canon 1086) but even by reason of the natural law. Such a consent is insufficient even *naturaliter,* and therefore there is no question of any marriage being effected. However, if they intend marriage, the element of indissolubility is inexorably connected with it, and, therefore, they intend the same implicitly. The objection that the Church must regard all civil marriages in such circumstances as sacraments is also not of much value. The "civil" element of the marriage is not canonized; it is the valid marriage which happened to be "civil" in its form. In itself, the argument is also weak because the Church recognizes as sacramental the valid marriage of baptized non-Catholics even though they may have been contracted before a civil official.

Article 2. The Presence of Two Witnesses

Having seen the dangers in and the difficulties arising from clandestine marriages, the legislator has demanded, ever since the Council of Trent, that matrimonial consent be manifested in the presence of at least two witnesses. This prudent provision of the decree *Tametsi* was continued in the discipline of the decree *Ne temere,* and has been retained in the Code of Canon Law.

The legislator has not laid down any requirements with reference to the capability of a person who is to act as a witness. Pallavicini (1607-1667) reported that the Council of Trent studiously omitted demanding any special qualities in the witnesses to the marriage contract. This it did, so he taught, to forestall any possible doubts or misgivings about marriages in which question could arise about the proper qualifications of the witnesses.[25]

[25] *Vera Concilii Tridentini Historia* (translated from the Italian by J. Bap-

The only requirements for a person to act as witness were those that were set by the law of nature, i.e., the use of reason and the capability of testifying about the fact of a marriage.[26] Accordingly, any man, woman or child, whether Catholic or non-Catholic, could act validly as a witness as long as he or she enjoyed the use of reason at the time the marriage was being contracted and was capable of testifying as to what had taken place.[27] If a person does not enjoy the use of reason permanently or even *in actu,* then the very notion of "witness" would imply his exclusion. Hence, an insane person, one who has not as yet reached the use of reason, a completely intoxicated person, or one who under the influence of drugs is asleep or unconscious, could not act as a witness. Likewise, the very fact of what is implied in being a witness would normally exclude a person who is both deaf *and* blind. If he is deaf but not blind, he may perceive signs or nods and thereby be able to testify; if blind but not deaf he may testify if he knows the voices of the parties well enough.

There were commentators who were of the opinion that the witnesses should have the qualities demanded of judicial witnesses as outlined in a negative way in Canon 1757. This is a gratuitous assumption, since the law makes no distinction in regard to witnesses for marriage. Unlike the position of the sponsor at baptism and confirmation, where designation of the person to act in such a capacity is necessary for the validity of the sponsorship, it is not required that the witnesses be designated or chosen beforehand.[28]

In fact, the Code of Canon Law does not enact any rules regu-

tista Giattino, S.J., 3 vols., Antuerpiae: ex Officina Plantiniana Baltasaria Noreti, 1670). lib. XXII, c. 4, n. 12.

[26] Sanchez, lib. III, disp. 41, n. 5.

[27] Benedictus XIV, *De Synodo,* lib. XII, c. 5, n. 5; Gasparri, n. 961; Cappello, *De Matrimonio,* n. 653; Wernz-Vidal, *Ius Matrimoniale,* n. 540.

[28] This is evident from the reply of the Sacred Congregation for the Propagation of the Faith to the Ordinaries in China and the Vicar Apostolic in Tunkin on July 2, 1827. The Congregation declared a marriage valid which was contracted apart from the presence of a qualified priest but which was contracted in the presence of the families, even though no witness had been formally designated. All that was required was that the witnesses were certain that the parties exchanged matrimonial consent. (Cf. *Collectanea S. C. de Prop. Fide* [ed. 1893], n. 1401; [ed. 1907], n. 794.)

lating the valid assistance of the witnesses at a marriage. It postulates only that the marriage take place *coram testibus*. Their assistance will be valid even though they are constrained to be present by force or fear or even though they are not aware of their position as witnesses, provided, however, that they can testify to the fact that a marriage has taken place. In each case the marriage has taken place *coram testibus*. The witnesses must be physically present and advert to what is taking place. Any sort of assistance by telephone or the like, e.g., being in another room and being able to hear by "straining one's ears," will be insufficient.[29]

An interesting problem presents itself in the question whether the parties contract validly if they are unaware that witnesses are present. The commentators distinguish. If the parties, knowing that witnesses are necessary, positively exclude witnesses by their action, the marriage will be invalid even though, by chance, witnesses may be present. Such a marriage will not be *coram testibus*. On the other hand, if the parties do not exclude witnesses by their actions when wishing to contract a valid marriage, the marriage will be valid if witnesses happen to be present, for the marriage will have taken place *coram testibus*.[30]

The number of witnesses required in the ordinary form of marriage is at least two (*coram saltem duobus testibus*). There may be more, but a smaller number never will suffice. From the wording of the law it is clear that it is an invalidating law (ea *tantum* matrimonia sunt valida). In the event that the law is not observed the act is juridically inefficacious. Ignorance of the necessity of having two witnesses will not excuse one from observing this law.[31] The Sacred Congregation of the Council declared that according to the law of the decree *Tametsi* a marriage was invalid for the simple reason that it was contracted, even though in good faith, in the presence of but one witness.[32] The same is to be held today, for

[29] Gasparri, n. 964.

[30] Payen, II, n. 1763; Cappello, *De Matrimonio,* n. 653, 5°; Coronata, *De Matrimonio,* n. 553.

[31] Canon 16, § 1.

[32] S. C. C., 14 ian. 1673—Schulte, p. 227, n. 40; Benedictus XIV, *De Synodo,* lib. XII, c. 5, n. 5.

the legislator has made no change in the requirement as to the number of witnesses.

The two witnesses must be simultaneously present along with the priest and the parties as the matrimonial consent is being exchanged according to the ordinary form. If at first but the one and only later the other witness is present, the marriage will be invalid, since thus it will not have been contracted *coram testibus*. It goes without saying that each of the two witnesses must in actual fact be naturally capable of being a witness. In the event that one of the two witnesses is asleep or drunk, then there would be present simply one witness, which would be insufficient.

As for licitness, one must always remember that matrimony is a sacrament and as such demands the greatest respect and reverence. Accordingly, non-Catholics, persons excommunicated, or public sinners should not be chosen to act as witnesses.[33] Still there is no general law of the Church to exclude these from acting validly in such a capacity. Acting as a witness at a marriage is not listed as a legitimately authorized ecclesiastical act in Canon 2256, 2°; therefore, the excommunicated are not barred on that ground. In regard to non-Catholics, the Congregation of the Holy Office has declared in a particular reply that they are not to be used as witnesses. However, it did not forbid the ordinary to tolerate their acting in such a capacity for a serious reason, as long as scandal would not be present.[34]

Such are the requirements in law for persons acting as witnesses in the ordinary form of marriage. The same must be said for witnesses who act in that capacity in the extraordinary form of marriage. Canon 1098 specifically states that the marriage in such circumstances is valid and licit *coram solis testibus*. The exact number of witnesses is not indicated, but the use of the plural number (*testibus*) postulates that at least *two* witnesses be present. It is not necessary that the witnesses ask and receive the consent of the parties to the marriage. This is an obligation only of a qualified witness in the ordinary form. The witnesses are not "qualified" witnesses and the law does not place this obligation on them. It may

[33] Gasparri, n. 962; Payen, II, n. 1763; Cappello, *De Matrimonio*, n. 653.
[34] S. C. S. Officii, 19 aug. 1891—*Fontes*, n. 1044.

be done, but it is not necessary for validity.[35] Since the canon does not set any requirements for the validity of the assistance of the witnesses at such a marriage, one must of necessity fall back on the requirements for witnesses as listed for the ordinary form. To demand more would be reading into the canon what is not there. To demand less would be going contrary to the mind of the legislator because less would be demanded in regard to witnesses in the exception than in the rule itself; the exception is not in regard to witnesses but rather in regard to the absence of a *qualified* witness.

Some difficulties have arisen in this very regard. There have been commentators who would exclude from the benefit of validity marriages contracted in such circumstances, even though a naturally valid consent would have been exchanged in the presence of witnesses, if this took place in a civil or non-Catholic religious ceremony. This problem arose in regard to marriages contracted in Russia and Mexico, where priests could not be had. The proponents of this view held that the words of the canon, *"coram solis testibus,"* must be understood in the strict sense in virtue of Canon 19. As witnesses in this regard only private persons are to be considered. Therefore *ministri ut sacris addicti* or civil officials are to be excluded for the reason that they are in official positions. Further, by the positive divine and ecclesiastical laws (Canon 1258), Catholics are forbidden to take part in non-Catholic ceremonies. The Code prescribes that another priest is to assist at such a marriage if he can be had; this would be impossible in such circumstances. Finally, the interpretation of the Code Commission given in regard to Canon 1078 on March 12, 1929, stated that a *civil* marriage without subsequent cohabitation would not induce the impediment of public propriety.[36] Since the reply was given in an absolute manner, with no limitations, it referred to all civil marriages, even those that may have been contracted under the conditions mentioned in Canon 1098. In view of all these arguments it

[35] Payen, II, n. 1825; Schönsteiner, *Grundriss des kirchlichen Eherechts,* p. 729; Wouters, *Manuale Theologiae Moralis* (2 vols., Brugis: Beyaert, 1933), II, 583; Aertnys-Damen, *Theologia Moralis,* II, n. 621.

[36] P.C.I., 12 mart. 1929—*AAS,* XXI (1929), 170; Bouscaren, *Digest,* I, 516-517.

was argued that one has to exclude as invalid the marriages contracted under circumstances mentioned in Canon 1098 if they had been contracted in a non-Catholic religious or civil ceremony.[37]

The purpose of the proponents of this view is indeed laudable; however, no matter how laudable, how elevated the purpose might be, no one is allowed to do violence to the wording of the canon by twisting its meaning to suit his purpose. The legislator did not say that marriages in such circumstances, if contracted before a non-Catholic minister or a civil official, would be invalid. To have that meaning the wording of the canon would have had to be changed to read "*tantum* coram solis testibus" or "*unice* coram solis testibus." This was not done. What the mind and purpose of the legislator was in framing this canon was to insist on the possibility of proving that a marriage had been contracted. If by chance a marriage had been contracted before a non-Catholic minister or a civil official, as long as two witnesses had been present to attest to the exchange of matrimonial consent, the marriage would be valid, the type of ceremony being completely without relevance to the element of validity. All that is necessary is the exchange of matrimonial consent in the presence of two witnesses.[38] Even under the *Tametsi* discipline, there were commentators who held that such marriages would be valid, even though they had taken place in the presence of a non-Catholic minister.[39]

It is a gratuitous assumption to say that the witnesses mentioned

[37] Močnik, "An canon 1098 comprehendat etiam matrimonii celebrationes acatholicas vel civiles," *Apollinaris,* IX (1936), 304-307; "Consultationes circa Pontificiam interpretationem c. 1078," *Apollinaris,* IX (1936), 444-446.

[38] S. R. R., *Nullitatis Matrimonii,* 7 dec. 1931, coram R.P.D. Andrea Jullien, dec. LV, n. 4: ". . . Siquidem comparendo coram magistratu civili et alio teste aut . . . aut nupturientes volunt, quantum in se est, praestare ac manifestare consensum matrimonialem; ita. . . . validum est matrimonium non ratione quidem actus civilis positi, sed ratione consensus naturalis praestiti et legitime manifestati coram solis testibus."—*Decisiones,* XXIII (1931), 474; Sipos, *Ius Pontificium,* XX (1940), 99; Dalpiaz, "An canon 1098 comprehendat etiam matrimonii celebrationes acatholicas vel civiles?" *Apollinaris,* X (1937), 277; Eichmann-Mörsdorf, *Lehrbuch des Kirchenrechts auf Grund des Codex Iuris Canonici,* II, 231.

[39] Laymann, lib. V, Pars II, c. 4, n. 7; Schmalzgrueber, lib. IV, tit. III, c. 2, n. 116.

in Canon 1098 have to be *privatae personae.* To state that Canon 1094 excludes civil officials and non-Catholic ministers and that therefore they are to be excluded in Canon 1098 does not quite follow. A non-Catholic minister or a civil official, *qua talis,* cannot take part in a Catholic ceremony in his official capacity. They are not excluded by law from acting as ordinary witnesses in the ordinary form of marriage. In marriages contracted according to the extraordinary form, at least as far as validity is concerned, there is nothing in the law that excludes them from acting in their official capacity. The law disregards their official capacity and takes cognizance merely of the exchange of matrimonial consent in the presence of two witnesses.

As for the argument that a non-Catholic ceremony was excluded by the legislator because of the divine law prohibiting participation in a non-Catholic religious service, one may say that such was not the *finis legis* of the legislator in framing this canon. Non-Catholic ceremonies are still forbidden, even in cases envisioned in Canon 1098. However, if the parties, whether in good or bad faith, do approach a non-Catholic minister and exchange matrimonial consent, otherwise naturally sufficient, in the presence of two witnesses, the marriage will nonetheless be valid. The Church has at times recognized marriages contracted before non-Catholic ministers. Pope Pius X, in his apostolic letter "Provida," dated January 18, 1906, declared that in Germany the parties in a mixed marriage would be exempt from the ordinary form of marriage. Marriages contracted before a civil official or a non-Catholic minister were to be considered valid in such cases.[40] This exemption was later extended also to Hungary. It had been a long-standing rule under the *Tametsi* matrimonial discipline that with reference to the form prescribed by the decree *Tametsi* there should be observed that part which could be observed. Hence matrimonial consent in the presence of two witnesses was all that was required. The fact that this took place in a non-Catholic ceremony was something irrelevant and could be abstracted from.[41]

[40] *Fontes,* n. 670.

[41] This is evident from the reply of the Sacred Congregation of the Sacraments to the Bishop of Pinsk on March 4, 1925. The Congregation stated

The argument that a priest should be called to assist at the marriage, if he could easily be had, overlooks the fact that the marriage is valid even without his presence. At most, the obligation of summoning him touches an element of licitness and not one of validity. One cannot demand something for validity if it is prescribed solely for licitness.

The proponents of this view, in using the interpretation of the Code Commission in regard to the impediment of public propriety, misinterpret the meaning of "civil" marriage. The Code Commission had in mind only an *attempted* civil marriage which *was invalid* by reason of lack of proper form. It was asked whether a *civil* marriage *qua* civil marriage (i.e., a mere, so-called civil marriage) would induce the impediment. It was not asked whether a marriage contracted in the circumstances mentioned in Canon 1098, which happened to be a civil marriage, was to be included. In the case presented the attempted marriage was null *ab initio* by the operation of law and in fact had no *"species matrimonii."* The same would be true even in the circumstances mentioned in Canon 1098 if the parties intended merely a civil marriage and nothing more. It would not be true if they intend a valid marriage, even in a civil ceremony, for in such circumstances, by the very operation of law, their matrimonial consent is rendered juridically efficacious. Therefore, the interpretation in regard to Canon 1078 does not pertain to a marriage contracted in accordance with Canon 1098, which perchance might happen to be a civil act.

As a final note in this regard, one should remember that a non-Catholic minister or a civil official, when acting in his official capacity is not excluded by law from acting validly as an ordinary witness. *Ubi lex non distinguit, nec nos distinguere debemus.* Therefore, in a non-Catholic or civil ceremony, if there is present at least one other witness besides the non-Catholic minister or the civil official when the valid matrimonial consent is exchanged, the marriage according to Canon 1098 would be valid since it was

that the fact that such marriages took place in a non-Catholic ceremony affected not the validity of such marriages but only their licitness. Cf. Dalpiaz, *Apollinaris,* IX (1936), 451. Similar replies were given by the same Congregation, under the *Ne temere* discipline, on February 23, 1909, and March 15, 1909. Cf. *Archiv für katholisches Kirchenrecht,* LXXXIX (1909), 717 and 722.

contracted in fact *coram testibus.* The law does not take cognizance of their official capacity; it regards them as ordinary witnesses.[42]

There have been others who held that persons acting as witnesses in accordance with Canon 1098 must not only know that they are taking part in a canonical marriage, but also intend witnessing a Catholic marriage.[43] It is claimed that this is done in a marriage contracted according to the ordinary form; the same would have to be done when marriage is contracted according to the extraordinary form.

This is a misunderstanding of the nature of the position of a witness as required by the law. In the ordinary form of marriage, the witnesses testify primarily to the fact of the exchange of matrimonial consent, and only secondarily to the fact that this took place in the presence of a priest. *De facto,* at times they may not even advert at the time to the fact that this taking place in the presence of a priest. To demand that the witnesses must intend taking part in a Catholic ceremony would lay the validity of marriage open to question. A non-Catholic can act validly as a witness; it would be precarious to demand that he intend taking part in a Catholic ceremony. The witnesses' official position is to testify to the exchange of consent wherever this took place. One cannot demand more in the extraordinary form of marriage, because this would restrict the use of Canon 1098 far beyond what the legislator intended. His purpose was to make possible and to safeguard the validity of marriages contracted in such circumstances.[44] To demand this on the part of the witnesses would defeat the very purpose of the law, since one might never know whether the witnesses had this intention. It would be illogical to demand that the witnesses must know that they are taking part in a canonical, ecclesiastically approved, sacramental marriage, when this knowledge is not demanded of the parties themselves. Consequently, all that

[42] S. R. R., *Nullitatis Matrimonii,* 7 dec. 1931, coram R.P.D. Andrea Jullien, dec. LV, n. 4—*Decisiones,* XXIII (1931), 474; Dalpiaz, *Apollinaris,* X (1937), 275-278; Sipos, *Ius Pontificium,* XX (1940), 99.

[43] Oesterle, *Apollinaris,* IX (1936), 446-462.

[44] S. R. R., *Decisiones,* XXIII (1931), 477.

is necessary is that the witnesses can testify that the parties did exchange matrimonial consent.[45]

The second part of Canon 1098 states that, whenever possible, another priest, i.e., one who is not a qualified witness, should be called, and that he should assist at the marriage *along with the witnesses.* A question naturally presents itself: does the legislator still demand the presence of two other witnesses, under pain of invalidity, even when such a priest is present? Or, in other words, if there is only one other witness present, may the priest function as the second witness, so that the marriage can take place *coram testibus.* At first glance it could seem that the legislator does demand the presence of at least two other witnesses, even though a priest may be assisting. To have such a priest and only one other witness, or just two priests and no one else, would be insufficient and would render the marriage invalid according to Mörsdorf.[46] In support of his position he cites Article VII of the decree *Ne temere,* which allowed marriage in danger of death, in the event that no qualified witness was available, to take place in the presence of any priest *and* two witnesses.

It seems to the writer that this opinion restricts the wording of the canon too much. If the *finis legis* is considered, it is readily seen that such a priest can testify as well as anyone else. He is neither directly nor indirectly excluded by the law from being a witness. From a consideration of the possible consequences, it seems absurd to think that he is to be excluded. If there were available just one other witness beside the priest, it would be better for the priest to hide the fact of his priesthood, for then the marriage could take place. Secondly, if no one knew of the fact that he was a priest and he acted as ordinary witness with just one other witness in attendance, one would be compelled to hold that marriage as invalid. Then, too, if only one other witness is available, the marriage could not take place. Consequently, the priest would not be a

[45] Eichmann-Mörsdorf, *Lehrbuch des Kirchenrechts auf Grund des Codex Iuris Canonici,* II, 231; Dalpiaz, *Apollinaris,* X (1937), 275; Mörsdorf, "Die Noteheschliessung (c. 1098)," *Archiv für katholisches Kirchenrecht,* CXXIV (1950), 91.

[46] Eichmann-Mörsdorf, *op. cit.,* II, 232; Mörsdorf, *Archiv für katholisches Kirchenrecht,* CXXIV (1950), 91.

priest assisting at a marriage according to the norm of Canon 1098. He could not avail himself of the faculties granted in Canons 1044 and 1045. Whereas, if he can act in the capacity of the second witness, there will be a marriage according to the norm of Canon 1098; being a priest at the same time, he will be able to make use of the powers of dispensing granted him in the above mentioned canons. There is nothing in the role of this assisting priest that will preclude the possibility of his acting as the second witness. He can in his dual role still lend dignity to the marriage, see to its valid celebration, dispense if necessary, and register the marriage, even when he acts as an ordinary witness.

The argument that the legislator demands two other witnesses because of the wording of the canon (*una cum testibus*) is not too strong. The legislator has in mind things and conditions as they generally happen. The normal state of affairs is that witnesses are readily available. If so, at least two other witnesses should be used. The legislator does not make laws about contingencies that rarely happen,[47] and that is why no mention is made in law for cases when *no* witnesses are available or when only one other witness besides the priest can be had. However, he does not exclude the priest from being one of the two necessary witnesses. It is not valid to argue that the decree *Ne temere* required a priest *and* two witnesses, and that therefore the same holds true today. The Code changed the law of that decree, dispensing with the necessity of having a priest at such a marriage under the pain of invalidity, acknowledging the validity of such a marriage if it is contracted solely in the presence of witnesses. A final argument can be taken from Canon 11, which states that only those laws are invalidating or incapacitating which expressly or equivalently state that the action is null or the person is incapable. This is not true of the circumstances in respect to the canon under consideration.

Thus far, the discussions pertained to cases in which witnesses could be had, A logical question at this point would be, for example, what provision is made for cases in which no witnesses or

[47] For laws ought to be adapted to events which frequently and readily occur rather than to such as rarely happen. In fact, what only happens once or twice, as Theophrastus says, legislators omit.—D. (1.3) 5, 6.

only one witness can be had. There is no provision in the law for such an eventuality, for it will rarely, if ever, happen, in consideration particularly of the fact that practically anyone can act as a witness. Still it is not out of the realm of possibility that such cases could occur. Gasparri listed two examples, namely, a party is constituted in danger of death, or he is detained in prison and a priest is present, or the civil law forbids the use of witnesses.[48]

The commentators are all in agreement that when there is a conflict between the ecclesiastical law as to the form of marriage and the natural right of marrying that a person possesses, the former has to give way to the latter. In the hypotheses considered, one must remember that, wherever possible, a competent ecclesiastical personage would have to be approached and a dispensation sought from the obligation of observing the form. If this is impossible and the prescripts of the ecclesiastical law requiring witnesses cannot be observed, the obligation ceases and a marriage would be valid if contracted in the presence of one witness or no witness at all.[49] Since the law makes no express provision for such cases, Canon 20 becomes operative in such a situation. Canonical equity would allow persons in such grave circumstances to contract marriage without witnesses, if otherwise they could never marry or could marry only after a long time. The same would be true if the parties are constituted in a proximate danger of eternal damnation.[50] Sipos [51] would extend this reasoning, and with merit, even to cases wherein parties, e.g., in Russia, although they may be bound to the juridical form of marriage, invincibly know nothing or could know nothing of the obligation of observing either the ordinary or extraordinary form of marriage. Normally, Canon 16 would not excuse from observing the law such persons who are ignorant of the invalidating effect of the law in question. However, the law of nature would supersede the ecclesiastical law (Canons 1094, 1098, 16) and a private marriage, i.e., even without witnesses,

[48] *De Matrimonio*, n. 999.

[49] Gasparri, n. 988; Coronata, *De Matrimonio*, n. 571; Wouters, *Manuale Theologiae Moralis*, II, n. 740; Cappello, *De Matrimonio*, n. 695; Sipos, *Ius Pontificium*, XX (1940), 100.

[50] Cappello, *loc. cit.*

[51] *Loc. cit.*

inasmuch as their necessity is not known by the parties, would be valid as long as matrimonial consent has been exchanged. Presuming upon the benign will of the legislator, it might be said that he would not wish to bind such people in such circumstances. Under the *Tametsi* discipline, the Congregations, in granting permission for marriages to take place apart from the presence of a priest, usually added that the form of *Tametsi* should be observed *as far as possible.* On certain occasions they also stated that the law of the Council of Trent remained suspended *quoad suum effectum* as often as it could no longer be observed because of insurmountable difficulties and dangers.[52] Finally, this is the common opinion of the commentators.

Such cases are indeed very rare and one need not fear abuse in such a matter. Usually the case will not be so urgent that witnesses cannot be summoned.

[52] *Vide supra,* p. 31.

CHAPTER VIII

OBLIGATIONS ARISING IN THE USE OF THE EXTRAORDINARY FORM OF MARRIAGE

THE three previous chapters treated of the postulated conditions for the valid use of the extraordinary form of marriage. In order that the form may be licitly used, there are certain duties incumbent on the parties who take part in a marriage contracted according to this form. They relate to (1) the contingent approval of the local ordinary; (2) the prenuptial investigation; (3) the assistance of another priest when obtainable; (4) the registration of the marriage, and (5) the subsequent observance of prescribed civil formalities.

ARTICLE 1. THE CONTINGENT APPROVAL OF THE LOCAL ORDINARY

The canon itself does not require the approval or the permission of the local ordinary for the licit use of the extraordinary form of marriage. However, the ordinary may with all due right reserve all such cases for his own judgment and approval. This right could be vindicated from the Code itself. It is the *mens legislatoris* that all difficult problems be referred to the local ordinary.[1] The Holy See has at various times stressed the prudence and necessity of the local ordinary's intervention in such cases.[2]

Realizing the need of such intervention, the Bishops of the Province of Malines decreed in Council that outside the danger of death these cases should be referred to the local ordinary.[3] Finally, this is the common opinion of the commentators.[4]

[1] Cf. Canons 336, 1023, 1026, 1028, 1031, 1032, 1034, 1063, 1065, 1066, etc.

[2] The Sacred Poenitentiary, in an instruction issued January 15, 1886 (*Fontes,* n. 6427; Gasparri, n. 1295) decreed that when a civil marriage is obligatory but cannot be performed, great prudence and caution should be observed and the advice of the ordinary sought. Cf. also S. C. de Sacramentis, 16 iun, 1922 (ad Ordinarium Brugensem)—apud De Smet, *De Sponsalibus et Matrimonio,* n. 136, footnote on page 110; 24 apr. 1935 (ad Episcopum Metensem)—*Periodica,* XXVII (1935), 45.

[3] *III Prov. Conc. Mechliniense* (1923), n. 214—apud De Becker, *Ephemerides Theologicae Lovanienses,* IX (1932), 290.

[4] Heylen, *Tractatus de Matrimonio,* 273; Claeys-Bouuaert—Simenon, *Man-*

Prudence suggests that such cases be not decided by the pastor himself. The ordinary can lay down certain rules which will preclude the possibility of abuses setting in. He can check to see that all the required conditions have been met, and can take the necessary steps to see that the marriage is properly recorded. At times it may be necessary for him to invoke the power given him by the Code of placing a ban for a period of time on the contracting of marriage by this couple.[5] This ban, however, will not have the force of an invalidating law, since it is only in the power of the Holy See to introduce an invalidating clause in such a ban.[6] If it be necessary to safeguard the validity of the marriage, he may have to call on the power of dispensing which he possesses either in virtue of a grant from the general law or from special faculties. In fact, in cases of doubt whether the facts as presented to him would allow the use of Canon 1098, he may, in virtue of Canon 15, dispense the parties and allow the use of the extraordinary form. In view of the foregoing it must be said that, even when the ordinary has made no ruling in this regard, the pastor would be most imprudent in venturing to act without consulting him.

As a general rule, when the parties are constituted in danger of death, there will be no opportunity of receiving the approval of the ordinary. Outside of these cases, if a qualified witness is, *de facto,* physically absent and unavailable, once again there will be no occasion for seeking the ordinary's approval. The cases in which such approval can easily and should be received obtain when the qualified witness is unavailable because of serious inconvenience threatened by the civil law. In cases of this sort the parties will invariably approach their parish priest for the purpose of contracting marriage. As a rule, they abide by his counsel and direction. There is absolutely no reason why the ordinary should not be consulted.

When the ordinary has made certain rulings in this matter, the parties are bound to obey him in view of the seriousness of the

uale Juris Canonici (3 vols., Vol. II, 3. ed., Gandae et Leodii: Dessain, 1947), II *(De Sacramentis),* n. 320; Vlaming-Bender, p. 430; *Periodica,* XXI (1932), 45.

[5] Canon 1039, § 1.

[6] Canon 1039, § 2.

matter. By disobeying him they would expose themselves to serious sin. One must not forget, however, that such disobedience, even in the event that the ordinary forbade the use of the extraordinary form, would not render the marriage invalid if all the postulated conditions in Canon 1098 are fulfilled. The law does not have an invalidating clause to that effect.

Article 2. The Prenuptial Investigation

Canon 1019, § 1, states that before *any marriage* is celebrated it must be clearly evident that there is no obstacle to its valid and licit celebration. This rule grants no exception in the use of the extraordinary form. One will note that the canon studiously omits mentioning to whom the facts mentioned therein must be evident. One explanation can be found in the fact that this state of the parties must also be known in the use of the extraordinary form.

When the parties are constituted in danger of death, there will be little if any time to conduct any sort of investigation. The Code makes provision for such an eventuality in the second paragraph of Canon 1019. It declares that if no other proofs are available, and there are no contrary indications, the sworn statement of the parties before witnesses that they have been baptized and that they are not bound by any impediment will suffice. A party would act temerariously, even if he felt in conscience that a former marriage was invalid or had been dissolved by death, as long as this fact had not as yet been established with certainty.[7]

Outside of the danger of death, if a qualified witness and any other priest is physically unavailable, some sort of investigation would have to be made. One cannot place this obligation on the witnesses, since they are not qualified witnesses in law; their sole obligation is to witness and to testify to the exchange of matrimonial consent between the parties. It can be said that in the event that they are aware of a diriment impediment between the parties, they must refuse their assistance. They may not participate in an invalid marriage. The obligation, then, of establishing the free state of the parties will devolve on the parties themselves. They must be certain that there is no obstacle to the mar-

[7] Canon 1069, § 2.

riage, otherwise they may not contract marriage. How far must this investigation go? All one can say is that they must establish that each is baptized and that they are not bound by any impediments. This they can do by producing relevant documents of proof and by furnishing sworn affidavits of witnesses. The question of whether the parties, even though bound by an impediment, could contract marriage according to the extraordinary form if there is no one who can dispense them from it will be discussed in the following chapter.

On the other hand, if a qualified witness is physically present but cannot assist at the marriage because of impending harm from the civil law, or if some priest is called to assist at the marriage as the canon prescribes, the obligation to establish the free state of the parties will fall to the priest. The obligation is primarily that of the pastor of the bride, i.e., the one whose right it is to assist at the marriage.[8] In fine, the Instruction of the Congregation of Sacraments, dated June 29, 1941, will have to be strictly observed. This responsibility is a grave one for the pastor, as is evident from the importance of the matter. The examination is to be made by the pastor personally, unless there is some reasonable cause that serves to excuse him. The pastor may not shirk this responsibility, even though the marriage will not take place according to the ordinary form. It would be his right to assist if it were to take place in the ordinary manner. Therefore it is his obligation to make the necessary investigation. The fact that the extraordinary form is to be used is only incidental to the marriage in this regard.

The priest who is called to assist at the marriage in accordance with the prescript of Canon 1098 will have an obligation to make this investigation only if no investigation has as yet been made. This is an obligation based not merely on the priest's duty to see that so great a sacrament be not exposed to nullity; one can say that it is implicitly stated in Canons 1044 and 1045, which give such a priest the power of dispensing from matrimonial impediments. The grant of this power presupposes an investigation from which it becomes evident that the use of this power is necessary.

[8] Canon 1097, § 2, cum c. 1020, § 1. Cf. also S. C. de Sacramentis, instr., 29 iun. 1941, n. 4, a—*AAS,* XXXIII (1941), 297 ff; Bouscaren, *Digest,* II, 255.

Article 3. The Assistance of Another Priest

The second part of Canon 1098 requires in both instances, i.e., in danger of death and also when it is foreseen that a qualified witness will be unavailable for at least a month, that wherever and whenever another priest, namely, one who is not a qualified witness, is at hand and can easily be had (*praesto sit*), he should be called and he should assist at the marriage along with the witnesses. However, lest the wrong impression be created, the canon hastens to remind the reader that his presence is not required for validity, the marriage being valid as long as it takes place in the presence of witnesses alone. The legislator calls for the priest's presence that the latter may lend dignity to the marriage ceremony; that he may contribute a religious note of reverence to the celebration of the marriage; that he may remind the people that the marriage is a sacrament; that he may offer the parties the opportunity of receiving a blessing; that he may safeguard the validity of the marriage, in the event that a dispensation from a diriment matrimonial impediment is necessary; and, finally, that he may make proper registration of the contracted marriage.

For the licit use of this form there rests on the parties the obligation of calling such a priest. This obligation is a serious one. It binds on the supposition that such a priest is readily available and can assist without serious inconvenience. If the parties disobeyed this law they would expose themselves to serious sin. The obligation ceases if the excusing cause is grave [9] and probably even if the cause is a reasonable one.[10] It will also cease if the priest is not readily available or can be had only with serious inconvenience on his part or that of the parties. The parties are not obliged to seek a priest in order to obtain his services; their obligation to use his services is predicated on his being readily available. When the priest is called, he must according to law (*debeat*) assist at that marriage. It is not a matter of choice for him, unless, again, a serious inconvenience would excuse him.

If he is present, must he assist actively, i.e., by asking and

[9] Wernz-Vidal, *Ius Matrimoniale,* n. 543.

[10] Cappello, *De Matrimonio,* n. 696.

receiving the consent of the contracting parties to the marriage? This is not required for validity, for he is not acting in the capacity of a qualified witness. Commentators do not consider the problem of whether his active assistance is required for licitness; one can say that it is not required.[11] Even though it is not required for the licitness of the act, it would be advisable for him to assist actively to safeguard the validity of the marriage. In the event that he does assist actively, it would be fitting (*convenit*) for him to follow the Roman Ritual,[12] although, once again, this cannot be urged as an obligation.

Inasmuch as the law does not distinguish, the parties may call for any priest, whether he be of the Latin or of some Oriental rite, whether he be a member of a religious order or a congregation or a member of the secular priesthood. Whether the phrase "any priest" points also to a priest who is under a censure of excommunication or suspension has long been disputed among the canonists. For the sake of clarity, one must note that in regard to excommunicates the Code distinguishes between those who are *tolerati* and those who are *vitandi*,[13] and, among the *tolerati*, between those who have incurred the censure but upon whom a declaratory sentence has not as yet been inflicted and those upon whom a condemnatory or declaratory sentence has been passed. Regarding the persons under the censure of suspension or interdict, the distinction is the same as for the *excommunicati tolerati*. Vlaming,[14] De Smet,[15] Vermeersch-Creusen,[16] Cappello[17] and Hyland[18] are of the opinion that if a priest is an *excommunicatus vitandus* he need not be called. Cerato,[19] on the other hand, felt that even if such a sentence has been passed on the priest he is to be called. In view of the probability of the

11 Payen, II, n. 1825, 4.

12 Sipos, *Ius Pontificium*, XX (1940), 102.

13 Canon 2258.

14 *Praelectiones Iuris Matrimonii*, II, n. 586.

15 *De Sponsalibus et Matrimonio*, n. 134, nota 1.

16 *Epitome Iuris Canonici*, II, n. 406.

17 *De Matrimonio*, n. 696.

18 *Excommunication*, The Catholic University of America Canon Law Studies, n. 49 (Washington, D. C.: The Catholic University of America, 1928), p. 106.

19 *Matrimonium a Codice Iuris Canonici integre desumptum*, p. 163.

first opinion, it may be said that there is no obligation of calling such a priest. May such a priest be called? In the event that the parties are constituted in danger of death, such a priest may certainly be called, because Canon 2261, § 3, allows the faithful to seek the ministrations of such men in the matter of sacramental absolution and, when no other priest is available, in the matter of the other sacraments and the sacramentals as well. Wishing to have their marriage blessed, the parties would be allowed to call him. Regarding his power of dispensing in the event that an impediment is present, a more detailed discussion will be found in the following chapter. When the danger of death does not obtain, it seems that he may not be called. One cannot fall back in such an eventuality on Canon 2261, § 3. There is no spiritual necessity great enough, or any utility, that would justify the assistance of such priests if they are under such a censure. De Smet, Hyland, and Cappello extend the same restrictions to priests upon whom has been passed a declaratory or a condemnatory sentence of excommunication or suspension of the type that forbids the exercise of orders or of jurisdiction. It seems that this restriction cannot be extended to a priest who is under personal interdict. This type of censure does not take away jurisdiction from the transgressor. He is forbidden to administer the sacraments and sacramentals,[20] the Code, making no mention of his being deprived of jurisdiction, except implicitly in Penance, for in its administration, jurisdiction would have to be used. Therefore, he would still possess the power of dispensing granted by the Code to priests mentioned in Canon 1044. It seems, then that, since some benefit might eventuate from his being called, it would be permissible to call him. Such assistance, as long as the blessing is excluded, could be allowed because it does not fall in the comprehension of the phrase *"divina officia,"* which are forbidden him by the law.[21] One must remember that not he but the parties themselves are the ministers of the sacrament. It is necessary that he have the power of orders, but in assisting at a marriage he doesn't exercise the power of orders.

As for the priest under censure upon whom no sentence has been

[20] Canon 2275.

[21] Canon 2275 cum c. 2256, § 1.

passed,[22] the Code forbids him to administer the sacraments and sacramentals except in cases wherein the faithful, by way of a reasonable request, seek from his hands the sacraments or the sacramentals, especially if no other priest is available. The censured priest may then, without asking the reason, accede to their reasonable requests.[23] Besides, if the censure is not notorious and its observance in the external forum would cause him to lose his good name, he need not observe the penalty until such time that a sentence has been passed.[24] The parties in wishing a priest to bless their marriage would be making a reasonable request. *Ergo*. Must he be called? Rossi [25] and Cerato [26] hold the affirmative view, while Leitner [27] is of the opinion that he should not be called.

Assisting at the marriage along with the witnesses, the priest is only a special, but not a qualified, witness. There have been commentators who have held that he was a qualified witness representing the Church. However, in view of the fact that his presence is not required under the pain of invalidity, and of the fact that he is not strictly required, even when present, to ask and receive the consent of the parties, it is difficult to see how this opinion can be sustained.[28]

The priest should remind the parties that they are receiving a sacrament, and that therefore it is necessary for them to be in the state of grace. After its celebration, it is his obligation to take care that the marriage is properly registered in the prescribed ecclesiastical registers.[29]

Article 4. Other Obligations

A valid marriage contracted according to the extraordinary form is as much a sacrament as is a marriage contracted according to

22 Except for a *vitandus* according to Canon 2343, § 1, who becomes such *ipso facto*. Cf. also C. 2266.

23 Canon 2261, § 1, § 2.

24 Canon 2232, § 1.

25 *De Matrimonii Celebratione iuxta Codicem Iuris Canonici*, pp. 113-114.

26 *Loc. cit.*

27 *Lehrbuch des katholischen Eherechts*, p. 207.

28 Schönsteiner, *Grundriss des kirchlichen Eherechts*, p. 729; Payen, II, n. 1825.

29 Canon 1103, § 3.

the ordinary form, if both parties are baptized. Since it is a sacrament of the living, it must be received in the state of grace. The Holy See has on various occasions insisted that this obligation be brought to the attention of the parties.[30] The reason is clear. The parties are likely not to advert to the fact that they will be receiving a sacrament when they contract marriage, and thus a sacrilege could possibly result. Furthermore, through a stressing of this obligation there will be impressed on the minds of the parties the fact of the sacredness of the marriage they are contracting, and the fact that it will be a true and binding sacramental marriage. If there is no priest at hand, the parties will have to provide for themselves. For the gaining of the state of grace an act of perfect contrition will be necessary. If a priest is available, whether he will be able to hear confessions will depend on whether he has faculties in that territory to hear confessions. If he has, then there is no problem. It must be remembered, however, that it cannot be insisted that the parties confess their sins. They may, if they so desire, but at their own peril, try to put themselves into the state of grace by means of an act of perfect contrition. If the priest has no faculties to hear confessions in that territory, faculties will be given him *a iure,* if the parties, one or both, be constituted in danger of death.[31] This faculty is given only for the benefit of the person in danger of death. The law makes no provision for the other party.

The local ordinary should bring this matter of the needed instruction of the people, in order that they must be in the state of grace to receive the sacrament of matrimony, to the attention of his priests. They in turn should then instruct the people when arranging for such a marriage. It will be primarily the duty of the priest who is arranging for the marriage. In the event that no qualified witness is available, the obligation will devolve on the priest who is called to assist at the marriage.

[30] S. C. de Propaganda Fide, instr. (ad Vic. Ap. Sin.), 23 iun. 1830—*Collectanea S. C. de Prop. Fide* (ed. 1907), n. 816; S. C. de Sacramentis, 16 iun. 1922 (ad Ordinarium Brugensem)—apud De Smet, *De Sponsalibus et Matrimonio,* n. 136, footnote page 110; 24 apr. 1935 (ad Episcopum Metensem)—apud *Periodica,* XXVII (1935), 45.

[31] Canons 882; 2252.

After the marriage is contracted, a very serious obligation of properly registering such a marriage remains. The Code states that, whenever a marriage is contracted according to the extraordinary form, the priest, if he assists at such a marriage, or otherwise the witnesses, are held *in solidum* with the contracting parties to see to it that the marriage is registered as soon as possible in the prescribed books.[32] The Holy See has ever been solicitous about this matter. In 1785, in its instruction to the Prefect of the Missions at Curaçao, the Congregation for the Propagation of the Faith advised the priest to tell the parties whom he permitted to contract marriage apart from his presence and solely in the presence of two witnesses that they should return as soon as possible after the celebration of the marriage to tell him of the contracted marriage so that he could make a proper annotation of it.[33] This solicitude is easily understandable because of the danger of subsequent marriages, or also of the danger that the offspring be considered as illegitimate, if the marriage is not properly recorded.

This obligation is indeed a serious one because of the possible consequences just mentioned.[34] The assisting priest will be well aware of this obligation. As for the parties, unless they have been informed of it, it is difficult to see how they will know of it. The priest arranging for this type of marriage will have the obligation of bringing this to their attention. This registration must take place *quam primum,* i.e., as soon as possible. To acquit oneself of this obligation within three or four days will fulfill the law. This obligation may demand immediate fulfillment if the party realizes that otherwise he may forget about it.

With reference to the subject of this obligation, two eventualities may emerge: Either a priest assists at the marriage, or the marriage is contracted in the presence solely of two witnesses. In the first instance, it seems from the wording of the canon that the entire obligation falls on the priest, the parties and witnesses incurring no obligation. Such is the common interpretation of the

[32] Canon 1103, § 3.

[33] *Collectanea S. C. de Prop. Fide* (ed. 1907), n. 571.

[34] Gasparri, n. 1013; Cappello, *De Matrimonio,* n. 720.

canonists.[35] However, there are a few who interpret the canon to mean that the obligation is that of the priest *and* of the contracting parties *in solidum,* i.e., all three are bound until one satisfies the obligation. The parties are always bound, even when a priest was present.[36]

This interpretation is not in strict conformity with the text of the canon.[37] In view of the common interpretation, one must hold that when a priest is present the obligation is solely his, neither the parties nor the witnesses having an obligation in such an eventuality. But if it were clearly evident that the priest will not have the marriage recorded, then there will be an obligation for the parties and witnesses. In the second instance, when marriage is contracted in the presence of two witnesses only, the obligation falls on the witnesses and the parties *in solidum.*

The canon does not specify which pastor is to be notified for the proper registration of the fact that such a marriage had been contracted. It could be the pastor of the place in which the marriage was contracted or it could be the proper pastor of the parties, i.e., the pastor who according to the law had the prior right and duty to assist at the marriage. The commentators are in disagreement. Cappello feels that it should be the pastor of the place.[38] Van der Acker [39] argued that, in view of the purpose of the law which seeks to facilitate proof of the fact that a marriage had been contracted, it should be the proper pastor of the parties. Because of the disagreement among authors, one is free to choose either of the two pastors. In consequence of the fact that the marriage is also to be annotated in the baptismal registers, practically it may make little difference which pastor is chosen.

[35] Gasparri, n. 1013; De Smet, *op. cit.*, n. 701; Cappello, *De Matrimonio,* n. 720; Ubach, *Compendium Theologiae Moralis,* II, n. 860, nota 2.

[36] Wouters, *Theologia Moralis,* II, n. 751; Noldin-Schmitt, *Summa Theologiae Moralis* (3 vols., 26. ed., Vol. III [*De Sacramentis*], Oeniponte/Lipsiae: Rauch, 1940), III, n. 653, 3°. Miceli (*Monitor Ecclesiasticus,* LXXV [1950], 236) holds that the priest, the contracting parties and the witnesses are held *in solidum.*

[37] Payen, II, n. 1921.

[38] *De Matrimonio,* n. 720.

[39] *Apud* Payen, II, n. 1922.

At first glance it may seem that Canon 1103, § 3 also demands that the obliged parties make the fact of the marriage known to the pastor or the pastors of the church or churches in which the contracting parties received baptism. It speaks of taking care that the marriage is recorded in the prescribed books, which besides the matrimonial registers can mean also the baptismal registers containing the record of the parties' baptisms.[40] There are commentators who like Cappello[41] actually place this double obligation on the parties and the witnesses. But there are others, like Vermeersch[42] and Van den Acker,[43] who believed that their obligation was fulfilled when the contracting of the marriage was made known to the pastor either of the place or to the proper pastor of the contracting parties. It then became his obligation to make provision that all proper annotations were made. This he could do by inquiring of the parties about the actual place of their baptism and also about

[40] The instruction of the Sacred Congregation of the Sacraments, dated June 29, 1941, in regard to the canonical investigation that is to be made before parties are admitted to the celebration of marriage (*AAS*, XXXIII [1941], 305-306; translated *apud* Bouscaren. *Digest*, II, 263) wisely counsels ordinaries to see to it that annotations of baptism should be made not only in the baptismal register of the actual place of baptism *(locus baptismi)*, if the baptism could not be deferred till the child could be taken to the proper pastor of the parents; but also in the baptismal register of the proper parish of the parents *(locus originis)* at the time of the birth (Canon 778 cum c. 738, § 2). The wisdom of this prescription is plainly evident from the fact that if the priests have observed the law, as they are presumed to have done, there will be two records of the baptism. To safeguard the provision that one's baptismal record furnish indication regarding one's free state in regard to marriage, the notice of the contracted marriage should be sent to both parishes. Since it cannot be assumed that the priest present at the contracting of the marriage knows of the fact that the baptism is registered in two different parishes, the obligation of forwarding a notice of the contracted marriage to the parish of origin seems to rest on the priest of the church where the baptism was actually conferred and where the primary record of baptism is preserved for it is likely that he will first receive the notice of the contracted marriage. Accordingly he should notify the pastor of the other church (parish of origin) where likewise a record of baptism is preserved.

[41] *De Matrimonio*, n. 720.

[42] *De Forma Sponsalium et Matrimonio post Decretum "Ne temere"* (Brugis, 1098), p. 82.

[43] *Apud* Payen, II, n. 1922, nota 4.

the place of their origin at the time of their baptism. This opinion has great intrinsic value. To place this obligation on the parties without ascertaining whether they are able to write or whether they have any knowledge of the further obligation of noting the contracted marriage in the baptismal registers seems contrary to the purpose of the legislator. The proper recording of the marriage will be duly safeguarded if the further obligation is acknowledged to rest with the pastor of the place where the marriage was contracted. Such an obligation could analogically be derived from the wording of paragraph two of the same Canon (1103) where the obligation of recording and notification is placed on the pastor even though the marriage took place in the presence of some other priest. Because of the extrinsic and intrinsic probability of this opinion, the parties and witnesses will be acquitted of this obligation if the contracting of the marriage has been made known either to the pastor of the place in which the marriage had been contracted or to the proper pastor of the parties. Gasparri noted that if such a marriage was contracted in a place where no parish or quasi-parish has as yet been erected, then the notification should be sent to the ordinary of the place.

The items comprised in the obligatory notification are the names of the parties, the date and place of their baptism, the names of their parents, the names and addresses of the witnesses, the date and place of the contracted marriage, annotations to the effect that the marriage was contracted in accordance with the prescripts of Canon 1098 and also to the effect that a dispensation had been granted if such was the case.

It was noted above that in such circumstances even a civil marriage would be valid as long as the parties had intended contracting a valid marriage. The purely civil effects of marriage, such as the right to an inheritance or to a pension would be duly safeguarded. There remains the question whether the parties who contracted a valid marriage in the presence of witnesses alone, without observing the formalities required by the civil law, are obliged to go through a "civil" ceremony in order to secure the civil effects of marriage once there is removed the civil impediment which originally stood in the way of the marriage. The same obligation would be present even where there was no civil impediment. It has been the constant practice of the Holy See and the teaching of the commentators to acknowledge that a civil marriage can indirectly become obligatory. The Sacred Penitentiary, in an instruction given on January 15, 1866,[44] declared that for various reasons it was opportune and expedient for the spouses who had contracted a valid marriage according to the laws of the Church to go through a civil ceremony demanded by the civil government. This was to be done for the avoidance of difficulties and penalties, for the good of the offspring which would otherwise be considered illegitimate by the civil law, and for the purpose of avoiding the danger of a subsequent marriage. D'Annibale (1815-1892) would not excuse one from a mortal sin if he or she should neglect the solemnities required by the civil law. In such a case the "civil" marriage was fully licit; its omission could lead to a serious danger of harm to the parties and to their offspring.[45] Gasparri was of the same opinion.[46]

It is no wonder that the Congregation of the Sacraments, in its reply to the Ordinary of Bruges on June 16, 1922,[47] insisted that the ordinary take care that the parties oblige themselves to fulfill the civil formalities as soon as this could be done. This insistence was so strong that the Congregation demanded that the promise of later compliance with the civil formalities be committed to writing, and that the document be kept in the episcopal curia. The ordinary or the priest who made the arrangement for the marriage to be contracted according to the extraordinary form was to exact this promise from the parties. True, the reply was only of a particular nature; nevertheless, it showed the mind of the Holy See, and accordingly should be followed in practice.

When a priest is also a civil official for the purpose of witnessing marriages, a "civil" marriage should be taken care of by him, when the parties are free to call for his service. If he is not, then the parties should look to a civil official to fulfill the requirements

[44] *Fontes,* n. 6427; Gasparri, n. 1295.

[45] *Summula Theologiae Moralis,* III, n. 467.

[46] *Loc. cit.*

[47] *Apud* De Smet, *De Sponsalibus et Matrimonio,* n. 136, footnote p. 110.

of the civil law. The Sacred Penitentiary, in the instruction mentioned above, prudently cautioned the parties not to forget that in complying with the civil law they were doing nothing more than going through a civil ceremony, since they were already married. In the event that a priest performs this civil ceremony he is to take care to warn the parties and the witnesses that the parties are already married. At all costs he is to preclude the possibility of having the sacrament of matrimony simulated. Simulation of a sacrament, i.e., placing the sacramental sign without having the sacrament come into existence, is never allowed, since it is an action that is intrinsically evil. It would be advisable that the compliance with the civil requirements take place privately.

CHAPTER IX

THE DISPENSING POWER OF A PRIEST ASSISTING AT A MARRIAGE ACCORDING TO CANON 1098

In allowing marriage to be contracted according to the extraordinary form, the legislator did not thereby relax the laws in regard to matrimonial impediments. The prescripts of Canon 1035 still obtain. Canon 1098 is so to be understood as to allowing this form of marriage in certain circumstances to parties who are not prohibited by law from entering marriage. The parties will still be bound, as parties are in contracting marriage according to the ordinary form, by Canon 1036 in regard to impedient and diriment impediments. If an impedient impediment is present and is not dispensed from by a competent ecclesiastical authority, the marriage would nonetheless be valid.[1] The use of the extraordinary form is not made dependent on the absence of impediments. Canon 1098 does not have a clause to that effect. In virtue of Canon 11, the use of the extraordinary form would not be invalid in the event that an impediment was present. However, if a diriment impediment is present and is not dispensed from, the marriage contracted according to the extraordinary form would be invalid, not by reason of the form of marriage employed, but by reason of the incapacitating effect of the impediment.[2]

It is not within the proposed scope of this dissertation to go into the problem of the cessation of law in regard to impediments. It may be briefly noted, though, that impediments of the natural or the positive divine law do not cease. As for ecclesiastical laws, the general rule is that neither a *grave incommodum* nor the impossibility of seeking a dispensation, whether the impossibility be of a private or of a common character, excuses one from the incapacitating effect of a diriment impediment. They may excuse one from a serious sin, but cannot restore capability which the law has taken

[1] Canon 1036, § 1.

[2] Canon 1036, § 2.

away. There is an exception to this general principle that is generally admitted by canonists. It is the case wherein the natural right of a person to contract marriage supersedes the ecclesiastical law constituting such an impediment. In such an eventuality, a person would otherwise have to abstain from marriage. The impediment, in such a case, as opposed to the natural law, would cease.[3]

The example given by Gasparri is taken from a problem presented to the Holy Office. A Chinese Catholic man lived among pagans in China and it was impossible for him to go anywhere else. There were no Christians in the region. He contracted marriage with a pagan woman. The Holy Office said that the parties were not to be disturbed. Considering the circumstances, one can readily see why commentators restrict this doctrine solely to the impediment of disparity of worship. It seems not to obtain in the case of any other impediments.

Some authors opine that an invalidating law would also cease *ex epikeia* in a case of a *gravissimum incommodum,* when it is a question of an impediment from which a dispensation is usually granted.[4] Cappello explains his opinion in the following manner:

1. If the purpose of the law becomes harmful to the common good, the law ceases to bind, because it may be presumed that the legislator would not want such harm to result.

2. If in a particular case the law would tend toward the *damnum animarum,* e.g., when a dying person involved in concubinage and being bound by an impediment from which he could not seek a dispensation with a view to contracting marriage would be in a proximate danger of sin and losing his soul. In such a case the law would not bind. This would also be probably true if the impediment was a diriment one.[5] All authors agree that after the use of *epikeia* in an invalidating law one must look, if possible, to the

[3] Gasparri, nn. 260 and 595; Cappello, *De Matrimonio,* n. 199; Wernz-Vidal, *Ius Matrimoniale,* n. 273, footnote 41; Payen, I, n. 567.

[4] E.g., Cappello, *loc. cit.;* De Smet, "Responsa," *Collationes Brugenses* XII (1907), 548-549.

[5] Ballerini-Palmieri, *Opus Theologicum Morale,* I, n. 318; Vlaming, *Praelectiones Iuris Matrimônii,* I, n. 198.

validity of the act by means of a subsequent dispensation or sanation.[6]

Foreseeing that at times such an impediment or impediments might be present and the concession in Canon 1098 would be meaningless, the legislator benignly granted certain faculties in the law itself to the priest who would be assisting at such a marriage.

When the parties are in danger of death, then, in order to provide for the consciences of the parties and, whenever the case demands it, for the legitimation of their offspring, and with reference both to the form to be observed in the celebration of marriage and to all of the impediments of the ecclesiastical law, public or occult, even multiple, except the impediments arising from the sacred order of priesthood and from affinity in the direct line when the marriage has been consummated, local ordinaries can dispense their subjects anywhere and everyone actually staying in their territory, provided that scandal be obviated and that when a dispensation is granted from the impediments of mixed religion and of disparity of worship, the usual promises are given.[7] This concession is extended by the Code, in the cases wherein the local ordinary cannot be reached, to a priest who assists at a marriage that is being contracted according to Canon 1098.[8]

Outside of the case of danger of death, whenever an impediment

[6] Van Hove, *Commentarium Lovaniense in Codicem Iuris Canonici* (1 vol. in 5 toms., Tom II [De Legibus Ecclesiasticis], Mechliniae: H. Dessain, 1930), Tom II, n. 294.

[7] Canon 1043: Urgente mortis periculo, locorum Ordinarii, ad consulendum conscientiae et, si casus ferat, legitimationi prolis, possunt tum super forma in matrimonii celebratione servanda, tum super omnibus et singulis impedimentis iuris ecclesiastici, sive publicis sive occultis, etiam, multiplicibus, exceptis impedimentis provenientibus ex sacro presbyteratus ordine et ex affinitate in linea recta, consummato matrimonio, dispensare proprios subditos ubique commorantes et omnes in proprio territorio actu degentes, remoto scandalo, et, si dispensatio concedatur super cultus disparitate aut mixta religione, praestitis consuetis cautionibus.

[8] Canon 1044: In eisdem rerum adiunctis de quibus in can. 1043 et solum pro casibus in quibus ne loci quidem Ordinarius adiri possit, eadem dispensandi facultate pollet tum parochus, tum sacerdos qui matrimonio, ad normam can. 1098, n. 2, assistit, tum confessarius, sed hic pro foro interno in actu sacramentalis confessionis tantum.

is discovered when everything is already prepared for the marriage and the marriage cannot, without probable danger of grave harm, be deferred until a dispensation is obtained from the Holy See, the ordinaries of places can, subject to the clauses at the end of Canon 1043, grant a dispensation from all the impediments mentioned in Canon 1043. This faculty may also be used when there is question of the convalidation of an invalid marriage.[9] These concessions also are extended to the priest assisting at a marriage that is being contracted according to Canon 1098. He may use this power only for occult cases and only in cases when even the local ordinary cannot be reached in time or, if he can be reached, it would involve the danger of violation of a secret.[10]

Article 1. The Subject of This Power

The wording of number 2 of Canon 1098, in prescribing the calling of another priest and his assistance at the marriage, is indeed very general. The legislator has laid down no restrictions, and therefore any priest, a member of a religious order or congregation, or a member of the secular priesthood, whether of the Latin or of one of the Eastern rites, who is not a qualified witness for the marriage in question, would fulfill the requirement in the canon. All that is called for is that he have received the sacred order of priesthood.

The mere fact that parties are constituted in danger of death does not suffice to bestow upon such a priest the acknowledged power of dispensing. The text of Canons 1044 and 1045, § 3, predicate the grant of this dispensing power on the supposition that such a

[9] Canon 1045, § 1: Possunt Ordinarii locorum, sub clausulis in fine can. 1043 statutis, dispensationem concedere super omnibus impedimentis de quibus in cit. can. 1043, quoties impedimentum detegatur, cum iam omnia sunt parata ad nuptias, nec matrimonium, sine probabili gravis mali periculo, differri possit usque dum a Sancta Sede dispensatio obtineatur.

Canon 1045, § 2: Haec facultas valeat quoque pro convalidatione matrimonii iam contracti, si idem periculum sit in mora nec tempus suppetat recurrendi ad Sanctam Sedem.

[10] Canon 1045, § 3: In iisdem rerum adiunctis, eadem facultate gaudeant omnes de quibus in can. 1044, sed solum pro casibus occultis in quibus ne loci quidem Ordinarius adiri possit, vel nonnisi cum periculo violationis secreti.

priest is *assisting* at a marriage that is being contracted in accordance with the norm enacted in Canon 1098, n. 2. It has been shown that the presence of two witnesses is always required even in a marriage contracted according to the extraordinary form. Therefore, it may be said that if no witnesses are present, a marriage cannot take place even according to the extraordinary form. Were a priest to be called and were he to be present, he would not be assisting at a marriage that is to be contracted *ad normam can. 1098, n. 2.* Hence, he would not enjoy, under such circumstances, the faculties mentioned in these canons.

This seems to be the only logical interpretation of the canons involved. The grammatical sense confirms this interpretation. The canon reads "sacerdos qui matrimonio, ad normam can. 1098, n. 2, assistit." It is a priest who assists at a marriage that is being contracted according to the norm of Canon 1098, n. 2, and not a priest who assists according to Canon 1098 at a marriage. This seems the only meaning the legislator could have intended. He has made no general provision for a form of marriage without witnesses. He is not to be considered as having done so here. Had the legislator wished to give *any* priest this faculty of dispensing, whether or not the priest assisted at a marriage according to Canon 1098, n. 2, he could have used a different mode of expression, e.g., sacerdos, de quo in can. 1098, or something similar. Further, such a priest would have by law more power than a parochial assistant, to whom a general delegation to assist at marriages could be given. The law gives such an assistant no power of dispensation, even in danger of death.

The burden of proof would fall on those who claim that this power could be exercised even though no witnesses are present. They cannot fall back on the *finis legis,* i.e., that the legislator wanted to make provision for cases of danger of death. Provision is made in the very same canon. Power of dispensing is given to a confessor, to whom the law also gives the faculty of hearing the confession of anyone constituted in danger of death. The priest could hear the party's confession and grant the necessary dispensation in the internal sacramental forum.[11]

[11] Canon 882 cum c. 1044.

In assisting at such a marriage, the priest does not necessarily have to take an active part. As long as he is present at the celebration of the marriage to be celebrated according to Canon 1098, in the presence of at least two witnesses, or, as has been explained above, probably even in the presence of one other witness besides himself,[12] he can be considered as assisting, and thus fulfills the requirement of Canons 1044 and 1045, § 3.

The general law has indeed given these priests wide faculties. Their use, however, must be accommodated to the rules of the Code on the loss of jurisdiction in priests who are under excommunication, under a general suspension, or under suspension from the power of jurisdiction, regardless of whether this disqualification is accompanied by a declaratory or a condemnatory sentence passed on the delinquent priest.[13] An act of jurisdiction—and the granting of a dispensation from a matrimonial impediment is an act of jurisdiction—whether placed in the internal or the external forum by an excommunicated cleric is unlawful. Once a declaratory or a condemnatory sentence has been passed, or if the cleric is a "*vitandus,*" such an act is invalid, except in the case wherein a party, in danger of death, requests sacramental absolution and, in the same circumstances, if other priests are unavailable, the other sacraments and sacramentals.[14] If no sentence has been passed and the priest is not a *vitandus,*[15] then an act of jurisdiction may even be lawful. This would eventuate where the faithful reasonably request sacraments and sacramentals, especially when other ministers cannot be had.[16] The same restrictions that circumscribe the jurisdiction of an excommunicated priest apply also to a priest under suspension *ab officio* or *a iurisdictione.*[17]

In wishing to contract marriage, the parties would be making a reasonable request of an excommunicated priest when they seek a dispensation. The canon does not state that a priest may exercise jurisdiction only in the *conferral* of a sacrament. He may use it

[12] *Vide supra,* p. 136 and p. 137.

[13] Canons 2232, § 1; 2258, § 2; 2261, 2264, 2278, 2279, § 2, n. 1; 2284.

[14] Canon 2264 cum c. 2261, § 3.

[15] Cf. Canons 2258, § 2; 2343; 2266.

[16] Canon 2264, cum c. 2261, § 2.

[17] Canons 2279, § 1; 2284.

whenever the faithful request (*petere*) a sacrament or sacramentals, as was noted above. The parties are the ministers of the sacrament of matrimony. However, if a diriment impediment is present, they cannot confer or receive the *sacrament* of matrimony. Requesting a dispensation in such a case is equivalent to requesting a sacrament.[18] It can be said, then that when a priest assists at a marriage that is being contracted according to the extraordinary form described in Canon 1098 he may:

1. if he is excommunicated or suspended *ab officio* or *a iurisdictione* and no sentence has been passed upon him to that effect, and if he is not a *vitandus,* validly use the faculties granted him both in Canon 1044 and in Canon 1045, § 3, and even do so licitly if requested by the parties;
2. if his excommunication or suspension is accompanied with a condemnatory or a declaratory sentence, or if he is a *vitandus,* validly use the grant of power conceded in Canon 1044 when he is requested by the parties, but not the power mentioned in Canon 1045, § 3.[19]

Article 2. The Nature of This Power

The Code itself defines a dispensation as the relaxation of a law in a special case.[20] Inasmuch as a dispensation has to do with releasing a subject from observing a law, it must stem from the legislator himself, from his successor, from his superior, or from one to whom this faculty has been given.[21] One can readily see, then, that a dispensation denotes an act of jurisdiction.

Jurisdiction, the Code tells us, can be ordinary or delegated. When the power of jurisdiction is attached to an ecclesiastical office by the law itself, it is called ordinary power. When it is committed to a person, it is known as delegated.[22] The office spoken

[18] Canon 19; Leges quae poenam statuunt . . . strictae subsunt interpretationi.

[19] Interdict has not been mentioned above because it does not entail the loss of jurisdiction. Consequently, a priest under interdict, assisting at a marriage being contracted according to Canon 1098, may validly use the power of dispensing in such circumstances.

[20] Canon 80.

[21] Canon 80.

[22] Canon 197, § 1.

of must be taken in the strict sense of the term, i.e., as it is defined in Canon 145, § 1, and not in the broad sense.[23] The power must be attached to an office which is constituted by divine or ecclesiastical ordination as a fixed entity, conferred according to the norms of the sacred canons, and contains in itself at least a participation in ecclesiastical power whether of orders or of jurisdiction. If the power is not ordinary, it must be delegated, because the Code has made the two mutually exclusive.[24] Ordinary power may be delegated to others unless there be a rule to the contrary. Delegated power, when shared *ad universitatem negotiorum*, may be subdelegated further. But delegated power when shared for the performance of a single act and when deriving from an authority lower than that of the Holy See, cannot be subdelegated further apart from a special provision to the contrary.

The question that must be determined here is whether the power of dispensing as enjoyed by a priest who is assisting at a marriage that is to be contracted according to the norm of Canon 1098 is, in virtue of the grant made by the general law of the Church, an ordinary or a delegated power. There is no doubt that this power is not ordinary, for such a priest does not have an office in the strict sense of the term. Since the power is not ordinary, it must be delegated. In view of the fact that it is not a delegation from a person, it must be a delegation *a iure*,[25] and, therefore, may not be subdelegated to others.[26]

Article 3. The Extent of This Power

The power given to the assisting priest may be exercised over anyone who calls him to assist at his or her marriage that is being contracted according to the extraordinary form. The person may belong to his rite or to another rite. In view of the grant made

[23] Kearney, *Principles of Delegation*, The Catholic University of America Canon Law Studies, n. 55 (Washington. D. C.: The Catholic University of America Press, 1929), p. 51.

[24] Kearney, *op. cit.*, p. 56.

[25] This prescinds from the possibility that the priest in question may have received a delegation of this power from the pastor or from the local ordinary, who hold it as ordinary power, attached to their offices.

[26] Canon 199, § 4.

by the supreme legislator in the Oriental Law on the matrimonial discipline, it may be exercised even over the faithful of the Oriental rites whenever a priest of the Latin rite assists at a marriage of the faithful of the Oriental rites which is being contracted according to the extraordinary form, as outlined in Canon 89 of the Oriental Code on Marriage Discipline.[27] Since the powers of dispensing granted by the Code to such priests are different according as it is a case of danger of death or not, it is indicated to treat the two cases separately.

A. *Dispensatory Power When Parties Are In Danger of Death*

The power that is granted may be used when either or both parties are in danger of death.[28] It may be exercised even when it is the party who is not bound by an impediment that is in danger of death.[29] Whereas formerly the use of the faculty had been restricted to cases in which the parties had been living in concubinage or in an invalid or civilly attempted marriage, this restriction no longer obtains in the present discipline. It may, therefore, be used even when marriage is being contracted for the first time.

This grant is made to the assisting priest for cases in which the local ordinary cannot be reached in time. At times this will be understood, for otherwise one is not free to employ the extraordinary form of marriage, since the ordinary can delegate the priest to assist at the marriage. However, in cases in which the extraordinary form is to be invoked and the local ordinary can be reached, the assisting priest will not enjoy this faculty. The Code Commission has decided that it is to be considered that the ordi-

[27] Pius XII, motu propr. *Crebrae Allatae Sunt*, cann. 89, 33, 34, 35—*AAS*, XLI (1949), 89-119.

[28] Since the *urgens mortis periculum* of Canon 1043 is to be understood in the same sense as the *mortis periculum* of Canon 1098 (O'Keeffe, *Matrimonial Dispensations—Powers of Bishops, Priests and Confessors*, The Catholic University of America Canon Law Studies, n. 45 [Washington, D. C.: The Catholic University of America, 1927], p. 111), *vide supra*, pp. 104-109.

[29] Gasparri, n. 393; De Smet, *De Sponsalibus et Matrimonio*, n. 759; Wernz-Vidal, *Ius Matrimoniale*, n. 413; Cappello, *De Matrimonio*, n. 231; Chelodi, *Ius Matrimoniale iuxta Codicem Iuris Canonici* (Tridenti, 1921), n. 41 (cited hereafter as *Ius Matrimoniale*); S. C. S. Off., 1 iul. 1891—*Fontes*, n. 1139.

nary cannot be reached if he can be reached only by telephone or telegraph.[30] As explained above, one must remember that the usual means of communication with the local ordinary is by letter or by personal approach. Therefore, one is not bound nor is one expected to use extraordinary means or to undergo serious inconvenience (*grave incommodum*) in order to contact the ordinary.[31] In this connection it should be noted that the use of the faculty is granted when the *ordinary* cannot be reached. Therefore, one does not have the obligation of approaching his delegate for a dispensation, even in the event that this delegate can easily be approached. This may be done, however.[32]

The scope of this power is as wide as the ordinary's power. The priest may dispense from all impediments of the ecclesiastical law, whether impediment or diriment, public or occult, whether single or multiple, with the exception of the diriment impediments arising from the sacred order of priesthood and from affinity in the direct line when the marriage has been consummated. In regard to affinity, it must be remembered that the restriction rests on the fact of the marriage's consummation. If the marriage had not been consummated, the dispensation could be granted. Oesterle [33] and Bender [34] reason that one may apply the provision of Canon 1019, § 2, in such a case. The canon accepts a sworn statement in certification of the free state of the parties if there is danger of death,

[30] P.C.I., 12 nov. 1922: Whether in cases mentioned in cc. 1044 and 1045, § 3, it is to be considered that the Ordinary cannot be reached when recourse can be had to him neither by letter, nor by telegraph nor by telephone; or also when it is impossible to reach him by letter, though he can be reached by telegraph or telephone. *R.* In the negative to the first part; in the affirmative to the second; that is, for the effect mentioned in cc. 1044 and 1045, § 3, it is to be considered that the Ordinary cannot be reached if recourse to him can be had only by telegraph or telephone.—*AAS, XIV* (1922), 662; Bouscaren, *Digest*, I, 502.

[31] *Vide supra*, pp. 89-94; Cappello, *De Matrimonio*, n. 237; Payen, I, n. 668, footnote 1, page 500; Gasparri, n. 397.

[32] De Smet, *op. cit.*, n. 792; Oesterle, *Consultationes de Iure Matrimoniali*, p. 110. Vlaming (*Praelectiones Iuris Matrimonii*, II, n. 412) holds the contrary opinion.

[33] *Consultationes de Iure Matrimoniali*, p. 118.

[34] Vlaming-Bender, *Praelectiones Iuris Matrimonii*, p. 299.

provided that there are no indications to the contrary, and as long as no further proof is available. The legislator knows that a solemn process to investigate the non-consummation of the marriage in question would be impossible in a case wherein danger of death threatens. If such were his purpose, the words *consummato matrimonio* would be superfluous and meaningless. Accordingly, as long as the party whose marriage caused the impediment of affinity swears that his or her marriage has not been consummated, the sworn statement can be accepted and the dispensation may be granted.

The faculty given to the local ordinary in Canon 1043 also includes the power to dispense from the formalities to be observed in the contracting of marriage. There are canonists who extend this power to the priest assisting at a marriage that is being contracted according to the norm of Canon 1098, n. 2.[35] This opinion seems to rest on a superficial reading of the two canons involved. True, Canon 1044 states that the same power is enjoyed by the priest assisting at a marriage that is being contracted according to Canon 1098 as is enjoyed by the local ordinary through Canon 1043. However, Canon 1044 states that this assisting priest is assisting at a marriage that is being contracted according to the norm of Canon 1098, n. 2. A closer inspection of the texts involved seems to deny to such a priest this power of dispensing from the form. If he were able to dispense from the form, he could dispense either from the presence of a qualified witness, or from the presence of the witnesses, or from both. There is no necessity of dispensing from the presence of a qualified witness, for his absence or unavailability is presupposed in Canon 1098 and it is on this absence that the use of the extraordinary form is predicated.

As for dispensing from the presence of the witnesses, this seems highly illogical. First, there is no reason to dispense from their needed presence, for they are already present. Then, his entire power is based on the fact that he is assisting at a marriage *una cum testibus*, as Canon 1098, n. 2, states. If there are no witnesses, he is not assisting at a marriage in the manner of the priest mentioned

[35] Cappello, *De Matrimonio*, n. 239; Payen, I, n. 668; Wernz-Vidal, *Ius Matrimoniale*, n. 426; Heylen, *Tractatus de Matrimonio*, n. 671, Gasparri, n. 397.

in Canon 1098, n. 2. Granted their presence, it seems that he cannot dispense from the need of their presence, for one may justly ask whether it is possible to dispose of the very basis of one's power and still retain that power.

The fact that Canon 1044 grants such a priest the same power that is granted to the ordinary in Canon 1043 is no argument for the grant of the power of dispensing from the form. The legislator did not have to expressly exclude this, for the very notion of a priest assisting at a marriage that is being contracted according to the extraordinary form presupposes the presence of witnesses and therefore precludes the possibility of dispensing from their presence. Not everything is always expressed; some things are to be understood from the context.[36] Canon 118 declares that only clerics can receive the power of jurisdiction. Yet, the Roman Pontiff upon his election obtains the fullness of jurisdiction. If one were to consider Canon 118 alone, then one would have to say that only a cleric can be elected pope. This is not true. The two canons must be understood together in the sense that, even though at his election the Roman Pontiff is not a cleric, he nevertheless automatically receives jurisdiction. For these reasons, then, it is the opinion of the writer that, even though the canon seems to imply that such a priest may dispense from the form, he does not have that power. On the other hand, because of the extrinsic probability of the opposite opinion, in consideration of the canonists who espouse it, it may, in virtue of Canon 15, be followed in practice till such time that the Holy See declares otherwise.

Every dispensation requires a just and reasonable cause, with due regard to the gravity of the law from which one is dispensing, otherwise the dispensation granted by a subordinate is illicit and invalid.[37] The faculty under discussion would also require a just and reasonable cause for its use. According to the common interpretation, the legislator has listed two causes in consideration of which the faculty can be used. They are: (1) the making of due provision for the consciences of the parties, and (2) the making of

[36] Canon 18: Leges ecclesiasticae intelligendae sunt secundum propriam verborum significationem *in textu et contextu consideratam*. . . .

[37] Canon 84.

due provision, should the case so require it, for the legitimation of the offspring.[38] The *et* joining the two causes or conditions is, according to the common opinion, to be taken disjunctively, even though at times it will be found that they are simultaneously present. Some commentators, and with merit, very expressly declare that either of these two must be in evidence for the validity of the dispensation. They base their argument on the text of the canon, viz., *ad consulendum*. . . . They argue that this denotes the reason for the faculties' use. A further argument can be found in the historical background, for in the original grant in 1888, in the Leonine Faculty, these clauses were inserted even though in the proposed draft submitted to the Holy Office they were lacking.

Recently an opinion has been proposed by Oesterle,[39] and espoused by Bender,[40] that the canonical cause is the *urgens mortis periculum*. The provision for the consciences of the parties and for the legitimation of the offspring is to be regarded simply the motive which the legislator had in granting this faculty. The argument is based on the verbal signification of the preposition *"ad"*; on a different interpretation of the Leonine Faculty and of the schema proposed to the Holy Office, and, finally, on the interpretation of Article VII of the Decree *Ne temere* taken in conjunction with the later replies which accorded the priest mentioned therein the power of dispensing.

The common opinion seems the better of the two. It is an axiom in jurisprudence that in every law each word must have some meaning, so that it is not superfluous. *Verba in legis interpretatione non debent esse superflua. Verba debent aliquid operari et non debent esse superflua.*[41] To espouse Oesterle's opinion would necessitate

[38] Gasparri, n. 394; Wernz-Vidal, *Ius Matrimoniale*, n. 413; Payen, I, n. 646 (where this interpretation is called certain); Coronata, *De Matrimonio*, n. 136; Cappello, *De Matrimonio*, n. 231; O'Keeffe, *Matrimonial Dispensations —Powers of Bishops, Priests and Confessors*, p. 59 (where it is held that either of these two causes is *required* for validity since the grant of this faculty was made precisely for that purpose); Heylen, *Tractatus de Matrimonio*, n. 658 (where the same opinion as O'Keeffe's is maintained).

[39] *Consultationes de Iure Matrimoniali*, pp. 105-106.

[40] Vlaming-Bender, *Praelectiones Iuris Matrimonii*, pp. 299-300.

[41] Barbosa, *De Axiomatibus Iuris usufrequentioribus* — apud *Tractatus Varii* (Lugduni, 1660), Axioma 222.

the view that the clauses which according to his claim simply reflect motives are totally unnecessary and add nothing to the law. The legislator does not need to account to his subjects for his law or to express the *finis legis* in the law itself. In practice, though, the discussion seems to be of a purely theoretical nature, since in every case either one or the other condition will be present. The wording is so general that it will encompass almost every case.

Ad consulendum conscientiae. Since no distinction is made, it may be for the peace of conscience even of the party who is not constituted in danger of death. This may eventuate from the removal of sin, the occasion of sin, or temptation. There have been some who claim that the unrest against which the provision is sought must arise from sins of impurity. However, the legislator does not distinguish; therefore, the source of the unrest is not to be considered. It may arise from any cause whatsoever, e.g., from hatred, enmity, or the lack of peace among the families; it may seek alleviation through the removal of scandal, through making good the damage that had been done, through precluding the possibility of future harm or through a restoration of the good name of the party or parties, or also of the families. All these can be considered as valid reasons. In a word, whenever the party's conscience would be soothed through the contracting of marriage which in conscience seems strongly urged, there would exist a sufficient reason for the granting of the dispensation.[42]

[*Ad consulendum*], *si casus ferat, legitimationi prolis.* Legitimacy has many beneficial juridic effects.[43] The legislator wishes to make a benign provision for these and therefore has granted this privilege of dispensing. The term *proles* was advisedly chosen. It pertains not only to the children already born but also to the children still unborn but already conceived at the time. For a child conceived but not yet born, the dispensation that is granted will in connection with the subsequent marriage produce the legitimacy of status since the child is born of a valid marriage.[44] The illegitimate status of a child at birth can indeed be regularized. But the consequent legitimation

[42] Gasparri, *loc. cit.;* Wernz-Vidal, *loc. cit.;* Payen, *loc. cit.*

[43] Cf. Canons 232, § 2; n. 1; § 1, n. 1; 504; 984.

[44] Canon 1114.

does not cancel out the earlier illegitimate status; at best, it simply abstracts from it, even in the case of a sanation. Among children born of unmarried parents canonists distinguish between the *naturales* and the *spurii.* In the former class is the child born of parents between whom from the time of conception of the child to its birth a valid marriage could have been contracted; in the latter category is the child born of parents between whom at no time a valid marriage could have been contracted because of a diriment impediment. Among the *spurii,* authors further subdistinguish between:

1. *adulterini*—born of parents of whom at least one was actually married to someone else;
2. *sacrilegi*—born of a union in which one or both parents were bound by solemn religious vows, or when the father was a cleric in major orders;
3. *incestuosi*—born of a union in which the parents were related either by affinity or by consanguinity in the collateral line;
4. *nefarii*—born of parents related in the direct line of consanguinity.

It is certain that Canons 1043 and 1044 legislate for children who are listed as *naturales;* such are legitimated by the very grant of the dispensation.[45] As for children termed *spurii* (except the *adulterini* et *sacrilegi*), it is certain that this legislation was intended for them, because, although they will not be legitimated by the subsequent marriage of the parents, their legitimation will be effected by the very grant of the dispensation.[46] The *nefarii* are definitely excluded from the benefit of legitimation by the way of

[45] Canons 1051 and 1116.

[46] Canon 1051. Cf. also Bender, "Legitimatio prolis sola dispensatione quin sequatur matrimonium. (Canon 1051.)"—*Monitor Ecclesiasticus,* LXXVII (1953), 102-108, who defends well the opinion which states that legitimation follows *upon the very grant of the dispensation* in accordance with Canon 1051, even though for any reason whatsoever the marriage does not take place. Normally, one would expect that the marriage will follow, and in view of this fact legitimation is granted to the offspring already conceived or even born. It is for this reason that there are others who would exclude from the benefit of legitimation the offspring of parents who do not contract marriage after the dispensation has been granted. The writer adheres to the opinion defended by Bender as being more in accord with the wording of Canon 1051.

dispensation since their parents can never entertain the hope of securing a dispensation, even in danger of death.[47]

A further question arises in regard to the *adulterini* and *sacrilegi*. May the legitimation of *adulterini et sacrilegi* be adduced as a reason for invoking the power of dispensing that is granted in Canons 1043 and 1044? The more common opinion holds that in such a case the power may not be invoked.[48] Their argument is based on the text of Canons 1051 and 1116 and on the reply of the Holy Office on July 8, 1903. Canon 1051 precludes from legitimation the *sacrilegi* and the *adulterini;* Canon 1116 provides for legitimation through the subsequent marriage of the parents only in a case when a valid marriage could have been entered between them at the time either of the conception, or of the gestation, or of the birth of the child in question. The Holy Office decreed that a legitimation of the *spurii* would follow from the use of the faculty granted on February 20, 1888,[49] without the need of a special rescript from Rome, except in the case of the *adulterini* or *sacrilegi.*[50]

There are others who unreservedly say that the faculty may be invoked, since the legislator makes no distinction in Canon 1043, and since, as Cappello contends, a peremptory argument cannot be drawn from the canons or from the reply of the Holy Office. Till the Holy See declares otherwise, this opinion, so it is claimed, may be considered safe in practice.

Still others, seeking a middle road between the strict opinion which denies the allowable use of the faculty, the opinion which allows its use without question, espouse what may be termed the *mediate opinion*. They allow the use of this faculty of dispensing in order that a marriage may subsequently be contracted. They reason that, with the parents married, a rescript of legitimation from

[47] Canon 1076, § 3.

[48] Wernz-Vidal, *Ius Matrimoniale,* n. 413, 2°; Vlaming, *Praelectiones Iuris Matrimonii,* II, n. 401; De Smet, *De Sponsalibus et Matrimonio,* n. 759, footnote 2,; Leitner, *Lehrbuch des katholischen Eherechts,* p. 324; Wouters, *Commentarius in Decretum "Ne temere" ad Usum Scholarum compositus* (2. ed., *Amstelodami-Galopiae,* 1909), p. 156; Vermeersch, *Theologia Moralis,* III, n. 758.

[49] *Vide supra,* p. 46; cf. also Canons 1043-1045 and 1051.

[50] *Collectanea S. C. de Prop. Fide* (ed. 1907), n. 2171; *Fontes,* n. 1267.

the Holy See is more easily obtainable. The reply of the Holy See did not say that the *adulterini* or *sacrilegi* could not be legitimated by means of a particular rescript from the Holy See. Therefore, a contracted marriage and consequently the antecedent dispensation could prepare the way for the legitimation of such children. For this reason the faculty may be invoked.[51] In view of the extrinsic as well as the intrinsic probability of this opinion, it may be followed in practice.[52] It may be said, then, that as long as there is question of the legitimation of the offspring, provided only the children are not *nefarii,* the faculty may be employed.

The legislator demands further that in the use of the faculty two precautions be taken, namely that scandal be obviated and that with reference to any needed dispensation from the impediments of disparity of worship and of mixed religion, the usual *cautiones* (promises) be given.

Scandal is to be obviated. This condition is required for the licit use of this power; one cannot claim that it is called for under the pain of nullity.[53] All possible means must be employed for warding off any possible scandal. This is required by the natural law itself. Past scandal must be repaired; future scandal precluded. Prudence will dictate how this is to be done. If it is a public impediment from which the parties must look to the dispensing agent for a dispensation, the dispensation should be given in the external forum, before witnesses, when this is possible. If it is occult, it should be taken care of in the internal, either sacramental or non-sacramental forum. The manner of repairing scandal when given by one in major orders or by one who is solemnly professed, through a life of concubinage, was suggested in the original grant of these faculties on February 20, 1888. Although the directive as

[51] Cappello, *De Matrimonio,* n. 231; Payen, I, n. 646; O'Keeffe, *op. cit.;* p. 70; Vermeersch, *De forma Sponsalium ac Matrimonio post Decretum "Ne temere,"* n. 73; Wernz-Vidal, *Ius Matrimoniale,* n. 413.

[52] Canon 15.

[53] Motry, *Diocesan Faculties According to the Code of Canon Law,* The Catholic University of America Canon Law Studies, n. 16 (Washington, D. C.: The Catholic University of America, 1922), p. 133; Cerato, n. 35; Payen I, n. 646, 3.

then given is not obligatory today,[54] it may be regarded as a norm that can be followed in the repairing of this and of other types of scandal. The original grant decreed that, if it proved necessary for the removal of scandal, the parties were to be enjoined to betake themselves to a place where they were not known; or, when this is not possible, a salutary penance was to be imposed with a view to repairing the harm already done. The dispensation could then be granted even when the scandal is irreparable.[55]

Usual Cautiones. When there is question of a dispensation from the impediment of mixed religion or of disparity of worship, it is necessary to recall the strict warning of Canons 1061 and 1071 to the effect that the Church does not dispense from these impediments unless the usual promises (*cautiones*) be given. The non-Catholic party must promise that all danger of perversion will be removed from the Catholic party. Both parties must promise that all the children will be baptized only in the Catholic church and raised in the Catholic faith exclusively. Further, there must be moral certitude that these promises will be kept. There is no reason to believe that Canons 1043 and 1044 excuse one from this obligation. One must hold that these *cautiones* are necessary for the validity of the dispensation.

Despite the fact that there have been commentators who held it as probable that a dispensation without these *cautiones* could still be valid, after the decree of the Holy Office, confirmed by Pius XI on January 14, 1932,[56] this opinion can no longer be sustained. The decree drew the attention of the bishops as well as the pastors and persons mentioned in Canon 1044 to the fact that dispensations from the impediments of mixed religion and of disparity of worship were not to be granted unless the parties had given in advance the promises whose faithful execution no one could prevent, even in virtue of the civil laws to which they were or would be subject; for *otherwise, the dispensation itself was to be entirely null and void.* Whenever possible, as a general rule, these should be given in writing.[57]

[54] Wernz-Vidal, *Ius Matrimoniale,* n. 413; De Smet, *De Sponsalibus et Matrimonio,* n. 762.

[55] O'Keeffe, *op. cit.,* p. 82.

[56] *AAS,* XXIV (1932), 25; Bouscaren, *Digest,* I, 505-506.

[57] Canon 1061, § 2.

After the dispensation has been granted, the priest assisting at a marriage that has been contracted according to Canon 1098 must take care that the dispensation is properly recorded. If it was granted in the external forum, the local ordinary is to be notified as soon as possible, and an annotation of it is also be made in the matrimonial register.[58] On the other hand, if it is granted in the internal non-sacramental forum, it should be noted in the secret book kept for this purpose in the diocesan curia.[59] At times, even a dispensation granted in the external forum should be noted there instead, in order to preclude the danger of scandal, whenever the dispensation and the celebration of the marriage have to remain secret.

B. *Dispensatory Power in Cases of Grave Necessity*

Prior to the publication of the Code, canonists discussed and disputed among themselves the course of action to be followed whenever a *casus perplexus* arose. This was the case in which a pastor learned at the last moment of the existence of a diriment impediment between the parties so that he was barred from assisting at the marriage despite the threat of grave evils and harm that argued for the contracting of the marriage. With the power given in Canon 1045, it definitely appears that the celebrated *casus perplexus* can no longer arise, that the legislator has dealt it a death-blow.[60]

Realizing that cases of grave necessity could likewise arise when marriage is to be contracted according to the extraordinary form, the legislator wisely provided in Canon 1045, § 3, for such an eventuality by extending the power granted to the local ordinaries

[58] Canon 1046.

[59] Cappello, *De Matrimonio,* n. 231, e; Payen, I, n. 646, *ad finem.*

[60] Chelodi, *Ius Matrimoniale,* n. 44; Cappello, *De Matrimonio,* n. 234; 11°; Vermeersch-Creusen, *Epitome Iuris Canonici,* II (6. ed., Mechliniae: Dessain, 1940), n. 308. There are authors, however, who insinuate that not all possible situations from which a *casus perplexus* could arise are covered in this canon, e.g., Arendt, "Dispensatio a forma matrimonii in casu perplexo,"—*Periodica,* XVI (1927), 1*-17*; De Smet, *De Sponsalibus et Matrimonio,* n. 837; Van Hove, *De Legibus Ecclesiasticis,* n. 294; Oesterle, *Consultationes de Iure Matrimoniali,* p. 126, footnote 67.

in the first two paragraphs of the same canon, to the priest assisting at such a marriage.[61]

The canon studiously omits mentioning the prescribed form of marriage. The fact that such mention was made in Canon 1043 but omitted in Canon 1045, leads one to believe that the legislator intended not to include it here. This is the interpretation of by far the greater number of canonists,[62] among whom there are some who discredit the opposite opinion to such an extent that they say it lacks all probability.[63]

The proponents of the opinion that a dispensation from the observance of the juridical form is also included in the faculty that is granted in Canon 1045 use the following arguments:

1. *ubi eadem est ratio, eadem esse debet legis dispositio;*
2. clandestinity was a diriment impediment before the Code and is still listed as an impediment in the alphabetical index to the Code;
3. the lack of the observance of the juridical form could eventuate as a *casus occultus* when people do not know of the lack of delegation or believe that the priest has complied with whatever the law calls for;
4. the *finis legis* is the same whether it is a question of impediments or of the form.[64]

[61] Canon 1045, § 3.

[62] Gasparri, n. 399; Wernz-Vidal, *Ius Matrimoniale,* n. 413; Claeys-Bouuaert—Simenon, *Manuale Iuris Canonici,* II, n. 252; Cappello, *De Matrimonio,* n. 234; Eichmann-Mörsdorf, *Lehrbuch des Kirchenrechts auf Grund des Codex Iuris Canonici,* II, 200; Knecht, *Handbuch des katholisches Eherechts,* p. 225; Triebs, *Praktisches Handbuch des geltenden kanonischen Eherechts in Vergleichung mit dem deutschen staatlichen Eherecht* (Breslau: Ostdeutsche Verlanganstalt, 1933), p. 178; Schäfer, *Das Eherecht nach dem Codex Iuris Canonici* (6. and 7. ed., Münster, 1921), p. 105; Cerato, n. 37; Chelodi, *Ius Matrimoniale,* n. 41; Vermeersch-Creusen, *Epitome Iuris Canonici,* II (6. ed.), n. 309; Payen, I, n. 648; Coronata, *De Matrimonio,* n. 137; O'Keeffe, *op. cit.,* pp. 145-146.

[63] Cappello, *De Matrimonio,* n. 234; Claeys-Bouuaert—Simenon, *loc. cit.;* Payen (I, footnote on page 483) denies that the opinion has any intrinsic probability whatsoever; however, he acknowledges the fact that it has extrinsic probability by reason of the authority of the men who espouse it; Wernz-Vidal, (*Ius Matrimoniale,* n. 413) calls the argument of De Smet weak.

[64] Arendt, *Periodica,* XVI (1927), 1*-17*; Oesterle, *Consultationes de Iure Matrimoniali,* pp. 135-138 Durieux, *Le mariage en droit canonique* (6. ed.,

Despite this intricate reasoning, it must be said that this opinion lack intrinsic probability, for as Claeys-Bouuaert—Simenon say, no opinion or interpretation of the commentators is equivalent to the law itself.[65] However, in view of the extrinsic probability, one must hold that in view of Canon 15 and Canon 209, until the Holy See settles the question, it cannot be said that the juridical form is excluded from Canon 1045 as an element susceptible of the granting of a dispensation.[66]

This dispute in no way affects the powers of the priest assisting at a marriage that is to be contracted according to Canon 1098. The writer maintains that, just as in Canon 1044, so also here in Canon 1045, § 3, the power of dispensing from the canonical form of marriage is excluded from the granted faculty by the very nature of his position.[67]

The use of the faculty in Canon 1045, § 3, is predicated on the following conditions:

1. its restriction simply to the impediments of the ecclesiastical law, with the exception of the impediments arising from the sacred order of priesthood and from affinity in the direct line when the marriage has been consummated;
2. the removal of scandal;
3. the exacting of the usual promises;
4. the fact that an impediment has been discovered when everything is prepared for the marriage;
5. the fact that the marriage cannot be deferred without probable danger of grave harm till the necessary dispensation is received from the Holy See;
6. the impossibility of reaching even the local ordinary in time;
7. the fact that the case is still occult in character.

Paris, 1928), n. 167; Arendt, "Ad Can. 1045 Iterum de Dispensatione a Forma Matrimonii in Casu Perplexo," *Ius Pontificium,* VII (1927), 147-150; "Casus de Forma Matrimonii eiusque Dispensatione," *Periodica,* XIV (1925), (122)-(124); Vermeersch, *Theologia Moralis,* III, n. 755.

65 *Op. cit.*, II, n. 252.

66 Payen, I, footnote 1 on page 483; D'Angelo, "In c. 1045 Codicis I.C. excursus," *Apollinaris,* I (1928), 255; Hanstein, *Kanonisches Eherecht* (2. Auflage, Paderborn: Ferdinand Schöningh, 1948), p. 69.

67 *Vide supra,* pp. 159-160, 165-166.

What has been said heretofore in regard to the impediments, the removal of scandal, the exacting of the usual promises and the means to be employed in reaching the local ordinary, also pertains here. Now it remains to consider the other conditions. The other three conditions must be in evidence together, conjunctively, otherwise the faculty cannot be invoked.

An impediment has been discovered when everything has been prepared for the Marriage. This must not be understood in the strict sense, i.e., as pointing only to a case in which the parties and the priest are completely unaware of the impediment until everything has been prepared for the marriage. Since the canon does not distinguish, there is comprehended also the case in which the impediment was previously known to the parties but only then became known to the priest.[68] In the event that the parties kept this information from the priest *mala fide* till this very moment, the canonists are in disagreement as to whether the faculty can still be operative. Vidal (1867-1938) [69] argued that no one should benefit from his deception, and that the parties are themselves responsible for their predicament. The faculty may not be invoked. Cappello [70] claims that the bad faith of the parties does not affect the dispensing power inasmuch as the Code does not discriminate against them. The purpose of the law is not only the welfare of the contracting parties but also the avoidance of public harm and scandal. The parties have need of the dispensation, and it matters little to them whence it will have its

[68] P.C.I., 1 mart. 1921: Whether, according to Canon 1045, § 1, the clause "*quoties impedimentum detegatur cum iam omnia parata sunt ad nuptias*" is to be taken in the strict sense; namely, as meaning that the impediment was before that entirely unknown and then becomes known: or is it rather to be understood in the sense that, although the impediment was known before, it is only then that it is reported to the pastor or to the ordinary? *R.* In the negative to the first part; in the affirmative to the second.—*AAS,* XIII (1921), 177; Bouscaren, *Digest,* I, 502.

[69] Wernz-Vidal, *Ius Matrimoniale,* footnote 59, page 535.

[70] *De Matrimonio,* n. 234 bis, 7°, Oesterle (*Consultationes de Iure Matrimoniali,* footnote on page 129) agrees with Cappello. Payen (I, n. 650) calls this opinion at least probable.

source. Creusen [71] steers a middle course in saying that, *servatis servandis,* in such a case the local ordinary may refuse to grant the dispensation. However, once he granted it, it would nonetheless be valid. In practice, then, one may grant a dispensation whether or not the bad faith of the parties was the reason why the knowledge of the impediment came to the priest only when everything was ready for the marriage.

Cum omnia parata sunt ad nuptias. This is not to be understood in the strict sense, as meaning that *everything* has been done, and that only the celebration of the marriage still awaits its fulfillment. This must be taken in the moral or equivalent sense. Therefore, if a day is set, the invitations mailed, the reception arranged, the vacations or furloughs planned and arranged, the banns already published, the presence of these factors would suffice.[72] Others wish to restrict the use of the dispensatory power simply to the cases in which all the *canonical* preparations have been attended to.

Cappello [73] and O'Keeffe [74] wisely note that the phrase *omnia parata* is not to be taken as a *conditio sine qua non* for the granting of the dispensation. It would be ridiculous to have the validity of a dispensation depend on different interpretations of the same phrase, with some commentators demanding more than others. Further, one would have to accept the word *omnia* in its full meaning, and that would restrict the canon too much. The phrase was used by the older commentators as an example rather than as a cause. Finally, the *mens legislatoris* undoubtedly seeks to make provision for cases of true, urgent necessity. He has done so in Canon 81 in regard to all ecclesiastical laws regarding which the Holy See customarily grants dispensations; in Canon 990, § 2, in regard to irregularities; in Canons 882, 2252, 2254 in regard to absolution from sins and censures. The same may logically be presumed in regard to the contracting of marriage. Provision was made for the grave necessity of danger of death in Canon 1043; provision is made for cases

[71] Vermeersch-Creusen, *Epitome Iuris Canonici,* II (6. ed.), n. 308.

[72] Chelodi, *Ius Matrimoniale,* n. 41, 3; Claeys-Bouuaert—Simenon, *Manuale Juris Canonici,* II, n. 252; Oesterle, *Consultationes de Iure Matrimoniali,* pp. 130-131.

[73] *Loc. cit.*

[74] *Op. cit.,* pp. 133-143.

of urgent necessity in Canon 1045. Vidal [75] and Oesterle [76] agree with this opinion. O'Keeffe wisely notes that one should not be scrupulous in the interpretation of this phrase, and that when the other condition, i.e., the probable danger of grave harm in the deferring of the marriage till a dispensation is obtained from the Holy See, is certainly fulfilled, the first (*cum omnia parata sunt ad nuptias*) need give little trouble, provided in the judgment of the dispensing agent there is real urgency in the case.[77]

Marriage cannot be deferred without probable danger of grave harm. The previous conditions taken alone would not allow the ecclesiastical personages mentioned in Canon 1045 to employ this faculty. It must be conjoined with the fact that the marriage in question cannot be deferred without probable danger of grave harm till such time that a dispensation could be received from the Holy See.[78] If the marriage can be deferred, this must be done, because this clause has an invalidating effect upon non-compliance with its demand. When there is question of a priest assisting at a marriage in accordance with the prescripts of Canon 1098, n. 2, it must be established that a timely approach is no longer possible, not only to the Holy See, but also to the local ordinary for the granting of the necessary dispensation or that every possible approach is attended with a danger of violation of a secret. Without doubt, it is not only the sacramental seal that is meant. It would have been superfluous for the legislator to mention it. Therefore, other secrets are to be honored and preserved in such a case. Secrets could arise from professional advice. A judge, a notary or other members of the diocesan tribunal, in regard to knowledge obtained through their offices, or ministers in the process instituted *super rato,* would be bound to secrecy. The same must be said of a priest who has been consulted in his priestly capacity. If there is danger of the violation

[75] *Loc. cit.*

[76] *Consultationes de Iure Matrimoniali,* page 131, footnote n. 72.

[77] *Op. cit.,* p. 143.

[78] If the local ordinary is the dispensing agent, it will be for him to decide whether the Holy See can be reached in time. In the event that the other ecclesiastical agents mentioned in Canon 1045 are to grant the dispensations, then it will be for them to decide whether the local ordinary can be reached in time.

of any of these secrets, the obligation of recurring to the local ordinary would cease. The parties are not obliged to betray themselves or to suffer harm from loss of good repute. As long as the impediment can remain occult and the parties reasonably request this, the secret must be preserved.[79] On the other hand, if indeed the impediment of its nature is public, i.e., it can be proved in the external forum, but *de facto* is occult, it seems that the obligation of preserving secrecy could not be rightly urged. The same would have to be said if the parties are willing to approach the local ordinary with their case.[80]

Since the Code does not state otherwise, one is not obliged to, although one may, seek a delegate of the Holy See or of the local ordinary, as the case might suggest. If the conditions are verified, the local ordinary or the priest enjoys the power in virtue of the general law.

The Code demands no more than a probable danger; the mere possibility of it will not suffice, but full certainty regarding it is not required. The measuring of the danger or of its probability is left to the prudent judgment of the dispensing agent. He is to judge all the facts at hand; then, if with warrant he fears that serious harm will follow, he may dispense. The harm spoken of can be of various kinds, e.g., the loss of a considerable sum of money; the danger of a civil marriage and of a subsequent public concubinage; the contingent illegitimacy of a child already conceived; the future loss of good name for the parties; the loss of a position; eventual difficulty with the civil officials; consequent enmity and hatred for the priest; the emergence of serious arguments; the resulting scandal, etc. If there is doubt as to the sufficiency of the reason, presumed of course that *de facto* there is a reason, Canon 84 allows a dispensation to be granted licitly and validly.

One must remember, however, that the danger of grave harm, spoken of in this canon and in Canon 81, does not include already existing evils. Hence, public concubinage, illegitimate children, or current grave scandals, may not be adduced as reasons for using

[79] Vermeersch-Creusen, *Epitome Iuris Canonici,* II, n. 311; Cappello, *De Matrimonio,* n. 237.

[80] Cappello, *loc. cit.*

the power that is accorded in these canons. The danger spoken of must be an impending danger or one that is feared for the future.[81]

As a final condition, the Code allows the use of this faculty to the priest assisting according to the norm of Canon 1098, n. 2, only in occult cases. Prior to the reply of the Code Commission, dated December 28, 1927, there was a great dispute among authors concerning the significance of the phrase *"casus occultus."* This interpretation settled the problem definitively. It was asked whether the words *"pro casibus occultis"* of Canon 1045, § 3, are to be understood only of matrimonial impediments which are by their nature and in fact occult, or also of those which are by their nature public and in fact occult. The reply was in the negative to the first part, and in the affirmative to the second part.[82]

Some had previously taken it as the equivalent of *impedimentum occultum* according to Canon 1037, i.e., an impediment that could not be proved in the external forum. Others had held that the word *casus* was of much wider import than and not to be confused with *impedimentum*. An impediment could be public in the sense of Canon 1037, but the case could nonetheless be occult. Canon 2197 defines a delict as public when it has been spread about or is constituted in such circumstances that one can prudently foresee that it will easily be made public knowledge. The term *public* in Canon 1037 and the term *public* in Canon 2197 do not have the same meaning. A delict would be occult if it is not public. By analogy, one could apply the meaning of the term public and occult as found in Canon 2197 to the phrase *casus occultus*. This latter position was upheld by the Code Commission.

As long as an impediment remains *de facto* occult, i.e., is not publicly known, even though legally it be public in the sense of Canon 1037 and the local ordinary cannot be reached in time, the priest assisting at a marriage in accordance with the norm of Canon 1098, n. 2, has power to dispense from it.[83]

[81] S. R. R., *Nullitatis matrimonii,* 4 martii 1927, coram R.P.D. Francisco Parrillo, dec. X, n. 6—*Decisiones,* XIX (1927), 74; cf. also Bouscaren, *Digest,* II, 278.

[82] P.C.I., 28 dec. 1927—*AAS,* XX (1928), 61; Bouscaren, *Digest,* I, 503.

[83] There are authors who hold it as probable that, in virtue of the reply of the Code Commission and the wide interpretation that should be given

According to the faculty, the power of dispensing may be used either when marriage is being contracted for the first time or when it is being undertaken as the convalidation of an illicit union.

The obligation of publishing the banns of marriage binds in all marriages in which two Catholics contemplate marriage. The only exceptions mentioned in the Code pertain to mixed marriages and to marriages of conscience.[84] One will notice that the power to dispense from the publication of the banns receives no mention in Canons 1043, 1044, 1045. The power has already been given to the local ordinaries in Canon 1028. The legislator has not given this power to the persons mentioned in Canons 1044 and 1045, § 3. Accordingly, in danger of death, if time permits, recourse should be had to the ordinary for delegation and a dispensation from the publication of the banns. If time does not permit—and this must usually be presupposed in the case of the priest who is assisting at a marriage according to the extraordinary form—the obligation to publish the banns ceases, inasmuch as the law itself makes provision for such an eventuality in Canon 1019, § 2.[85] Outside of the danger of death, it would indeed be a rare case for the emergency to be so great that it justified the omission of the banns without a dispensation.[86] As for marriages contracted according to the extraordinary form, two possibilities present themselves, namely, the local ordinary cannot be had or approached, or he is unavailable in view of the harm threatened by the civil law. In the first case, the assisting priest, assured of the free state of the parties from other sources, may declare that the obligation of the banns no longer urges in such a case.[87] Strict compliance with the law in such a case

Canon 1045, even in a case wherein an impediment is public by its nature and the fact inducing the impediment is public knowledge, the case could still be a *casus occultus,* namely, if the people do not know that such a fact induces the impediment in question. Cf. Vromant, *De Matrimonio,* n. 116; Payen, I, n. 669; Oesterle, *Consultationes de Iure Matrimoniali,* p. 143, footnote 100.

[84] Canons 1022; 1026; 1104; Payen, I, n. 468.

[85] Roberts, *The Banns of Marriage,* The Catholic University of America Canon Law Studies, n. 64 (Washington, D. C.: The Catholic University of America, 1931), p. 96.

[86] Vermeersch-Creusen, *Epitome Iuris Canonici,* II (6. ed.), n. 291.

[87] Cappello, *De Matrimonio,* n. 162; Wernz-Vidal, *Ius Matrimoniale,* n. 123; Payen, I, n. 468; Roberts, *op. cit.,* p. 97.

would not only be useless but also positively harmful. The legislator is not to be presumed as insisting upon its observance.[88] Finally, to demand that this obligation be fulfilled would make Canon 1098, which allows the extraordinary form, inoperative.

In the other eventuality, when it is possible to reach the local ordinary, this must be done. True, the very purpose of the use of the extraordinary form in such circumstances would preclude the very idea of publishing the banns. Nevertheless, the ordinary is to be consulted. He may declare that the law no longer obliges in such circumstances or, if he chooses, he may grant a dispensation from the publication of the banns. The pastor should not take it upon himself to pass judgment in such a case. The ordinary is the competent authority in passing judgment in such cases.[89]

[88] Van Hove, *De Legibus Ecclesiasticis,* n. 291.
[89] Roberts, *op. cit.*, p. 97.

CONCLUSIONS

1. Prior to the Council of Trent, at which for the first time a juridical form of marriage had been instituted to be observed under the pain of nullity, there was no need of an "extraordinary form" of marriage. A mere exchange of consent, even when accomplished clandestinely, sufficed for validity (pp. 20, 22).

2. Under the Tridentine discipline, provision had been made for eventualities in which a qualified witness could not be had. The Sacred Congregations on various occasions declared that in a place where the decree *Tametsi* was binding and a qualified witness could not be had, a couple could contract marriage validly by observing that part of the form prescribed by *Tametsi* which could be observed, namely, the exchange of consent *de praesenti* in the presence of at least two witnesses (pp. 29-39).

3. In the *Ne temere* discipline, provision was made for the first time for an "extraordinary form" of marriage to be employed when the contracting parties or party was constituted in danger of death or in other cases of grave necessity. There was a disagreement among canonists as to whether Article VIII of *Ne temere* included the case in which a qualified witness could be considered as morally absent because of harm threatened by the civil law. Some demanded recourse in each case to the Holy See under pain of nullity. Others held that this was merely a directive norm to be observed when there was time for recourse. A definitive decision had not been given by the Holy See (pp. 50-58).

4. Under the present discipline of the Code, the use of the extraordinary form is predicated on the actual (not presumed) unavailability of any qualified witness who could assist validly at the marriage in question. The qualified witness is to be considered unavailable if he cannot get to the parties, or they cannot get to him, without serious inconvenience. To excuse the parties the serious inconvenience must be personal. It may affect the priest, the parties or the common good. The use of extraordinary means would normally constitute a serious inconvenience and consequently may be

disregarded. The simple refusal of assistance on the part of a qualified witness will not constitute him as unavailable (pp. 85-96).

5. Serious harm threatened by the civil law may be considered a serious inconvenience and is and always has been comprehended in the text of the canon allowing the use of the extraordinary form (pp. 96-103).

6. The mere actual unavailability of a qualified witness will not suffice. There must be conjoined to it a probable danger of death which could arise from any source and could affect either of the contracting parties. Any danger that would allow the administration of Holy Viaticum would suffice here. It suffices that parties wish to contract marriage; no other reason is necessary. Where there is no danger of death, the fact of unavailability must be such that anyone can prudently foresee that it will perdure for at least a full month, as it is found in the calendar. The *terminus a quo* is the period of time when one can say that *omnia parata sunt ad nuptias* because only then would serious inconvenience result (pp. 104-119).

7. The matrimonial consent exchanged between the parties must have the same qualities as the matrimonial consent exchanged by parties when they contract marriage according to the ordinary form. All that is required is that the parties intend a real, true, valid marriage and exchange consent *de praesenti*. Even though they know nothing of the extraordinary form, the law recognizes the consent exchanged in such circumstances as juridically efficacious (pp. 124-127).

8. Two witnesses are required for validity. As long as they witness the exchange of the consent between the parties, they fulfill the requirements for their position. Even a civil official or non-Catholic minister in his official capacity can be considered as one of the two witnesses who are necessary for validity. The priest who is called to assist is not excluded by law from serving as a witness, especially if only one witness be present and no other witness is available. When no witness at all or at most only one witness is available, even though there is no provision in law for such a rare occurrence, marriage could be validly contracted in the pres-

ence of the one available witness or also in the absence of any witness at all (pp. 127-139).

9. Wherever this can easily be done, another priest, i.e., one who is not qualified to act as an official witness according to Canons 1094 and 1095, if he is available, should be called no assist at such marriages. If it should happen that the priest is under excommunication or suspension ***post sententiam*** or is a ***vitandus,*** he should not be called, for the parties are relieved of the obligation of calling him. He may be called if the parties are constituted in danger of death, because he may be of service to them if a dispensation should be necessary or if the parties wish their marriage blessed. In any other circumstances an excommunicated or suspended priest need not be called. He may, however, be called to assist because he too may prove helpful (pp. 144-147).

10. Approval of the local ordinary in allowing the use of the extraordinary form of marriage cannot be demanded under pain of nullity if all the conditions required by the canon are verified (p. 142).

11. The dispensing power of a priest called to assist at a marriage that is to be contracted according to the extraordinary form as depicted in Canon 1098 depends on his assistance at such a marriage that is to be contracted in accordance with the norm of Canon 1098, n. 2. Hence, if there are no witnesses, he does not assist according to Canon 1098, n. 2, and has no dispensing power as assisting priest. Because of his peculiar position, he has all the powers mentioned in Canons 1044 and 1045, § 3, except the power of dispensing from the form of marriage (pp. 158-160; 165-166).

APPENDIX

LETTER OF INSTRUCTIONS TO THE PRIEST ARRANGING FOR A MARRIAGE TO BE CONTRACTED ACCORDING TO THE EXTRAORDINARY FORM

DEAR FATHER:

Enclosed you will find a formulary which is to be used by N.N. and N.N. in the convalidation of their civil marriage (or in the contracting of marriage) according to the extraordinary juridical form of marriage as prescribed in Canon 1098, § 1.

N.N. and N.N. should with two witnesses assemble in one room of the rectory and you should instruct them in the procedure to be followed in the contracting (or convalidation) of this marriage. You should then retire from the room and return only after they have completed the ceremony. While N.N. and N.N. clasp right hands, the groom should read aloud the first paragraph and the bride the second paragraph in the presence of the two witnesses. Once this is done, the groom and the bride are to affix their signatures. The witnesses likewise are to affix their signatures and date the document.

After this is done, the contracting parties should then read aloud paragraphs three, four and five, insert the date and add their signatures. The two witnesses should then read aloud the concluding paragraphs, insert the date and affix their signatures.

The record of this marriage should be inserted in the matrimonial registers of your parish with the annotation that it was contracted without the presence of the priest, according to the extraordinary form. The enclosed formulary should then be returned to the Chancery for filing.

Thanking you for your cooperation in the matter, and with every best wish, I remain

Sincerely yours in Xto.,

....

, Chancellor.

MATRIMONIUM IUXTA FORMAM EXTRAORDINARIAM

§ 1. I, N.N., take thee, N.N., for my lawful wife, to have and to hold from this day forward, for better, for worse, for richer, for poorer, in sickness and in health, until death do us part.

§ 2. I, N.N., take thee, N.N., for my lawful husband, to have and to hold from this day forward, for better, for worse, for richer, for poorer, in sickness and in health, until death do us part.

....

Date

(Signature of groom) ....

(Signature of bride) ....

(Signature of witnesses) ....

....

§ 3. We, the undersigned, do hereby certify in writing, in the presence of each other, that we realize and accept the fact that, by using the above mentioned form of marriage, we have effected an indissoluble and sacramental union by virtue of which we incur all the obligations and responsibilities which are the effects of a valid, sacramental matrimonial contract.

§ 4. Secondly, we do hereby certify in writing in the presence of each other that we understand and accept the fact that this marriage contract can have and will have no civil effects of any kind before the law of the State of ....nor in any other civil jurisdiction and, moreover, that this marriage contract into which we have entered may never be adduced as evidence in any civil court. We likewise promise that, as soon as it is legally possible, we will comply with the ceremonies required by the civil law, so that our marriage will be recognized also by the civil law.

§ 5. In testimony of this fact that we accept each and every one of these conditions, we do hereby affix our signatures in the presence of each other at ...., ..., on this .... day of ...., 19.....

(Signature of groom) ....

(Signature of bride) ....

We, the undersigned, do hereby declare in the presence of each other that we have seen and heard N.N. and N.N., Catholics, exchange matrimonial consent in our presence according to the following form:

"I, N.N., take thee, N.N., for my lawful wife, to have and to hold from this day forward, for better, for worse, for richer, for poorer, in sickness and in health, until death do us part."

and

"I, N.N., take thee, N.N., for my lawful husband, to have and to hold from this day forward, for better, for worse, for richer, for poorer, in sickness and in health, until death do us part."

In testimony whereof, we have simultaneously affixed our signatures at ...., ..., on this, the .... day of ...., 19.....

(Signature of witnesses) ....

....

BIBLIOGRAPHY

Sources

Acta Apostolicae Sedis, Commentarium Officiale, Romae, 1909-1929; Civitate Vaticana, 1929- .

Acta Sancta Sedis, 41 vols., Romae, 1865-1908.

Bouscaren, T. Lincoln, *The Canon Law Digest,* 2 vols. and Supplement through 1948, Milwaukee, Wis.: The Bruce Publishing Co.. 1934-1943-1949.

Bruns, H., *Canones Apostolorum et Conciliorum Saeculorum IV-VII,* 2 vols., Berolini, 1839.

Codex Iuris Canonici Pii X Pontificis Maximi iussu digestus, Benedicti Papae XV auctoritate promulgatus, Praefatione, Fontium Annotatione et Indice Analytico-Alphabetico, ab Emo Petro Card. Gasparri Auctus, Romae: Typis Polyglottis Vaticanis, 1917; reimpressio. 1934.

Codicis Iuris Canonici Fontes, cura Emi Petri Card. Gasparri editi, 9 vols., Romae (postea Civitate Vaticana): Typis Polyglottis Vaticanis, 1923-1939 (Vols. VII-IX, ed. cura et studio Emi Iustiniani Card. Serédi).

Collectanea Sacrae Congregationis de Propaganda Fide, Romae: Typographia Polyglotta S. C. de Propaganda Fide, 1893.

Collectanea Sacrae Congregationis de Propaganda Fide, 2 vols., Vol. I, ann. 1622-1866, NN. 1-1299; Vol. II, ann. 1867-1906, NN. 1300-2317, Romae: Typographia Polyglotta S. C. de Propaganda Fide, 1907.

Corpus Iuris Canonici, ed. Lipsiensis secunda, post Aemilii Richteri curas... Instruxit Aemilius Friedberg, 2 vols. in 3, Lipsiae, 1879-1881.

Corpus Iuris Civilis, 3 vols., Vol. I, *Institutiones,* quas recognovit P. Krueger, ed. stereotypa 15., 1928; *Digesta,* quae recognovit T. Mommsen et retractavit P. Krueger, ed. stereotypa 15., 1928; Vol. II, *Codex Iustinianus,* quem recognovit et retractavit P. Krueger, ed. stereotypa 10., 1929; Vol. III, *Novellae.* recognovit Rudolphus Schoell, opus Schoellii morte interceptum, absolvit Gulielmus Kroll, ed. stereotypa 5., Berolini, 1928.

Cursus Scriptorum Ecclesiasticorum Latinorum, 71 vols. incomplete, Vindobonae, 1866- .

Decretales D. Gregorii Papae IX, suae integritati una cum glossis restitutae, cum privilegio Gregorii XIII, Pont. Max., et aliorum Principum, Romae, 1582.

Decretum Gratiani emendatum et notationibus illustratum cum glossis, Gregorii XIII, Pont. Max., iussu editum, 2 vols., Romae, 1582

Denziger, H.-Bannwart, C., *Enchiridion Symbolorum et Definitionum,* editio decima, emendata et aucta, Friburgi Brisgoviae: Herder, 1908.

Hardouin, J., *Acta Conciliorum et Epistolae Decretales ac Constitutiones Summorum Pontificum,* 12 vols., Parisiis, 1714-1715.

Hinschius, P., *Decretales Pseudo—Isidorianae et Capitula Angilramni,* Lipsiae, 1863.

The Holy Bible, Duoay Version, New York: Wildermann, 1938.

Jaffé, P., *Regesta Pontificum Romanorum ab condita Ecclesia ad annum post Christum natum MCXCVIII,* ed. 2., correctam et auctam auspiciis Gulielmi Wattenbach curaverunt S. Loewenfeld, F. Kaltenbrunner, P. Ewald, 2 vols., Lipsiae, 1885-1888.

Mansi, J., *Sacrorum Conciliorum Nova et Amplissima Collectio,* 53 vols. in 60, Parisiis, 1901-1927.

Monumenta Germaniae Historica, Epistulae, Vol. VI (*Karolini Aevi IV*), pars prior, curante Ernesto Dümmler, Hannoverae, 1902; pars II, fasc. I, curante Ernesto Perels, Berolini, 1925.

———, *Leges,* 5 vols., Vols. I-IV, ed. G. Pertz; Vol. V, edd. G. Pertz, G. Waitz, H. Brunner, Hannoverae, 1835-1889.

———, *Legum Sectio I,* Tomus I, *Lex Visigothorum,* ed. K. Zeumer, Hannoverae, 1902.

Pii VI, Pontificis Maximi, Acta Quibus Ecclesiae Catholicae Calamitatibus in Gallia consultum est, 2 vols. in 1, Romae: Typis S. C. de Propaganda Fide, 1871.

S. Romanae Rotae Decisiones Recentiores, edd. Pr. Farinacius, Paulus Rubeus, Ioannes Baptista Compagnus, pro annis 1518-1684, 25 vols., Romae, 1618-1703.

S. Romanae Rotae Decisiones seu Sententiae ab anno 1909, Romae: Typis Polyglottis Vaticanis, 1912- .

Schulte, F.-Richter, A., *Canones et Decreta Concilii Tridentini.* Lipsiae, 1853.

Thesaurus Resolutionum Sacrae Congregationis Concilii, 167 vols., Urbini, 1718-1741; Romae, 1741-1908.

Reference Works

Aertnys, J.-Damen, C. A., *Theologia Moralis,* 2 vols., 14. ed., 6. post Codicem Torino: Marietti, 1944.

The Babylonian Talmud, Kiddushim, London: Sancino Press, 1936.

Ballerini, A.-Palmieri, D., *Opus Theologicum Morale,* 3. ed., 7 vols., Prati, 1898-1901.

Barbosa, A., *Tractatus Varii,* pars 1, *De Axiomatibus Iuris usufrequentioribus,* Lugduni, 1660.

Benedictus XIV (Prospero Lambertini), *De Synodo Dioecesana,* 2 vols., secunda Parmensis editio, Parmae, 1744.

Buckland, W. W., *Textbook of Roman Law from Augustus to Justinian,* 2. ed., Cambridge: University Press, 1932.

Cappello, F., *Tractatus Canonico-Moralis de Censuris.* 4. ed., Romae: Marietti, 1950.

———, *Tractatus Canonico-Moralis de Sacramentis,* Vol. III, *De Matrimonio,* Taurinorum Augustae: Marietti, 1923.

———, *Tractatus Canonico-Moralis de Sacramentis,* 5 vols., Romae: Marietti, 1942-1947 (Vol. I, *De Sacramentis in Genere,* 5. ed., 1947; Vol. V, *De Matrimonio,* 5. ed., 1947).

Carberry, J., *The Juridical Form of Marriage,* The Catholic University of America Canon Law Studies, n. 84, Washington, D. C.: The Catholic University of America, 1934.

Cerato, P., *Matrimonium a Codice I.C. integre desumptum,* ed. 4., Putavi, 1927.

Chelodi, I., *Ius Matrimoniale iuxta Codicem Iuris Canonici,* Tridenti, 1921.

Chelodi, I.-Ciprotti, P., *Ius Canonicum de Matrimonio,* 5. ed., Vicenza: Società Anonima, 1947.

Chrétien, P., *De Matrimonio (Praelectiones),* 2. ed., Metis: Typis Imprimerie du Journal "Le Lorrain," 1937.

Ciesluk, J., *National Parishes in the United States,* The Catholic University of American Canon Law Studies, n. 190, Washington, D. C.: The Catholic University of American Press, 1944.

Claeys-Bouuaert, F.-Simenon, G., *Manuale Iuris Canonici,* 3 vols., Vol. II, 3. ed., Gandae et Leodii: Dessain, 1947.

Coronata, Matthaeus Conte a, *Institutiones Iuris Canonici—De Sacramentis Tractatus Canonicus.* 3 vols., Romae: Marietti, 1943-1946.

Corbett, P., *Roman Law of Marriage,* Oxford: Clarendon Press, 1930.

Cronin, Charles J., *The New Matrimonial Legislation,* 2. ed., revised and corrected, London: Washbourne, 1909.

D'Annibale, J., *Summula Theologiae Moralis,* 5. ed., 3 vols., Romae, 1908.

De Becker, I., *De Sponsalibus et Matrimonio Praelectiones Canonicae,* 2. ed., Lovanii, 1903 (cum appendice *Commentarius in Legem Novam, de Forma Sponsalium et Matrimonii,* a. 1913).

De Smet, A., *De Sponsalibus et Matrimonio,* Brugis, 1909.

———, *Tractatus Theologico-Canonicus de Sponsalibus et Matrimonio,* 4. ed., Brugis: Bayaert, 1927.

Diana Coordinatus seu Omnium Resolutionum Moralium eius ipsissimis verbis ad propria loca et materias per v.p. Martinum de Alcolea fideliter dispositarum tomi I-X, 10 vols. in 5, Venetiis, 1728.

Durieux, P., *Le Mariage en droit Canonique,* 6. ed., Paris, 1928.

Eichmann, E.-Mörsdorf, K., *Lehrbuch des Kirchenrechts auf Grund des Codex Iuris Canonici,* 3 vols., Vol. II. *Sachenrecht,* Paderborn: Schöningh, 1950.

Engel, L., *Collegium Universi Iuris Canonici,* Beneventi, 1670.

Esmein, A., *Le Mariage en Droit Canonique,* 2 vols., Paris, 1891.

Fagnanus, Prosp., *Commentaria in secundum librum Decretalium,* 5 vols. in 8, Romae, 1661.

Feije, H., *De Impendimentis et Dispensationibus Matrimonialibus,* 3. ed., Lovanii, 1885.

Feine, H., *Kirchliche Rechtsgeschichte,* 2 vols. (Vol. I, 1950), Weimar: Herman Böhlaus Nachfolger, 1950- .

Friedberg, E., *Das Recht der Eheschliessung,* Liepzig, 1865.

Freisen, J., *Geschichte des canonischen Eherechts bis zum Verfall der Glossenliteratur,* 2. ed., Paderborn, 1893.

Gasparri, P., *Tractatus Canonicus de Matrimonio,* 3. ed., 2 vols., Parisiis. 1904; nova editio ad mentem Codicis I.C., 2 vols., Romae: Typis Polyglottis Vaticanis, 1932.

Gennari. C., *Breve Commento della Nuova Legge sugli Sponsali e sul Matrimonio,* 2. ed., Romae, 1908.

Gury, I.-Ballerini, A.. *Compendium Theologiae Moralis,* 9. ed., 2 vols., Romae, 1887.

Hanstein, H., *Kanonisches Eherecht,* 2. Auflage, Paderborn: Schöningh, 1948.

Hörmann, W. von, *Quasi-Affinität,* 2 vols., Innsbruck, 1897-1906.

Hostiensis, Cardinalis (Henricus de Segusio), *Summa Aurea,* Venetiis. 1570.

Heylen, V., *Tractatus de Matrimonio,* 9. ed., Mechliniae: Dessain, 1945.

Hyland, F., *Excommunication,* The Catholic University of American Canon Law Studies, n. 49. Washington, D. C.: The Catholic University of America, 1928.

Joyce, G., *Christian Marriage,* 2. ed., London: Sheed & Ward, 1948.

Kearney, R., *Principles of Delegation,* The Catholic University of America Canon Law Studies, n. 55, Washington, D. C.: The Catholic University of America, 1929.

Knecht, A., *Handbuch des katholischen Eherechts,* Freiburg im Breisgau: Herder, 1928.

Laymann, P., *Theologia Moralis in quinque libros distributa,* Venetiis, 1630.

Leitner, M., *Lehrbuch des katholischen Eherechts,* 3. ed., Paderborn, 1920.

Leurenius, P., *Ius Canonicum Universum,* 3 vols., Venetiis, 1729.

Linneborn, I., *Grundriss des Eherechts nach dem Codex Iuris Canonici,* 2. and 3. Auflage, Paderborn, 1922.

Migne, J. P., *Patrologiae Cursus Completus, Series Graeca,* 161 vols., Parisiis, 1857-1866.

———, *Patrologiae Cursus Completus, Series Latina,* 221 vols., Parisiis, 1844-1855.

Motry, L., *Diocesan Faculties According to the Code of Canon Law,* The Catholic University of America Canon Law Studies, n. 16, Washington, D. C.: The Catholic University of America, 1922.

Neufeld, E., *Ancient Hebrew Marriage Laws,* New York: Longmans, 1944.

Noldin, H.-Schmitt, A., *Summa Theologiae Moralis,* 3 vols., 26. ed., Vol. III, *De Sacramentis,* Oeniponte/Lipsiae: Rauch, 1940.

Oesterle, G., *Consultationes de Iure Matrimoniali,* Romae: Officium Libri Catholici, 1942.

Ojetti, B., *Synopsis Rerum Moralium et Iuris Pontificii,* 3. ed., 3 vols. and Index, Romae, 1909-1914.

O'Keeffe, G.. *Matrimonial Dispensations—Powers of Bishops, Priests and Confessors,* The Catholic University of America Canon Law Studies, n. 45, Washington, D. C.: The Catholic University of America, 1927.

Pallavicinus, P. S., *Vera Concilii Tridentini Historia,* translated from the Italian by J. Baptista Giattino, S.J., 3 vols., Antuerpiae: ex Officina Plantiniana Baltasaria Noreti, 1670.

Pallotini, S., *Collectio omnium conclusionum et resolutionum quae in causis propositis apud Sacram Congregationem Cardinalium S. Concilii Tridentini interpretum prodierunt ab eius institutione anno MDLXIV ad MDCCCLX, distinctis titulis alphabeticis ordine per materias digesta,* 17 vols., Romae, 1868-1893.

Payen, G., *De Matrimonio in Missionibus ac Potissimum in Sinis Tractatus Practicus et Casus,* 2. ed., 3 vols., Zi-ka-wei: Typographia T'ou-Se We, 1935-1936.

Perez, M., *De Sancto Matrimonii Sacramento—Opus Morale-Theologicum,* Lugduni, 1646.

Petrus Lombardus, *Libri Sententiarum Quatuor,* 2. ed., 2 vols., cura et studiis PP. Collegii S. Bonaventurae, ad Claras Aquas (Florence), 1916.

Pirhing, E., *Ius Canonicum Novo Methodo Explicatum,* 5 vols. in 4, Dilingae, 1674-1678.

Pollock. F.-Maitland, F., *History of English Law Before the Time of Edward* I, 2. ed., 2 vols.. Cambridge: University Press, 1895.

Pontius, B., *De Sacramento Matrimonii Tractatus,* Venetiis, 1756.

Regatillo, E., *Interpretatio et Iurisprudentia Codicis Iuris Canonici,* Santander: Sal Terrae, 1949.

Reiffenstuel, A., *Ius Canonicum Universum,* 5 vols. in 6, Romae. 1831-1834.

Rossi, J., *De Matrimonii Celebratione iuxta Codicem Iuris Canonici,* Rome: Pustet, 1924.

Sägmüller, J., *Lehrbuch des katholischen Kirchenrechts,* 2 vols., Freiburg im Breisgau, 1900.

Sanchez, T., *Disputationum de sancto matrimonii sacramento tomi tres,* 3 vols., Antuerpiae, 1626.

Schäfer, T., *Das Eherecht nach dem Codex Iuris Canonici,* 6. and 7, ed., Münster, 1921.

Schmalzgrueber, F., *Ius Ecclesiasticum Universum,* 5 vols. in 12, Romae, 1843-1845.

Schmier, F., *Iurisprudentia Canonico-Civilis seu Ius Canonicum Universum,* 2 vols., Venetiis, 1754.

Schönsteiner, F., *Grundriss des kirchlichen Eherechts,* 2. ed., Wien: Auer, 1937.

Schulte, J. F. von, *Summa Paucapalea über das Decretum Gratiani,* Giessen: Roth, 1891.

Singer, H., *Summa Decretorum Rufini,* Paderborn, 1902.

Soto, D.. *Commentarium in Quartum Sententiarum,* 2 vols., Venetiis, 1584.

Suarez, F., *Opera Omnia,* 26 vols. (Vols. V and VI—*De Legibus et Legislatore Deo,* Parisiis, 1856).

Thaner, Fr., *Anselmi Lucensis Collectio Canonum,* Oeniponte, 1906.

Thomas Aquinas, St., *Opera Omnia,* 25 vols., New York: Misurgia, 1948-1950.

Triebs, F., *Praktisches Handbuch des geltenden kanonischen Eherechts in Vergleichung mit dem deutschen staatlichen Eherecht,* Breslau: Ostdeutsche Verlagsanstalt, 1933.

Ubach, J., *Compendium Theologiae Moralis,* 2 vols., Friburgi Brisgoviae: Herder, 1926-1927.

Van Espen, B., *Opera Omnia Canonica in sex partes distributa—Ius Ecclesiasticum Universum,* 6 partes in 3 vols., Lovanii, 1732.

Van Hove, A., *Commentarium Lovaniense in Codicem Iuris Canonici,* 1 vol. in 5 tomes, Tom. II, *De Legibus Ecclesiasticis,* Mechliniae: H. Dessain, 1930.

Verde, F., *Institutionum Canonicarum Libri Quatuor,* 2 vols., Neapoli, 1735.

Vermeersch, A., *De Forma Sponsalium et Matrimonii post decretum "Ne Temere,"* Brugis, 1908.

———, *Theologia Moralis,* 4 vols., Romae-Brugis: Dessain, 1922-1924.

Vermeersch, A.-Creusen, J., *Epitome Iuris Canonici,* 2. ed., 3 vols., Mechliniae-Romae: Dessain, 1923-1925; Vol. II, 6. ed., Mechliniae: Dessain, 1940.

Vlaming, T., *Praelectiones Iuris Matrimonii,* 3. ed., 2 vols., Bussum, 1919-1921.

———, *Praelectiones Iuris Matrimonii,* 4. ed., a L. Bender, Bussum in Hollandia: Brand, 1950.

Vromant, G., *Ius Missionarium,* Tom. V, *De Matrimonio,* Louvain: Museum Lessianum, 1931.

Wernz, F., *Ius Decretalium,* 6 vols., Romae, 1898-1914; Vol. IV, *Ius Matrimoniale Ecclesiae Catholicae,* Romae, 1904.

Wernz, F.-Vidal, P., *Ius Canonicum ad Codicis Normam Exactum,* 7 vols. in 8, Romae: Apus Aedes Universitatis Gregorianae, 1923-1938; Vol. V, *Ius Matrimoniale,* ed. 2., 1928; ed. 3., a Philippo Aguirre recognita, 1946.

Wouters, L., *Commentarius in Decretum "Ne temere" ad Usum Scholarum compositus,* 2. ed., Amstelodami-Galopiae, 1909.

———, *De Forma Promissionis et Celebrationis Matrimonii,* ed. 5., ad Codicem Iuris Canonici accommodata, Bussum in Hollandia, 1919.

———, *Manuale Theologiae Moralis,* 2 vols., Brugis: Beyaert, 1933.

Zitelli, Z., *Apparatus Iuris Ecclesiastici,* ed. altera novis curis auctior et emendatior, Romae, 1888.

Articles

Aguirre, P.. "Annotationes," *Periodica,* XXXIV (1945), 281-285.

Arendt, G., "Ad Can. 1045. Iterum de Dispensatione a Forma Matrimonii in Casu Perplexo," *Ius Pontificium,* VII (1927), 147-150.

———, "Dispensatio a forma matrimonii in casu perplexo," *Periodica,* XVI (1927), 1*-17-*.

Bender, L., "Legitimatio prolis sola dispensatione quin sequatur matrimonium (C. 1051)," *Monitor Ecclesiasticus,* LXXVII (1953), 102-108.

Dalpiaz, V., "An canon 1098 comprehendat etiam matrimonii celebrationes acatholicas vel civiles," *Apollinaris,* X (1937), 275-278.

———, "De validitate aut nullitate matrimoniorum a captivis ex bello in Russia initorum," *Apollinaris*, X (1937), 272-275.

D'Angelo, S., "In C. 1045 Codicis I.C. excursus," *Apollinaris*, I (1928), 245-262.

De Becker, I., "De Recta Canonis 1098 Codicis Iuris Canonici Interpretatione," *Ephemerides Theologicae Lovanienses*, IX (1932), 284-291.

De Smet, A., "Responsa," *Collationes Brugenses*, XII (1907), 547-549.

Jelicic, V., "Consultationes," *Ius Pontificium*, XV (1935), 126.

König, F., "Eine interessante Ehenichtigleitsklage zu Can. 1098," *Osterreichisches Archiv für Kirchenrecht*, III (1952), 274-285.

Marbach, J., "The Recent Instruction of the Sacred Consistorial Congregation Regarding Military Ordinariates," *The Jurist*, XII (1952), 141-155.

Maroto, P., "Animadversiones ad responsa ad proposita dubia 10 martii, 1928," *Apollinaris*, I (1928), 334-339.

Miceli, J., "De Forma Celebrationis Matrimonii iuxta c. 1098," *Monitor Ecclesiasticus*, LXXV (1950), 234-237.

Močnik, V., "An canon 1098 comprehendat etiam matrimonii celebrationes acatholicas vel civiles," *Apollinaris*, IX (1936), 304-307.

———, "Consultationes circa Pontificiam interpretationem c. 1078," *Apollinaris*, IX (1936), 444-446.

Mörsdorf, K., "Die Noteheschliessung (c. 1098)," *Archiv für katholisches Kirchenrecht*, CXXIV (1950), 78-91.

Oesterle, G., "Elucubratio Historica circa Declarationem Authenticam C. 1098," *Ius Pontificium*, VIII (1928), 174-182; IX (1929), 141-158.

———, "De Validtate aut Nullitate Matrimoniorum a Captivis ex Bello in Russia Initorum,," *Apollinaris*, IX (1935), 446-462.

Sipos, S., "Forma Celebrationis Extraordinaria Matrimonii extra Mortis Periculum," *Ius Pontificium*, XX (1940), 93-102.

———, "Casus de Forma Matrimonii eiusque Dispensatione," *Periodica*, XIV (1925), (122)-(124).

Toso, ., "Consilia et Responsa," *Ius Pontificium*, X (1930), 341-342.

Periodicals

Apollinaris, Romae, 1928- .

Archiv für katholisches Kirchenrecht, Innsbruck, 1857-1861; Mainz, 1862- .

Collationes Brugenses, Brugis, 1896- .

Ephemerides Theologicae Lovanienses, Lovanii-Brugis, 1924-

Ius Pontificium, Romae, 1921-1940.

Jurist, The, Washington, D. C., 1941- .

Monitore Ecclesiastico, Il, Romae, 1876-1948; ab anno 1949: *Monitor Ecclesiasticus*.

Osterreichisches Archiv für Kirchenrecht, Wien, 1950-

Periodica de Religiosis et Missionariis, Brugis, 1905-1919; ab anno 1920: *Periodica de Re Canonica et Morali utilia praesertim Religosis et Missionariis*, Brugis, 1920-1927; *Periodica de Re Morali, Canonica, Liturgica*, Brugis, 1927-1936, et Romae, 1937- .

Abbreviations

AAS—*Acta Apostolicae Sedis.*
ASS—*Acta Sanctae Sedis.*
Bruns—*Canones Apostolorum et Conciliorum Saeculorum IV-VII.*
C.—Causa.
c.—canon or caput.
Cerato—*Matrimonium a Codice I.C. integre desumptum.*
CSEL—*Corpus Scriptorum Ecclesiasticorum Latinorum.*
Chelodi-Ciprotti—*Ius Canonicum de Matrimonio.*
D.—*Digestum Iustinianum* or Distinctio.
De Synodo—*De Synodo Dioecesana.*
Digest—*The Canon Law Digest and supplement through 1948.*
Fontes—*Codicis Iuris Canonici Fontes.*
Gasparri—*Tractatus Canonicus de Matrimonio.*
Hardouin—*Acta Conciliorum et Epistolae Decretales ac Constitutiones Summorum Pontificum.*
Jaffé—*Regesta Pontificum Romanorum.*
JE—Jaffé, *Regesta Pontificum Romanorum*, ed. curavit P. Ewald.
JK—Jaffé, *Regesta Pontificum Romanorum*, ed. curavit F. Kaltenbrunner.
Laymann—*Theologia Moralis in quinque libros distributa.*
Leurenius—*Ius Canonicum Universum.*
Mansi—*Sacrorum Conciliorum Nova et Amplissima Collectio.*
MGH—*Monumenta Germaniae Historica.*
MPG—Migne, *Patrologiae Cursus Completus, Series Graeca.*
MPL—Migne,*Patroligiae Cursus Completus, Series Latina.*
N.—*Novellae.*
Pallottini—*Collectio omnium conclusionum et resolutionum quae in causis propositis apud Sacram Congregationem Cardinalium S. Concilii Tridentini interpretum prodierunt ab eius institutione anno MDLXIV ad MDCCCLX, distinctis titulis alphabeticis ordine per materias digesta.*
Payen—*De Matrimonio in Missionibus ac Potissimum in Sinis Tractatus Practicus et Casus.*
P.C.I.—Pontificia Commissio ad Codicis Canones Authentice Interpretandos.
Perez—*De Sancto Matrimonii Sacramento.*
Periodica—*Periodica de Religiosis et Missionariis*, etc.
Pontius—*De Sacramento Matrimonii Tractatus.*
Reiffenstuel—*Ius Canonicum Universum.*
Rossi—*De Matrimonii Celebratione iuxta Codicem Iuris Canonici.*

S. C. C.—Sacra Congregatio Concilii.
S. C. de Prop. Fide—Sacra Congregatio de Propaganda Fide.
S. C. de Sacramentis—Sacra Congregation de disciplina Sacramentorum.
S. C. S. Off.—Sacra Congregatio Sancti Officii.
S. R. R.—Sacra Romana Rota.
Sanchez—*Disputationum de sancto matrimonii sacramento tomi tres.*
Schmalzgrueber—*Ius Ecclesiasticum Universum.*
Schmier—*Iurisprudentia Canonico-Civilis seu Ius Canonicum Universum.*
Schulte—*Canones et Decreta Concilii Tridentini.*
Thesaurus Resolutionum—*Thesaurus Resolutionum Sacrae Congregationis Concilii.*
Verde—*Institutionum Canonicarum Libri Quatuor.*
Vlaming-Bender—*Praelectiones Iuris Matrimonii,* ed. 4. a L. Bender.

ALPHABETICAL INDEX

BIOGRAPHICAL NOTE

EDWARD A. FUS was born on April 22, 1919, in Brooklyn, New York. After receiving his elementary school education at Our Lady of Consolation Parochial School in Brooklyn, N. Y., he entered St. John Kanty Preparatory School in Erie, Pa. in September, 1931, graduating therefrom in June 1935. The degree of Bachelor of Arts was conferred on him by St. John's University in Brooklyn, N. Y., at the commencement exercises in June, 1939. In September of the same year he entered the Diocesan Seminary of the Immaculate Conception at Huntington, L. I., N. Y. The Most Reverend Thomas E. Molloy, Bishop of Brooklyn, ordained him to the Holy Priesthood on April 27, 1943. Before being assigned to chancery and parochial duties in Brooklyn in June, 1948, he had been engaged in parochial work at Our Lady of Poland Parish in Southampton, L. I., N. Y. In February, 1951, he entered the School of Canon Law of the Catholic University of America, Washington, D. C., where he received the degree of the Baccalaureate in Canon Law in February of the following year, and the degree of the Licentiate in Canon Law in February of 1953.

CANON LAW STUDIES *

337. BOURQUE, REV. JOHN R., S.T.L., J.C.L., The Judicial Power of the Church—Canon 1553, § 1.
338. CORNELL, REV. CHARLES E., A.B., S.T.B., J.C.L., The Juridical Status of Heretics and Schismatics in Good Faith.
339. FITZGERALD, REV. WILLIAM FRANCIS, A.B., S.T.L., J.C.L.. The Parish Census and the *liber status animarum*.
340. KUBIK, REV. STANISLAUS J., S.T.L., J.C.L., Invalidity of Dispensations According to Canon 84, § 1.
341. NUGENT, REV. JOHN GERARD, C.M., J.C.L., Ordination in Societies of the Common Life.
342. PETERSON, REV. CASIMIR MELVYN, S.S., A.B., S.T.L., J.C.L., Spiritual Care in Diocesan Seminaries.
343. REISS, REV. JOHN CHARLES, A.B., S.T.L., J.C.L., The Time and Place of Sacred Ordination.
344. SHEEHAN, REV. JOSEPH GEORGE, J.C.L., The Obligation of Respect and Obedience of Clerics to Their Ordinary.
345. SHEKLETON, REV. MATTHEW M., O.S.M., J.C.L., Doctrinal Interpretation of Law.
346. VIAU, REV. ROGER. S.T.L., J.C.L., Doubt in Canon Law.
347. WALSH, REV. DONNELL A., A.B., J.C.L., The New Law on Secular Institutes.
348. FUS, REV. EDWARD A., A.B., J.C.L., The Extraordinary Form of Marriage According to Canon 1098.

* For a complete list of the available numbers of this series apply to the Catholic University of America Press, 620 Michigan Avenue, N.E., Washington (17), D. C.

www.ingramcontent.com/pod-product-compliance
Lightning Source LLC
LaVergne TN
LVHW050241080826
844660LV00012B/570

* 9 7 8 0 8 1 3 2 2 5 1 6 6 *